MANAGEMENT EXCELLENCE

PRODUCTIVITY THROUGH MBO

McGraw-Hill Series in Management

Fred Luthans and Keith Davis, *Consulting Editors*

MANAGEMENT EXCELLENCE

PRODUCTIVITY THROUGH MBO

Heinz Weihrich
University of San Francisco

McGRAW-HILL BOOK COMPANY

New York   St. Louis   San Francisco   Auckland   Bogotá
Hamburg   Johannesburg   London   Madrid   Mexico   Montreal   New Delhi
Panama   Paris   São Paulo   Singapore   Sydney   Tokyo   Toronto

This book was set in Helvetica by Black Dot, Inc. (ECU).
The editors were John R. Meyer and Ellen W. MacElree;
the production supervisor was Marietta Breitwieser.
The drawings were done by Danmark & Michaels, Inc.
The cover was designed by Suzanne Haldane.
R. R. Donnelley & Sons Company was printer and binder.

MANAGEMENT EXCELLENCE
Productivity through MBO

1 2 3 4 5 6 7 8 9 0 D O C D O C 8 9 8 7 6 5

ISBN 0-07-069002-2

The model shown on the inside of the front and back covers has been adapted from H.
Weihrich, "A New Approach to MBO: Updating a Time-Honored Technique," *Manage-
ment World* (April 1977), pp. 7–12. Used with permission from the Administrative
Management Society, Willow Grove, PA 19090. Copyright © 1977 AMS.

Library of Congress Cataloging in Publication Data

Weihrich, Heinz.
    Managment excellence.

    (McGraw-Hill series in management)
    Includes bibliographies and index.
    1. Management by objectives. I. Title. II. Series.
HD30.65.W45 1985   658.4'012   84-26130
ISBN 0-07-069001-4

ABOUT THE AUTHOR

HEINZ WEIHRICH is Professor of Management at the University of San Francisco. He received his doctorate degree from the University of California at Los Angeles (UCLA), where he conducted the first comprehensive research study on management by objectives (MBO) as a comprehensive, integrated management system. He taught at Arizona State University, the University of California at Los Angeles, and in France and Austria.

Professor Weihrich has published six books including *Management* (translated into 15 languages) and *Essentials of Management,* both with Professors Harold Koontz and Cyril O'Donnell. Over 70 of his articles have been published in the United States and abroad. His extensive business and consulting experiences in the United States and Europe include working with firms such as Volkswagen and Hughes Aircraft Company.

To Peter F. Drucker
George S. Odiorne
Eugene J. Seyna

CONTENTS

PREFACE

One of the most pressing problems in our society is the productivity dilemma. Although there is wide agreement about this problem, there are many different views on what to do about it. Whatever the proposed solution, however, most people would agree that any intelligent approach to improving productivity requires the systematic setting of goals and monitoring progress toward these aims.

This book is about managerial excellence. It is about personal and organizational effectiveness, which requires setting and achieving objectives. The book is also about efficiency, that is, accomplishing these aims at the least cost. Simply stated, this is what productivity is all about: effectiveness and efficiency for individuals, teams, and organizations.

The book title includes the term "MBO," which is the acronym for management by objectives. I am using this term with some hesitation because my approach differs from that of traditional MBO programs, which usually focus on selected and limited aspects of managing such as performance appraisal, goal setting, or controlling. In fact, the various approaches to MBO and the different labels used for such programs are often quite confusing. Over 20 years ago, the late Professor Harold Koontz of UCLA wrote what has become the most widely reprinted and quoted article, "The Management Theory Jungle," in which he analyzed the many different, and often divergent, approaches to general management, thereby creating a semantic jungle. Today, with the great expansion of knowledge in MBO, many articles and books frequently focus only on some selected managerial concepts rather than on managing as a whole. Therefore, we encounter difficulties by having created a kind of "MBO Jungle." The purpose of this book is to untangle this jungle by introducing a comprehensive and integrated goal-oriented management system for improving managerial productivity. I would have liked to give the suggested system a name other than MBO, but dropped the idea as new terminology would have contributed to the already thick semantic jungle.

FEATURES OF THE BOOK

The primary purpose of this text is to promote excellence of all persons in organizations, but especially managers, aspiring managers, and other professionals. Excellence requires aiming at high but achievable goals that are integrated in a systematic manner. On the inside of the front and back covers of the book and at the end of the first chapter you will find a model that highlights the topics examined in the various chapters. These include:

• Achieving managerial excellence through a comprehensive, goal-oriented system of managing
• Measuring the productivity of managers and subordinates
• Developing a strategic plan that focuses on the long-term success of the enterprise
• Measuring organizational productivity
• Getting action into plans
• Motivating people for greater productivity
• Controlling organizational performance and appraising managers
• Making organizations and people productive through human resource planning, training, and development
• Managing careers for greater job satisfaction
• Improving productivity by learning from the Japanese
• Taking advantage of the megatrends by preparing for the future with goal-oriented management

Other features of the book are as follows:
1 It is written in a readable style using vocabulary familiar to managers and potential managers who should become acquainted with terms they need to know for career success.

2 The emphasis is on the practice of managing, based on sound theory. Scholarly documentation facilitates further studies for those interested in theory.

3 People are the most important part in productivity improvement. Therefore, emphasis is given to behavioral science topics.

4 Many examples are given to illustrate concepts and to serve as models.

5 The goal-oriented approach applies to any kind of organization. But the special situation of government is discussed in considerable detail.

Productivity is the concern of both practicing managers and business schools. For this reason, the American Assembly of Collegiate Schools of Business (AACSB) held a conference on U.S. Porductivity and International Competitiveness in Washington, D.C. Deans, faculty members, and representatives of corporations and government agreed that the deterioration of productivity is a national problem and should be a special focus of business schools. They urged that topics of productivity be included in business school curriculums. At this time, very few schools do so, partly because of the lack of a suitable textbook. This book is designed to fill this need to some extent as it aims to assist managers and college students preparing for managerial excellence through productivity.

ACKNOWLEDGMENTS

I am indebted to the many people who generously shared their ideas about managerial excellence through a goal-oriented management approach. Practicing managers, seminar participants, colleagues, and students all helped directly or indirectly in formulating and reformulating management-by-objectives concepts and integrating them into a system to improve managerial productivity. Contributions of scholars are also acknowledged through footnotes and references. In addition, there are individuals who contributed in a very special way.

First there are those to whom this book is dedicated: Peter F. Drucker and George S. Odiorne contributed most to the development and the popularity of management by objectives (MBO) through their perceptive writings and teachings. Eugene J. Seyna, as president of the MBO Institute, has done much to promote the state-of-the-art thinking on goal management. James L. Hayes, chairman; John W.

Enell, vice-president for research; and Ernst C. Miller, editor in chief, all of the American Management Association, supported my initial study of MBO. Professors Harold Koontz, Anthony P. Raia, and George A. Steiner, all at UCLA, generously shared their time to discuss goal-oriented management. I also appreciate the many ideas presented at the various MBO Conferences by members of the MBO Institute. These persons include Bonnie MacLean Abney, Richard D. Babcock, Arthur C. Beck, Jr., Donn Coffee, Ellis D. Hilmar, John W. Humble, Brendan M. Keegan, Dale D. McConkey, R. Henry Migliore, George L. Morrisey, Thomas S. Roberts, and Glenn H. Varney.

I am especially grateful for the reviews by Stephen J. Carroll, Jr., University of Maryland; Wayne F. Cascio, University of Colorado at Denver; F. Theodore Helmer, University of Hawaii at Manoa; George S. Odiorne, University of Massachusetts; Gene Seyna, Eastman Kodak Company; Paul E. Thomsen, Public Service Company of Colorado; Jerry Wofford, University of Texas at Arlington; and my colleagues Thomas P. Cullen and Marvin M. Okanes, both at the University of San Francisco. Professors Keith Davis and Fred Luthans, consulting editors for McGraw-Hill, have both made valuable suggestions throughout the preparation of the manuscript. To them and to John Carleo, Kathi Benson, John Meyer, and Ellen W. MacElree at McGraw-Hill I owe my special gratitude. Dean Bernard L. Martin at McLaren College of Business at the University of San Francisco has been very supportive while I wrote this book. I also would like to thank Ms. Elizabeth Demesa and Ms. Nancy.Six for assuming the task of preparing the manuscript for publication. Finally, my wife Ursula has helped greatly with her critique and her cooperative spirit.

Heinz Weihrich

ACHIEVING MANAGERIAL EXCELLENCE THROUGH THE SYSTEMS APPROACH TO MANAGEMENT BY OBJECTIVES

In the late 1960s the French journalist Servan-Schreiber warned Europeans about the economic invasion by American multinational companies.[1] The organizational genius of American managers was considered superior. The Japanese, too, admired American management approaches and regularly sent—and still do send—their managers to the United States to attend its business schools. After World War II, the United States clearly was the productivity leader. But in the late 1960s the deceleration of productivity growth began. In times of prosperity, productivity is taken for granted. During economic distress the concern for productivity improvement is constantly in the news, as illustrated by the following sample of headlines, announcements of seminars, and suggestions of solutions to the productivity crisis.

"How Deadly is the Productivity Disease?"
"Productivity: The Difficulty of Even Defining the Problem"
"Public Sector Productivity in an Era of Retrenchment"
"In 30 Years, Productivity Has Helped Raise Japan's GNP by 300%"

Several reasons given for the productivity crisis are contained in such articles as:

"Many Culprits Named in National Slowdown of Productivity Gains"

"Productivity Debate is Clouded by Problem of Measuring Its Lag"

"Many Businesses Blame Governmental Policies for Productivity Lag"

"Study Disputes View That Growth of Service Jobs Crimps Productivity"

"The Psychological Component in Productivity"

"Knowledge Worker Measurement Needed Quickly"

"Productivity Drop Not Fault of Workers, Study Says"

And here are some of the headlines that propose solutions to the problems:

"Training: The Key to Productivity"

"Try Treating All Your Workers as 'White Collars' "

"HRD's (Human Resource Development) Crucial Role in Productivity Improvement"

"Increasing Productivity Through Performance Appraisal"

"U.S. Firms, Worried by Productivity Lag, Copy Japan in Seeking Employees' Advice"

"Japanese Cited as Productivity Experts"

"Overhauling America's Business•Management"

And what will the benefits of increased productivity mean? Try this headline:

"Productivity and Prosperity"

If headlines do not impress, let us look at the report issued by the U.S. Department of Labor and the Bureau of Labor Statistics. Figure 1-1 shows that between 1950 and 1981 the real gross domestic product (GDP) per employed person grew about 1.5 percent per year in the United States. Compare this with the other five major industrialized countries, especially Japan, which grew at 6 percent per year. To be sure, the chart shows productivity growth rates— rather than absolute productivity—yet the fact that the United States trailed the other listed major industrial countries should be of great concern.

The concern for productivity led to the establishment of the National Productivity Advisory Committee in 1981 by President Reagan, which, in turn, resulted in legislation calling for a White

Index, 1950 = 100   Ratio scale

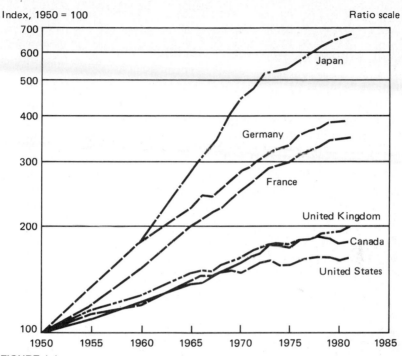

FIGURE 1-1
Trends in real gross domestic product per employed person, selected countries and
years, 1950-81. [Productivity and the Economy: A Chart Book, *U.S. Department of
Labor, Bureau of Labor Statistics, Bulletin 2172 (June 1983), p. 21.*]

House conference on productivity. The objectives of the conference
were to:

• Develop recommendations for stimulating productivity.
• Increase public awareness of the productivity problem.
• Promote private initiatives for increasing productivity growth.
• Facilitate public debate that may result in fundamental reforms
in government policies.

To achieve these aims, four preparatory conferences were held in
various parts of the country with the final conference held in
Washington in September 1983. One attending such a conference
had to be impressed by the productivity concern of government,

private industry, and academic circles. It was interesting to note frequent references to Japanese approaches for productivity improvements, which suggests the need to compare Japanese and United States managerial practices. This will be done later in this book.

THE NATURE OF PRODUCTIVITY PROBLEMS AND SOME SOLUTIONS

Although there is general agreement about the need for improving productivity, there is little consensus about the fundamental causes of the problem and what to do about them.[2] The blame has been placed on many different factors. Some people place it on the greater proportion of less skilled workers in respect to the total force, but others disagree.[3] There are those who associate the productivity problem with the high costs of energy, and economists often attribute inadequate investment in capital goods as a major factor inhibiting productivity growth. Still others see the cutback in research and the emphasis on immediate results as the main culprit. Other reasons given for the productivity dilemma are the growing affluence of people that makes them less ambitious, the breakdown in family structure, the workers' attitudes, and the government. Increasingly, the attention shifts to management as the cause of the problem—as well as the solution.

Some time ago the director of a productivity center located at a major U.S. university attended a conference on productivity in Tokyo and visited six Japanese plants with the aim of finding the key to Japanese productivity. The three outstanding factors contributing to the high level of productivity were: (1) the Japanese concern for quality, (2) participative management, and (3) the relationship between engineering and manufacturing, resulting in excellent teamwork between people from these functional areas. During my visit to Japan I was not impressed by modern machinery nor by automation. Rather it was the attention given to details that resulted in high-quality products.

Japanese observers frequently comment on two shortcomings in American management. First, there is too much concern for short-term profits. Second, there is too little concern for workers. Let us take the short-term orientation first. American companies are heavily dependent on the stock market to raise capital. Consequently, managers have to produce quarter-to-quarter profit increases to please financial investors. This is why one hears talk about the Wall Street tyranny. Perhaps too many top managers today are financial geniuses who are not sufficiently concerned about the fundamentals of marketing, technology, production, and the motivation of the labor force. While U.S. managers have to perform to please Wall Street, in Japan and Germany the banks play a major part in supplying capital and they have an interest in the long-term welfare of the companies. John Naisbitt in *Megatrends* reports that in Japan 80 percent of permanent capital is supplied by the banks.[4] In Germany, the situation is similar although to a lesser degree.

Also, top U.S. executives are typically about sixty years old and have perhaps five more years to stay on the job. Will they make decisions that have a payout long after they have retired? Unfortunately, they often invest in projects that show a favorable return in the near future. This short-term orientation pervades not only top management but all levels in the organizational hierarchy. Most managerial systems are designed to reward short-term performance with bonuses and promotions and actually discourage investment in projects that increase productivity in the distant future. Some managers do not invest in effective and efficient machines, but rather keep the old ones to improve the return on investment in the short run. This may result not only in financial rewards for them but also in their successors' inheritance of inefficient machines prone to breakdowns. If such practices pervade the whole organization, the long-term effect on declining productivity can only be estimated. The need for a system that rewards investment in the organization's long-term productivity seems obvious.

Another aspect of the productivity problem is the way people are utilized. Some managers give lip service to the value of people. Most people want to contribute to the aims of the organization. They want to participate in the decision-making process, but in many organizations few opportunities are provided for using employees' potential.

Many other reasons are suggested for the productivity problem and there is disagreement on the total list of causes. However, there is agreement that a general shift from skilled work to knowledge work, such as that carried out by managers, has occured. At TRW Inc. the shift is predicted as being quite dramatic. While approximately 40 percent of the labor force were in manufacturing in 1983, the number is expected to decrease to 5 percent in seventeen years. This shift from skilled to knowledge work creates difficulties in defining, measuring, and improving productivity of managerial work.

Knowledge workers use concepts, principles, ideas, and theories to plan, organize, and control resources and to make people productive through effective leadership. In one study, for example, it was found that there was hardly any research dealing with the productivity of the knowledge worker.[5] Yet it is this area that probably has the greatest potential for productivity improvement. In his best-selling book *Theory Z,* Professor William G. Ouchi of the University of California at Los Angeles suggests that, "Productivity is a problem that can be worked out through coordinating individual efforts in a productive manner and giving employees incentives to do so by taking a cooperative, long-range view."[6] This is congruent with the aims of this book, which emphasize:

• A balanced concern for profit and people through the integration of organizational demands with individual needs.
• A concern for long-term productivity through comprehensive, long-range, and strategic planning, supported by medium- and short-range planning.
• A management system that stresses self-control and self-direction without the loss of organizational control.
• The establishment of an organizational environment conducive to motivating knowledge workers.
• Results that are measurable, but with careful consideration given to intangible factors—such as the quality of working life—because they contribute, although indirectly, to long-term productivity.
• Productivity that can only be obtained by managing effectively and efficiently the interrelationships of people. Organizations, then, are viewed as open systems with interactions among people within the organization and between the organization and its environment.

Kenneth Blanchard and Spencer Johnson, authors of *The One Minute Manager,* propose three "secrets" for making managers more effective: goal setting, praising, and appropriately reprimanding subordinates.[7] While most experienced managers would consider this an oversimplification of their difficult job, it nevertheless points out that goal setting is one of the most important keys to managerial effectiveness.

In their book *In Search of Excellence,* Thomas J. Peters and Robert H. Waterman, Jr. identify the 7-S framework used by McKinsey, the well-known management consulting firm.[8] The framework, further discussed by Richard Pascale and Anthony Athos in

The Art of Japanese Management,[9] consists of strategy, structure, systems, style, staff, skills, and shared values. Let us briefly look at the seven "S"s that were used as the basis by Peters and Waterman in their search for excellent companies. We will note the relationship of these variables to the topics discussed on productivity in this book.

1 *Strategy* requires not only the determination of the mission and direction, but also a systematic determination of the organization's strengths and weaknesses and their relationship to the external opportunities and threats, aspects discussed in Chapters 2, 3, and 4 in this book.

2 *Structure* is the second "S" in the McKinsey framework. Although organization structure is not emphasized in this book,[10] action planning (Chapter 5) will aid in deciding on the appropriate structure.

3 *Systems* concepts have been emphasized throughout the book and the model introduced later in this chapter shows the goal-oriented systems model for improving managerial productivity.

4 *Style* pertains to the way managers behave while working toward organizational goals. The productivity improvement process is carried out in different styles as shown in Chapters 6 and 10. Contrasting managerial styles of Japanese and United States managers are discussed in Chapter 11.

5 *Staff* refers to personnel and to the process by which employees are integrated with the organizational culture. As you will note later, the importance of teaching the nature and philosophy of the goal-oriented approach to managerial productivity permeates the whole book. Special attention is given to improving human resources in Chapter 8.

6 *Skills,* a term somewhat stretched by the authors because it starts with an "S," pertains to the distinct capabilities of the firm, an aspect treated extensively in Chapter 3.

7 *Shared values* is the final variable in the 7-S framework. As will be seen, Peter F. Drucker, who popularized the management-by-objectives (MBO) concept, provided the philosophical underpinning by emphasizing self-control, teamwork, and a way of directing all organizational activities toward a common goal. This is certainly one key to managerial and organizational success. Whenever the mechanics of an MBO program conflict with the underlying MBO values, failure is most likely to occur.

We can conclude, then, that the 7-S framework used and tested by the highly respected consulting firm of McKinsey is similar to the thrust of this book. Both methods aim at integrating key managerial activities in a systematic manner toward the achievement of both organizational as well as individual objectives.

To improve managerial productivity is the purpose of this book. We will suggest a goal-oriented management system such as that practiced in a comprehensive management-by-objectives (MBO) program. But this approach is also different from traditional MBO programs (which clearly are in need of updating) because it integrates many key managerial activities in a systematic way. Specifically, it incorporates strategic planning and the hierarchy and network of aims into the process. It shows how behavioral knowledge facilitates the processes of setting of objectives, planning for action, implementation of action plans, and appraising, as well as controlling performance. Finally, a comprehensive MBO system, as viewed by leading MBO proponents, includes subsystems such as human resource planning, management development, and career planning.

Before we deal in greater detail with MBO as a way of improving managerial productivity, we will first discuss some concepts of productivity, the difficulties in measuring the productivity of managers, and attempts made to improve productivity. Then a brief review of the history of MBO will indicate that it underwent considerable changes before becoming a system of managing by objectives. Finally, this chapter introduces a conceptual model that will become the framework for organizing knowledge discussed in this book.

PRODUCTIVITY

Productivity is the buzzword of the 1980s and perhaps even beyond, yet the concern for productivity is not new. Frederick Winslow Taylor, generally considered the "father of scientific management," aimed at increasing the productivity at the production level. He recognized that there was a lack of knowledge of what was a fair day's work as well as a fair day's play. Frank and Lillian Gilbreth put into practice some of the principles of scientific management by studying the motions required in doing the work. By reducing wasted motions, they doubled the productivity of bricklayers without increasing the effort. Although time and motion studies contributed to improved productivity, even a time-study expert will admit that the standards are often subject to question. The worker, while being observed by the time-study person, will often not perform in the most efficient way. Measuring the productivity of managers is even more difficult. Yet, as Peter F. Drucker, one of the most perceptive writers on management, observed: "The greatest opportunity for increasing productivity is surely to be found in knowledge work itself, and especially in management."[11]

Toward a Definition of Productivity

There is no agreement on the true meaning of productivity. One frequently used definition describes productivity as "output per employee-hour, quality considered."[12] This definition may be too narrow because it does not, for example, include nonemployees such as entrepreneurs. Furthermore, the hourly time frame is too restrictive, especially since the soundness of managerial decisions often cannot be known for a long time. Others have defined productivity as "a systematic concept concerning the conversion of inputs to outputs by the system under consideration."[13] Although this definition may sound abstract, it decisively points at the system's nature of productivity that includes both inputs and outputs. It also draws attention to the fact that productivity involves a process of transforming the inputs into outputs. In its basic form, and used as a working definition in this book, *productivity is the Input-output ratio within a time period with due consideration for quality;* in short, productivity = outputs/inputs (within a time period; quality considered), or $P=O/I$. This concept of productivity implies effectiveness and efficiency of individual and organizational performance. Effectiveness pertains to the achievement of objectives and efficiency is the achievement of the ends with the least amount of resources.[14]

Measuring Productivity of Knowledge Workers

In the United States there is a trend away from blue-collar skills work to white-collar knowledge work. The difference between the two kinds of work is the relative use of knowledge and skills. Thus, a white-collar typist would be considered a skill worker while the assistant to the manager with planning as his or her main function would be a knowledge worker. Thus, managers, engineers, and programmers may be knowledge workers because the relative amount of their work does not consist of utilizing skills, as would be the case for bricklayers, mechanics, and butchers. But the job title cannot be the sole guide for making distinctions. The owner of a small gas station may schedule the day's tasks, determine priorities, and direct subordinates, but this same owner may also change the brakes, adjust the carburetor, or realign the front wheels on a car. Thus the distinction between the skill worker and the knowledge worker is the relative amount of skill or knowledge used. In general, the knowledge worker, such as a manager, may plan the direction of the company and make decisions, organize the activities to achieve the company's aims, staff the organization structure with competent people, create an environment for motivation and effective communication, and control the operation by measuring performance against standards.

It is clear that, in general, the productivity of the knowledge worker is more difficult to measure than that of the skill worker (note also that worker productivity measurement is somewhat artificial because it often ignores the cost of capital). Little is known about how to measure knowledge work accurately. Peter F. Drucker admits that, "we do not know how to measure either the productivity or the satisfaction of the knowledge worker."[15] At the same time, Drucker also provides the most promising solution for measuring productivity of knowledge workers through the application of MBO. What makes it so difficult to measure the productivity of knowledge workers or managers? First, some outputs are really activities that contribute to end results. Thus, the engineer contributes indirectly to the final product. This does not mean that this effort cannot be measured. Activities can be stated so that they are verifiable and thus can be measured. We can say, for example, that the objective of the engineer is to redesign a product with certain specifications by a specific time at a stated cost and a specified quality. But, this measure is only valid when we know that the product design does indeed make the product more effective or less expensive. Often it is also difficult to link the inputs to outputs. Thus, the efforts expended and the resources used will presumably improve many different outputs over a long period of time. To allocate the inputs (say, costs) to the future outputs can, in many cases, only be estimated and making this calculation may be prohibitively expensive.

Another difficulty in measuring the productivity of knowledge workers is that they contribute to other organizational units. The advertising manager's efforts should contribute to increased sales. But it is difficult to know for sure the exact contribution. Similarly, knowledge workers often depend on the inputs from others to produce the outputs. For example, the sales manager depends on the product manufactured by another department which, in turn, depends on the product design prepared by the engineer. Still another difficulty is that the quality of the knowledge workers' outputs are usually difficult to measure. For example, the effects of a strategic decision may not be evident for several years, and even then the success or failure of the new strategic direction may depend on external factors beyond the control of the manager.

The difficulties in measuring the productivity are not insurmountable. In fact, Chapter 5 will suggest in great detail how to set measurable objectives for knowledge workers.

There is Not One Best Approach to Productivity Improvement

Productivity may be increased in many different ways.[16] The Nucor Company, which manufactures various steel products, emphasized job security (also an important aspect of Japanese management) and group incentives. But to distribute rewards in a fair manner, operational performance must be defined and measured—key aspects of typical MBO programs. Kaiser Aluminum and Chemical Corporation emphasized stating improvement objectives, a way to measure performance against these objectives, an effective reporting system, and frequent reinforcement of good performance. The Beatrice Foods Company's productivity improvement program emphasized being aware of the productivity problem, providing the tools necessary for improved performance, and giving incentives to increase productivity. Hughes Aircraft Company, with a very large portion of their employees being knowledge workers, provided principles and guidelines for productivity improvement covering many areas such as recognition of good performance, use of work modules, design of meaningful work, emphasis on goals, and development of the ability to work with people.

But the concern for productivity is not restricted to profit-oriented firms. Frederic V. Malek, who was a special assistant to the President at the White House and later became deputy director of the Office of Management and Budget, sees MBO as a common sense approach to providing new direction to government. He states: "If the executive government is to be managed effectively, it clearly needs a system for setting priorities, pinpointing responsibility for their achievement, requiring follow-through, and generating enough feedback that programs can be monitored and evaluated from the top."[17] We can see that many of these programs imply a goal-oriented approach to management such as that suggested by management by objectives, which first was used for performance appraisal but is now evolving as a system of managing.

STAGES IN THE DEVELOPMENT OF MANAGEMENT BY OBJECTIVES

Management by objectives started as a philosophy of managing, soon became a tool for performance appraisal, then a way for integrating individual and organizational objectives, and now is also a part of strategic planning in several companies. But it is suggested that MBO must become a system of managing to be truly productive.

MBO as a Philosophy of Managing

The term "management by objectives" was popularized by Peter F. Drucker, a consultant, prolific writer, and professor of management, who stated that, "Objectives are needed in every area where performance and results directly and vitally affect the survival and prosperity of the business."[18] He emphasized the importance of participative goal setting, self-control, and self-evaluation, stating that:

> . . . management by objectives and self-control may legitimately be called a philosophy of management. It rests on a concept of the job of management. It rests on an analysis of the specific needs of the management group and the obstacles it faces. It rests on a concept of human action, behavior and motivation. Finally, it applies to every manager, whatever his level and function, and to any organization whether large or small. It insures performance by converting objective needs into personal goals. And this is genuine freedom.[19]

Although Drucker saw MBO as a way of managing, it was not immediately practiced this way. Instead, selected aspects of MBO were singled out and applied to performance appraisal.

The Appraisal Approach

Douglas McGregor, a major contributor to the behavioral sciences, called attention to the shortcomings of conventional appraisal programs, which focused primarily on personality traits.[20] Managers, mistrusting the validity of the appraisal instrument, resisted because they did not like to judge other human beings like physical objects. Consequently, a new appraisal format—utilizing Drucker's MBO concepts—was suggested. In this approach the subordinates set their short-term performance goals for themselves; these goals are then discussed with their superiors. Later, the individuals' performances are evaluated against these goals, but this is done primarily by self-appraisal.

The MBO approach to appraisal was certainly a step in the right direction. However, it dealt with only a small, although important, part of the managerial job.

Integration of Organizational and Individual Objectives

In the mid-1960s, consultants and line managers became interested in the concept of self-control for involving subordinates in the decision and control process. They saw MBO as a vehicle for integrating individual and organizational objectives.[21] Moreover, the underlying premise of this approach is that top managers do not necessarily "know best," but rather, that individuals at all levels are capable of contributing to the success of the organization. Consequently, participation is a key aspect of this orientation.

Another characteristic of this approach is the concern not only for organizational objectives but also for personal development objectives. MBO recognizes that learning does not stop at the time a diploma or degree is earned. Learning is a continuing process, and developmental and growth objectives should be an important part of the MBO process. People in organizations are better educated than ever before. They do not want to accept orders blindly; they demand a part of the action; they want to be involved; they want more control over their job and their life; and they also want to know where the company is going, so that they can contribute to the aims of the organization. The needs of the organization and the individual are not necessarily incongruent; they can be integrated.

The Long-Term, Strategic View

Although the emphasis on the needs of individuals creates a favorable environment for managing, there are still some problems.

One is that the focus of many programs is still primarily on short-term objectives. This, unfortunately, often results in undesirable consequences. By focusing on the one-year cycle, individuals may neglect important decisions necessary for the long-term health of the organization. This points to the need to integrate long-range and strategic plans with medium- and short-range objectives.

The implication of the new long-term orientation has a greater impact than we may realize at first. Previously, MBO programs were primarily implemented by the personnel departments. It was not unusual to find top management saying that such a program was valuable, but only for middle and lower managers. The new orientation of relating MBO to long-range and strategic planning demands the attention and involvement of top managers. Their commitment has to go beyond the issuance of a policy statement endorsing MBO for the company. Instead, top executives must become active participants in the managerial process. MBO, then, welds together not only short-term goals with long-term aims, but it also integrates the efforts of managers at all levels of the organization.

The Systems Approach to Management by Objectives for Improving Productivity

MBO has come a long way, from a performance appraisal tool to an integrative device for individual and organizational objectives, and finally to a long-range planning instrument. This goal-oriented management approach has survived as an effective managerial approach because it has changed, grown, and developed. But the development must not stop now if it is to remain viable. Increasingly, writers and practitioners share the view that MBO, to be really effective, has to be a system of managing that integrates many key managerial activities. George S. Odiorne, widely regarded as the most vocal spokesperson for MBO today, wrote a book entitled *Management by Objectives—A System of Managerial Leadership.*[22] The subtitle recognized the systems nature of MBO. But it was not until the early 1970s that a research study investigated the implications of the integration of key managerial activities into an MBO system.[23]

Several years after this study, Hughes Aircraft Company, a research and development firm, undertook a comprehensive study on productivity, using the services of thirteen consultants.[24] Interestingly, this study identified several factors thought to contribute to productivity that are similar to the MBO study previously mentioned. Specifically, the Hughes study found that all organizations have unused potential for improvement. Second, resources are underutilized. Third, the greatest improvement in productivity can be obtained through the systems approach. Fourth, an effective way to improve productivity is to identify factors that are counterproductive. Fifth, even small improvements can have a great impact on productivity. Sixth, small increases in overall productivity can greatly impact profits. The study also suggests that productivity can be improved through effective planning (long-range, medium-range, and short-range), organizing (organization structure, span of control, clarity in responsibility and accountability), staffing (hiring practices, compensation, promotion, and management development), directing (motivation, job environment, leadership, communication), and controlling (control techniques).

In this book, we will introduce a new MBO model building on the effective concepts of earlier approaches, but adding at least three new dimensions:

1 MBO is viewed as a system of managing in which *many* key managerial activities are integrated.

2 Systems concepts are used to emphasize the interdependency of the organization with its environment.

3 Inputs, which are transformed into outputs, are considered.

So, whenever tenable, objectives are stated in terms of inputs (resources) used and outputs (results) produced. This makes productivity measurement possible.

**The Systems Approach to
Management by Objectives Defined**

Management by objectives has been defined in different ways. One of the most frequently quoted definitions is by George S. Odiorne, who describes MBO as follows:

> . . . a process whereby the superior and subordinate managers of an organization jointly identify its common goals, define each individual's major areas of responsibility in terms of the results expected of him (her), and use these measures as guides for operating the unit and assessing the contribution of each of its members.[25]

John W. Humble, a consultant in England and author of several MBO books, defines management by objectives as "a dynamic system which seeks to integrate the company's need to clarify and achieve its profit and growth goals with the manager's need to contribute and develop himself (herself)."[26] Since MBO is also used to make nonprofit organizations more productive, one probably should change the word "profit" to "surplus" since it is the aim of all managers (whether they work in business, government, or not-for-profit organizations) to create surplus value in which the value of all outputs is greater than the values of all inputs.[27]

In this book we define management by objectives as:

> . . . a comprehensive managerial system that integrates many key managerial activities in a systematic manner consciously directed toward the effective and efficient (that is, being productive) achievement of organizational and individual objectives.

To be complete yet not too cumbersome, a definition has to be abstract. Therefore, we need to elaborate on our definition. Specifically, then, the comprehensive approach to management by objectives includes:

- Forecasting the external and internal environment of the enterprise.
- Developing a hierarchy and a network of aims ranging from the determination of the purpose and the mission of the enterprise to setting of objectives throughout the organization, down to the lowest level.
- Preparing a strategic plan that becomes the basis for intermediate- and short-term plans.
- Emphasizing setting of verifiable objectives.
- Developing action plans to achieve the objectives, coordinating of tasks, clarifying the organization structure, authority, responsibilities, and roles for individual positions.
- Creating a flexible and dynamic organization that can respond to changes in the environment.
- Integrating MBO with a human resource system that provides for determining the workforce requirements, selecting, appraising, compensating, and developing managers.
- Establishing an environment of open communication, conducive to effective leadership, motivation, and commitment to agreed-upon results.
- Measuring performance against verifiable objectives.
- Combining MBO with organizational development (OD), devel-

oping a philosophy of management that taps the potential of individuals by encouraging self-direction and self-control.

Perhaps only a few programs may have integrated all these aspects into a system. But whatever the degree of sophistication of the program, it is important to remember that to be effective, all organizational units, all managers, all nonmanagers, even all managerial tools and techniques should contribute toward the common goal of the organization.

The modern MBO approach views the organization in its totality and the relationship of its parts to the whole. It is like the story of the blind men who were asked to describe an elephant. The one who touched the leg of the elephant described the animal as a trunk of a tree. Another one, touching the body, viewed the elephant as a large, soft wall. But neither understood the whole. Unfortunately, in the past the focus on MBO was too often on selected aspects of the managerial process. MBO is more than an appraisal tool; it is more than a budgeting system; it is also more than a way of integrating individual and organizational objectives. Instead, MBO must become a system of managing that integrates the organization with its environment and the various key managerial activities, so that the whole is more than simply the sum of its parts.

A word of caution must be added to avoid misunderstandings. The systems approach to MBO does not advocate a complex program with unnecessary, overwhelming paperwork. This would be the fastest way to elicit resistance to the program. Instead, the systems approach requires that the various systems are integrated (if necessary, even informally) into a whole with a minimum of incongruencies. The systems approach, then, is not a gimmick, but a managerial style; and, above all, a way of managing.

A MODEL FOR THE SYSTEMS APPROACH TO MANAGEMENT BY OBJECTIVES AND THE ORGANIZATION OF THIS BOOK

The model shown in Figure 1-2 is an overview of the systems approach to management by objectives. It identifies the important parts and their relationships in the system. The model is also the framework for organizing knowledge in this book. Therefore, the numbers in the model indicate the chapters in this book in which the topics are discussed in greater detail.

Managers have to be aware that an enterprise does not exist in a vacuum. Rather, it is mutually dependent on its external environ-

18

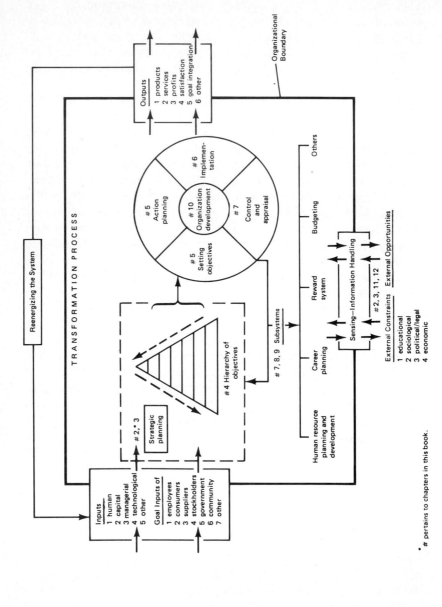

Inputs
1 human
2 capital
3 managerial
4 technological
5 other

Goal inputs of
1 employees
2 consumers
3 suppliers
4 stockholders
5 government
6 community
7 other

#2,* 3

Strategic
planning

#4 Hierarchy of
objectives

7, 8, 9 Subsystems

Human resource
planning and
development

Career
planning

Reward
system

Budgeting

Others

Sensing—Information Handling

External Constraints
1 educational
2 sociological
3 political/legal
4 economic

#2, 3, 11, 12   External Opportunities

TRANSFORMATION PROCESS

#5
Setting
objectives

#5
Action
planning

#10
Organization
development

#6
Implemen-
tation

#7
Control
and
appraisal

Reenergizing the System

Outputs
1 products
2 services
3 profits
4 satisfaction
5 goal integration
6 other

Organizational
Boundary

* # pertains to chapters in this book.

ment. The enterprise receives inputs from the external environment, transforms them, and exports the outputs to the environment. First, we discuss the interaction between the enterprise and its environment with emphasis on organizational inputs. Second, we focus on the transformation process. Third, we indicate that the communication system links the organization with its external environment. Fourth, we identify and specify the outputs. Finally, we close the discussion by showing how to reenergize the managerial system.

Inputs

The inputs from the external environment—as shown in Figure 1-2—include people, capital, and managerial skills, as well as technical knowledge and skills. In addition, various groups of people make demands on the enterprise. Unfortunately, many of the goals of these claimants are incongruent with each other and it is the manager's job to integrate these divergent needs and goals.

Employees, for example, want higher pay, more benefits, and job security. *Consumers,* on the other hand, demand safe and reliable products at a reasonable price. *Suppliers* want assurance that their products are bought. *Stockholders* want not only a high return on their investment but also security of their money. Federal, state, and local *governments* depend on taxes paid by the enterprise, but they also expect the enterprise to comply with their laws. Similarly, the *community* demands that enterprises not only be "good citizens," providing the maximum number of jobs with a minimum of pollution, but that they also take an active part in community affairs by participating in social activities, making donations, and helping to beautify the environment. *Other claimants* to the enterprise may include financial institutions and labor unions; even competitors have a legitimate claim for fair play. It is clear that many of these claims are incongruent with each other and it is management's job to integrate the legitimate objectives of the claimants, while at the same time improve organizational productivity.

FIGURE 1-2
Systems approach to management by objectives. [The model and its discussion have been adapted from H. Weihrich, "A New Approach to MBO: Updating a Time-Honored Technique," *Management World* (April 1977), pp. 7–12. Used with permission from the Administrative Management Society, Willow Grove, PA 19090. Copyright © 1977 AMS.]

The Transformation Process

Management by objectives is a process that involves the transformation of inputs in an effective and efficient manner to produce outputs. Although the steps may vary somewhat for the individual company, the following provides a logical framework for the transformation process.

1 *Improving productivity through strategic planning and the hierarchy of objectives.* Strategic planning and the hierarchy of objectives are closely interwoven and are consequently discussed together here, but separately in the chapters that follow.

Strategic planning is concerned with overall concepts of the operation. It involves determining major objectives of the company as well as the acquisition and disposition of the resources necessary to achieve the objectives. In strategic planning, external opportunities and constraints are analyzed and matched with the internal strengths and limitations of the organization. This part of the strategic planning process is discussed in Chapters 2 and 3. The situational analysis is the basis for determining the *hierarchy of aims,* especially the strategic objectives. In discussing megatrends, John Naisbitt states that the question for the 1980s is: "What business are you really in?"[28] The answer to this question helps to identify the fundamental purpose, the mission, and the general overall objectives as well as the more specific objectives which, of course, are normally determined by top management, with inputs from lower-level managers. These objectives are then further broken down into divisional, departmental, unit, and individual objectives. The process of setting objectives, however, is not one way; communication and planning efforts must go in *both* directions (down and up), as indicated by the arrows in the hierarchy of aims shown in Figure 1-2. The hierarchy and network of aims will be discussed in Chapter 4.

2 *Setting objectives helps measurement of productivity.* Objectives should generally be set jointly by the superior and subordinate. The emphasis is on verifiable objectives; that is, at the end of a specified period one knows whether an objective has been achieved. An objective such as "To produce 500 units per month at the current quality level without additional costs" can be verified. But the objective "to improve communication" is open to different interpretations and can hardly be verified.

Objectives should be measurable (later we will see that this is not always possible), contribute to objectives of the next higher organizational unit, focus on results rather than on activities, indicate performance and personal development, be challenging, yet reasonable, and emphasize results, but not to the neglect of other important aspects of a job that cannot be quantified. You can see that it is not easy to set objectives that meet all of these criteria. Yet, the effort of setting objectives with these criteria is necessary to measure productivity. How this can be done is discussed in Chapter 5.

3 *Planning action for individual and organizational productivity.* Action planning determines *what* functions, tasks, and activities must be carried out to accomplish the objectives; *how* to achieve the objectives most effectively and efficiently; *when* the tasks and activities must be done; and *who* will do them.

Action planning is therefore concerned with identifying and grouping activities; coordinating—vertically and horizontally—the efforts of groups and individuals; defining roles, authority, and responsibilities for each individual; scheduling the activities; and determining the need for human, financial, and other resources required to achieve the objectives. Critical and interdependent objectives frequently demand fairly elaborate plans, as will be pointed out in Chapter 5.

X **4** *Implementing plans and programs.* Objectives and action plans give direction for organizational efforts. Both, however, must be implemented. To be effective, a number of conditions must be met. First, top managers must not simply give lip service to MBO; they must be personally involved in the process. Second, the organizational climate must be congruent with the MBO philosophy that emphasizes self-control. Third, objectives do not exist in isolation; they are interrelated and form a network. Therefore, coordination and a team approach must be used where appropriate. Fourth, objectives are based on premises that may change. A premise is an assumption, such as that the gross national product may increase by 4 percent this year. We know, however, that forecasts are often incorrect. Therefore, alternate plans must be prepared that are based on different assumptions. Objectives must also be reviewed from time to time and may have to be adapted to unforeseen changes in the environment. Fifth, managers must be taught the concepts and philosophy of MBO and how the program works. Sixth, in most organizations, the implementation of the program requires changes in the organization as well as changes in managing. Success in the implementation does not happen by chance; it must be planned. How this can be done will be shown in Chapter 6.

✗ **5** *Measuring productivity through control and appraisal.* Control refers to the measurement of organizational performance, whereas appraisal emphasizes the evaluation of individual performance.

Control, simply stated, involves the measurement and, if necessary, the correction of performance. Verifiable objectives set in the planning process become the standards against which performance and productivity are measured. Based on the analysis of performance, positive steps can be taken to correct deviations from standards and to prevent them from occuring in the future.

Performance appraisal has several important characteristics. First, the focus is on performance and productivity, not on personality. Second, the emphasis is on self-control rather than autocratic control by the boss. Third, responsibility for evaluation and development should be shared by both the subordinate and the superior. Of course, the superior still retains the veto power in setting performance criteria and in measuring performance. But in the proper environment, this power may not have to be exercised. Fourth, appraisal is viewed as an opportunity to learn from the past, and to focus on the future, rather than being a judgment. This means that during the appraisal meeting, a great amount of time should be spent to find ways to improve productivity in the future and to set new objectives. Fifth, the emphasis is shifted from judging a subordinate by the superior to a shared, rational analysis of performance. In short, MBO appraisal is not a fault-finding session that both the superior and subordinate dislike; instead, the meeting is positive, constructive, and oriented toward the future. Both control of organizational performance and appraisal of individual contribution will be discussed in Chapter 7.

6 *Subsystems.* Several managerial subsystems can be integrated with the MBO process for greater productivity, depending on the specific needs of the organization. They may include human resource planning, management development, and career planning. Sometimes even other subsystems such as compensation, budgeting, and safety programs may be included in the process. Let us look more closely at some of these subsystems.

Human resource planning and management development should be an integral part of the total management system. Specifically, the strategic and operational plans should be the basis for determining the number and qualifications of managers required. These requirements are then compared with the people available. Before IBM moved into the personal computer field, it had to assess the number and qualifications of its employees. Based on this analysis, people are recruited, selected, promoted, and developed. Human resource management will be discussed in Chapter 8.

The training and development plan of the organization is then linked with *career planning* of individuals. Individual aspirations and abilities are matched with the needs of the organization as identified through the human resource plan. Specifically, organizational requirements are translated into personal and professional development objectives and action plans. Such an objective may be stated as follows: "To obtain the master of business administration degree from an accredited local university within two years, graduating with a grade point average of 3.5 (on a 4.0 scale)." The detailed aspects of career planning and how to improve individual productivity will be discussed in Chapter 9.

The *compensation* program, another MBO subsystem, is often linked to the appraisal against verifiable objectives. Although there should be a basic congruency between the performance and compensation levels, there are some questions about how directly MBO should be linked to compensation. It requires great skill to develop a compensation system that is perceived as being fair and that does not result in unintended managerial decisions in which self-interest may interfere with the welfare of the organization.

Budgeting, that is, expressing plans in numerical terms, is another subsystem that can be integrated with MBO. Jim Hayes, the past president of the American Management Association, stated that "the budget is the price of the plans." Zero-base budgeting is especially pertinent to the measurement of productivity because the programs are expressed as packages that show the goals, activities, and resources needed. Specifically, the requested resources (inputs) must be justified, rather than adhering to the widespread practice of simply increasing last year's expenditures by a certain percentage.

7 *Removing obstacles to productivity through organization development.* Organization development (OD) is concerned with the total organization, or a major part of it, and involves systematic, planned, long-range efforts to make the organization more productive by improving human and social processes within the organizational culture. Some of the specific approaches of OD include problem solving, work team development, collaboration, and organizational renewal. But there are many other ways of making organizations more productive. Organization development is the dynamic aspect that makes MBO effective and will be discussed in Chapter 10.

Communication System and External Factors

Communication pervades the total managerial process; it integrates the managerial functions, and it links the enterprise with its environment. For example, the objectives set in planning are communicated so that an appropriate organization structure can be devised. To fill the organizational roles, communication is essential in the selection, appraisal, and training of managers. Similarly, effective leadership and the creation of an environment conducive to motivation depends on communication. Moreover, it is through communication that one determines whether events and performance conform to plans. Thus, it is communication that makes managing possible.

The second function of the communication system is to link the enterprise with its external environment, which is where many of the claimants are. One should never forget that the customers, who are the reason for the firm's existence, are outside the company. It is through the communication system that the needs of consumers are identified. These needs then become opportunities for the firm by providing products and services at a profit, as exemplified by IBM when it identified the opportunities for marketing personal computers.

Effective managers will constantly scan the external environment. While it is true that managers may have little or no effect in changing many of these forces, they have no alternative but to respond to them. In the *educational* and *economic environments,* for example, managers must be cognizant of the availability of capital, labor, and entrepreneurial talent, all important inputs to the organization. They are also concerned about price levels, fiscal and tax policies of the government, and, of course, the economic and personal desires and needs of customers. Similarly, *technological* developments affect productivity and the way the managerial functions are carried out. Increasingly, computer technology is used in planning and controlling, which requires an understanding of what computers can and cannot do in making the operations of the firm more effective through communication.

There are also other forces in the external environment: social, political, and ethical considerations. *Social* attitudes, beliefs, and values certainly have an effect on the social interaction within the firm. When people come to work, they bring with them influences from other social systems such as schools, families, and church groups. Similarly, the *political* environment creates a massive web of laws and regulations within which the manager has to operate. Finally, *ethics,* which are sets of generally accepted and practiced standards of personal conduct, influence the various key managerial activities such as leadership, the determination of objectives, and the plans to achieve them. In all, managers have to respond to, and at times even influence, the external variables in a socially responsive manner. Clearly, an enterprise that hopes for a long-term survival must be an open system through active communication and interaction with its environment.

Outputs

It is the task of managers to secure and utilize inputs to the enterprise and transform them through managerial and other processes to produce outputs.

Although the kinds of outputs will vary with a specific enterprise, they usually include several of the following: products, services, profits, satisfaction, and goal integration of claimants to the enterprise. Most of them require no elaboration, and only the last two will be discussed, because they are often overlooked. The organization must indeed provide many kinds of satisfaction if it hopes to retain and elicit contributions from its members. This pertains not only to the satisfaction of lower-order needs (for example, employees earning money to buy food and shelter; having job security), but it also includes needs for affiliation, acceptance, esteem, and perhaps even self-actualization. Most volunteer workers would not contribute to the enterprise were it not for the satisfaction of fulfilling some of their higher-order needs.

Another output in the model (Figure 1-2) is goal integration. As noted above, the different claimants to the enterprise have very divergent—and often directly opposing—objectives. It is the task of managers to resolve conflicts and integrate these aims. This is not easy, as one of the earlier executives of Volkswagen discovered. In his case, economics dictated the construction of an assembly plant in the United States. This plan, however, was opposed by labor, an important claimant, because of fear of the elimination of some jobs. The conflict was so deep that it contributed to the executive's resignation and a change in leadership. Clearly, harmony among claimants is essential for organizational productivity.

Reenergizing the System

The final aspect of the management model (Figure 1-2) is that some of the outputs become inputs again. Thus, the satisfaction of employees becomes an important human input. Similarly, profits, which are the surplus of income over costs, are reinvested in capital goods such as machinery and equipment, buildings, inventories of goods, tools, and cash.

This chapter provided an overview of the book by introducing the model of the systems approach to MBO. A model, by its very nature, is abstract because it focuses only on the key aspects of a complex process and their relationships. The following chapters will deal with these aspects in a more practical way. In the last two chapters we discuss the future of MBO, which may evolve into a comprehensive goal-oriented managerial system that includes a systematic integration of many key managerial activities, rather than just a selected few. In addition, a key for productive organization is the effective management of people. Japanese management is often seen as a way to solve the productivity crisis. We will carefully assess which aspects of the Japanese approach may be successfully employed by managers in the United States.

NOTES

1 J. J. Servan-Schreiber, *The American Challenge* (New York: Avon Books, 1969). More recently, the author views the aggressive Asian unions, moving into the computer age through their microchip technology, as being a major challenge to developed nations. See "Servan-Schreiber's New Challenge," *Wall Street Journal,* Dec. 26, 1980 and D. A. Heenan, *The Re-United States of America* (Reading, Mass.: Addison-Wesley, 1983).

2 See, for example, V. M. Buehler and Y. K. Shetty, eds., *Productivity Improvement—Case Studies of Proven Practice* (New York: AMACOM, 1981), reporting on the experiences of companies in improving their productivity. Also see I. C. Magaziner and R. B. Reich, *Minding America's Business* (New York: Harcourt Brace Jovanovich, 1982); B. J. Reilly and J. P. Fuhr, Jr., "Productivity: An Economic and Management Analysis with a Direction Towards a New Synthesis," *Academy of Management Review,* vol. 8, no. 1 (January 1983), pp. 108–117; and *The Productivity Problem: Alternatives for Action,* Congress of the United States, Congressional Budget Office, a CBO Study, January 1981. The Soviets have passed the first "labor reform" law since World War II, which gives the proletariat the opportunity to participate in running the production with the aim of improving productivity; see "Moscow Tries to Light a Fire Under Its Workers," *Business Week,* Aug. 1, 1983.

3 For a discussion of the possible causes of the productivity problem, see

"Many Culprits Named in National Slowdown of Productivity Gains," *Wall Street Journal,* Oct. 21, 1980; *The Collegiate Forum,* Fall 1980; "Study Disputes View that Growth of Service Jobs Crimps Productivity," *Wall Street Journal,* June 19, 1981; Ron Aemke, "HDR's Crucial Role in Productivity Improvement," *Training,* January 1979.

4 J. Naisbitt, *Megatrends* (New York: Warner Communications Company, 1982) chap. 4.

5 W. A. Ruch, "Measuring Knowledge Worker Productivity," *Conference on Productivity Research,* American Productivity Center, April 1980. See also W. A. Ruch, "The Measurement of White-Collar Productivity," *National Productivity Review,* Autumn 1982, pp. 410–420.

6 W. G. Ouchi, *Theory Z—How American Business Can Meet the Japanese Challenge* (Reading, Mass.: Addison-Wesley, 1981), p. 5.

7 K. Blanchard and S. Johnson, *The One Minute Manager* (New York: Berkley Books, 1982).

8 T. J. Peters and R. H. Waterman, Jr., *In Search of Excellence* (New York: Harper & Row, 1982).

9 R. T. Pascale and A. G. Athos, *The Art of Japanese Management* (New York: Simon & Schuster, 1981).

10 Aspects of organizing have been discussed in great detail in H. Koontz, C. O'Donnell, and H. Weihrich, *Management,* 8th ed. (New York: McGraw-Hill, 1984). Chaps. 11 to 16.

11 P. F. Drucker, *Management: Tasks, Responsibilities, Practices* (New York: Harper & Row, 1973), p. 69.

12 R. A. Sutermeister, *People and Productivity,* 3d ed. (New York: McGraw-Hill, 1976), p. 5.

13 E. E. Adam, Jr., J. C. Hershauer, and W. A. Ruch, *Measuring the Quality Dimension of Service Productivity* (Tempe, Ariz.: College of Business Administration, Arizona State University, and sponsored by the National Science Foundation, 1978).

14 *R & D Productivity, Study Report,* 2d ed. (Culver City, Calif.: Hughes Aircraft Company, 1978).

15 P. F. Drucker, "Managing the Knowledge Worker," *Wall Street Journal,* Nov. 7, 1975.

16 Buehler and Shetty, op. cit.

17 F. V. Malek, *Washington's Hidden Tragedy* (New York: The Free Press, 1978), p. 148. The concern of government for productivity is also shown by the enacted Public Law 97-367, Oct. 25, 1982 which establishes a White House conference on productivity.

18 Drucker, *Management.* Actually, Drucker was influenced by Harold Smiddy who put MBO into practice at the General Electric Company. Drucker even suggested that Smiddy was the godfather of the classic book *The Practice of Management,* in which Drucker popularized the MBO concepts. For a detailed history of the origins of management by objectives see Ronald G. Greenwood, "Management by Objectives: As

Developed by Peter Drucker, Assisted by Harold Smiddy," *The Academy of Management Review,* vol. 6, no. 2 (April 1981), pp. 225–241. Also, in a personal discussion with the author, Drucker stated that he did not specifically see strategic planning as a part of MBO, although he advocated MBO as a way of managing.

19 Drucker, *Management,* p. 442.

20 D. McGregor, "An Uneasy Look at Performance Appraisal," *Harvard Business Review,* vol. 35, no. 3 (May–June, 1957), pp. 89–94.

21 R. A. Howell, "Managing by Objectives—A Three Stage System," *Business Horizons,* vol. 13, no. 1 (February 1970), pp. 41–45.

22 G. S. Odiorne, *Management by Objectives—A System of Managerial Leadership* (New York: Pitman, 1965).

23 H. Weihrich, "A Study of the Integration of Management by Objectives with Key Managerial Activities and the Relationship to Selected Effectiveness Measures," Ph.D. dissertation, University of California, Los Angeles, 1973.

24 R & D Productivity, op. cit.

25 Odiorne, op. cit., pp. 55–56.

26 J. W. Humble, *Improving Management Performance* (London: Management Publications Ltd., 1965, 1970). This book describes an integrated approach to management development and planning to increase profitability. It was first published in 1965 when the approach was described as "improving management performance," but in the revised edition (1969) the term "management by objectives" (MBO) was used.

27 Koontz et al., op. cit., p. 5.

28 Naisbitt, op. cit.

CHAPTER 2

MAKING STRATEGIC PLANNING THE BASIS FOR LONG-TERM PRODUCTIVITY*

The previous chapter introduced the systems approach to management by objectives. An important part of the comprehensive MBO model used in this book is strategic planning. This and the next chapter deal in greater detail with this important managerial activity. Specifically, in this chapter the concept of strategy and a model showing the strategic planning process are introduced. In the next chapter, a conceptual framework is suggested for an analysis of the situation, that is, the threats and opportunities in the external environment and the organization's weaknesses and strengths. Chapter 4, which deals with the hierarchy of aims, is also to some extent a part of strategy formulation, especially as it relates to determining the organization's purpose and mission.

STRATEGIC PLANNING AND PRODUCTIVITY

Productivity usually implies measurement. Yet, as you will see in this chapter, strategic planning does not lend itself very well to quantifica-

*This and the next chapter have been adapted from H. Weihrich, "The TOWS Matrix—A Tool for Situational Analysis," *Long Range Planning,* vol. 15, no. 2 (1982), pp. 54–66. Used with permission from Pergamon Press Ltd.

tion. It does not follow, however, that strategic planning does not contribute to productivity. In fact, strategy formulation and especially implementation may be the most neglected factors in the managerial process. Some criteria for evaluating the effectiveness of a strategy may be that it provides clarity, an internal consistency of aims, integration of the internal strengths and weaknesses with the external opportunities and threats, appropriate direction in light of the available resources, assessment of the acceptable degree of risk, compatibility of objectives with the values of top managers, an appropriate time frame, clear objectives, concentration on the critical factors for success, flexibility to cope with changes in the environment and the competition, securing of important resources (such as raw material), and the communication of broad plans.[1] Clearly, these characteristics cannot be measured by simple input-output analysis, and the contribution of strategic planning to increased productivity can only be inferred. It is not the measurement that makes organizations productive, but rather the actions managers and nonmanagers undertake to achieve the organizational purpose effectively and efficiently. It is for this reason that strategic planning is included in this book on productivity.

Increasingly, business enterprises engage in strategic planning, although the degrees of sophistication and formality vary considerably. Conceptually strategic planning is deceptively simple: Analyze the current and expected future situation, determine the direction of the firm, and develop the means for achieving the mission. In reality, this is an extremely complex process that demands a systematic approach for identifying and analyzing factors external to the organization and matching them with the firm's capabilities.

STRATEGIC PLANNING

The term "strategy" (which is derived from the Greek word "strategos," meaning "general") has been used in different ways. Authors differ in at least one major aspect. Some focus on both the end points (purpose, mission, goals, objectives) and the means of achieving them (policies and plans). But other writers emphasize the means to the ends in the strategic process rather than the ends *per se*. The great variety of meanings of the word "strategies" is illustrated in the glossary of one book:

> [Strategies are] general programs of action and deployment of emphasis and resources to attain comprehensive objectives; the program of objectives of an organization and their changes, resources used to attain

these objectives, and policies governing the acquisition, use, and disposition of these resources; the determination of the basic long-term objectives of an enterprise and the adoption of courses of action and allocation of resources necessary to achieve these goals.[2]

This chapter does not emphasize the ends because the purpose and the mission of the organization are discussed in detail in Chapter 4. You will recall that the MBO model, Figure 1-1, shows arrows going in both directions between strategic planning and the hierarchy of aims, indicating that they are closely interwoven. On the one hand, the mission and purpose have to be clarified before the means to achieve them can be determined. On the other hand, one must first recognize the various organizational inputs (such as stockholders' expectations), assess the strengths and weaknesses of the organization, and match them with opportunities and threats in the external environment before the mission can be finalized. At any rate, this situational analysis must be directed toward the purpose and the overall aims of the enterprise.

Although specific steps in the formulation of the strategy may vary, the process can be built, at least conceptually, around the following framework:

1 Recognition of the various organizational inputs, especially the goal inputs of the claimants to the enterprise
2 Preparation of the enterprise profile
3 Identification of the present external environment
4 Preparation of a forecast with predictions of the future environment
5 Preparation of a resource audit with emphasis on the company's internal weaknesses and strengths
6 Development of alternative strategies, tactics, and other actions
7 Evaluation and choice of strategies
8 Consistency testing
9 Preparation of contingency plans

These steps (shown in Figure 2-1) serve as the framework for the discussion that follows.

Inputs for Strategic Planning

Strategic planning, to be effective, must carefully consider the inputs into the system. These inputs, deemphasized in this discussion, are enclosed by broken lines, as shown in Figure 2-1. They include people, capital, managerial and technical skills. In addition, various

32

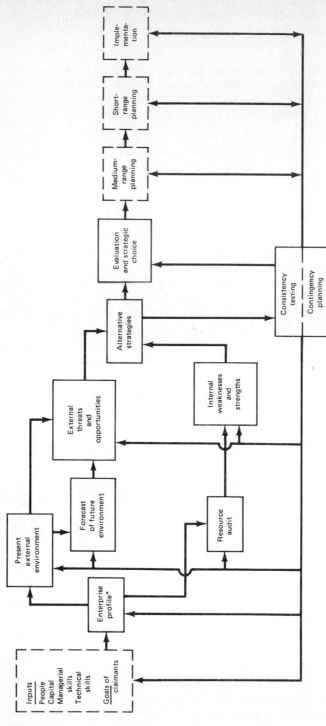

*The enterprise profile should be developed in conjunction with the mission statement (or organizational purpose) discussed in chap. 4.

FIGURE 2-1
Strategic planning process.

groups of people make demands on the enterprise. Unfortunately, many goals of these claimants are incongruent with each other and it is the manager's task to integrate these divergent needs and goals as was discussed in the previous chapter.

The Enterprise Profile

The way an enterprise has operated in the past is usually a starting point to determine where it will go and where it should go. In other words, top executives wrestle with such fundamental questions as:

"What is our business?"
"Who are our customers?"
"What do our customers want?"
"What should our business be?"

These and similar questions should provide answers about the basic nature of the company, its products and services, geographic domain, its competitive position, and its top management orientation and values. These topics demand elaboration.

Geographic Orientation A company must also answer questions such as:

"Where are our customers?"
"Where are those who should be our customers, but are not at present?"

Companies need to develop a profile of their geographic market. While some firms may restrict themselves to the eastern part of the United States, others view the whole country as their region of operations. Many large companies, of course, conduct their business on different continents.

Competitive Situation Business firms usually do not have an exclusive market; instead, they compete with other firms. At times, an enterprise even has to take steps to prevent competitors from gaining a large market share, as illustrated by International Business Machines (IBM), which made efforts to gain rather early a strong position in the main frame computer market in Japan. This, in turn, restricted the cash generation of Japanese competitors, which would have enabled them to get a strong foothold in the United States. Current market share, often an important factor, is not necessarily a sufficient indicator of a firm's long-range potential. One must also consider other factors and competitive items such as price, quality, cost, service, product innovation, distribution systems, facilities, and locations.

The assessment of the competitive situation involves several steps. First, key success factors must be identified. Then the relative importance of these factors needs to be estimated. Next, the firm's competitive position in respect to these key success factors must be evaluated and ranked. Thus, a careful analysis of the current competitive position provides an indication of the company's future growth and profits.

The competitive analysis, especially for large firms, is done for individual business units, product lines, or even specific products. Moreover, the competitive analysis focuses not only on the present situation, but also looks into the more distant future.[3] Strategies may be designed to prevent potentially threatening moves of competitors, as illustrated by General Electric (GE), a company that foresaw competition from AEG, a similar firm in Germany. Thus, General Electric arranged for licensing agreements that, in turn, prevented competition of AEG in the large United States market.[4] The situation analysis becomes intricate for firms that compete in national and international markets.

Top Management Orientation   An enterprise profile is shaped by people, especially executives. They set the organizational climate, they influence the atmosphere in the organization, and they determine the direction of the company. For example, management may not pursue opportunities in the casino business because of a conflict with top management's values, which may be against gambling. Another example of the influence of values may be management's commitment to socially responsible actions, believing that these activities will benefit the enterprise in the long run.

An understanding of the past and the present postures of the enterprise and its policy, as well as the values of managers, are important factors in the development of the enterprise profile. The next step in the strategic planning process is the analysis of threats, opportunities, weaknesses, and strengths.

The External Environment: Threats and Opportunities

In the analysis of the external environment, many diverse factors need to be considered. The threats certainly may include the problems of inflation, energy, technological change, and government actions. The diverse factors—which can be either threats or opportunities—can be grouped into the following categories: economic, social, and political factors; products and technology; demographic factors; markets and competition; plus others.

Economic Factors   The general state of the economy certainly affects strategy formulation. For example, the expansion phase of the business cycle in the 1960s created an abundance of business opportunities while the recession in the first half of the 1970s required many industries to change their strategy and drastically reduce their business activities. Inflation, another critical economic factor, may result in consumer price-consciousness. In the early 1970s the major catalogue retailers committed themselves not to raise their printed prices for a certain time. With rapid inflation in the retail business, this resulted in brisk sales for catalogue companies such as J.C. Penney Co., Sears Roebuck, and Montgomery Ward. Eventually, however, this commitment could also cause a cost-price squeeze for these companies. The strategist, of course, takes other economic factors besides inflation and the business cycle into account, such as the level of employment, the availability of credit, and the level of prices. Also, individual companies are affected differently by economic factors. What is a threat to one firm is an opportunity for another.

Social and Political Factors   Social developments also influence business strategy. For instance, consumerism and consumer protection movements require the firm's attention to product safety and truth in packaging. Similarly, managers are confronted by a host of federal, state, and local laws and regulations. As an example, consider container firms such as American Can Company and the Continental Group, which are faced with great uncertainties caused by state and local antican and antibottle legislation. Oregon and Vermont had such laws for some time, and later similar laws in Maine and Michigan required a deposit for many beverage containers. Chances are that other states may place similar restrictions on the sale of cans. The public's demand for clean air, clean water, and a clean environment is also often considered a threat to business. At the same time, these factors can become opportunities, as shown by the car emission test requirements in many states that presented opportunities for companies to develop, produce, or operate such test equipment.

Products and Technology   Products need to be adjusted to technological changes. For example, the astonishing success of the Volkswagen Beetle in the 1960s diminished in the 1970s. New customer demands for optional equipment, safety requirements, and competition, along with new technology, gave rise to a new generation of VWs. It must be remembered that in almost all situations success is only temporary and product innovation is needed to ensure a competitive advantage for the firm. Of course, innovation is also costly and risky and the failure rate of new products is high; yet a policy of no innovation at all may not be good and cause the demise of a company.

Demographic Factors   Demographic changes significantly affect business. In the United States there are geographic shifts such as the movement of many people to the sun belt. An interesting case is Marshall Field. The company, which was well established in Chicago, faced strong competition from stores such as Saks Fifth Avenue, Neiman-Marcus, and I. Magnin. At the same time, Chicago also had a declining population. Rather than diversifying into different businesses, Marshall Field now expands into areas with population growth, planning to add four more stores in Texas to the already opened store in Houston. Angelo R. Arena, the chief executive officer, describes the strategy as follows: "Our premise has been to lessen our concentration in the Midwest and expand into areas where there will be more growth. We could have looked at some nonretail areas, but I felt that first and foremost we were retailers, and that our strategy would be better served expanding in something we already knew."[5]

Besides population changes, white-collar jobs tend to increase proportionally to blue-collar occupations. Income levels are expected to change, although the direction is less clear and may vary for different sectors of the labor market. The age composition will also change with elderly people making up an increasing proportion of the population. The strategist must take these and other factors into account because they influence the preferences for the kinds of products and services demanded by consumers.

Markets and Competition   In the United States, coping with competition in the marketplace is a corporate way of life. The following questions and the answers to them are crucial for formulating a strategy:

"Who are our competitors?"
"How does our company compare with the competition?"
"What are the strengths and weaknesses of our competitors?"
"What are their strategies?"
"How do we best compete?"

Strategic moves by big and successful competitors can even have a great impact on large companies. In the 1970s companies such as General Electric and RCA found that the high cost of developing new computers made it difficult to compete against IBM and, consequently, they sold their computer businesses to Honeywell and Sperry Univac, respectively. In the personal computer field, Apple Computer certainly is a success story. Yet, the entrance of large companies such as IBM, Xerox, and Japanese firms will make it very difficult for Apple to continue its phenomenal success in the microcomputer market.

Other Factors There are, of course, many other factors that might be particularly important to a specific firm. The availability of raw materials, suppliers, and the transportation system are a few examples. The everchanging environment demands continuous scanning for opportunities and threats. A company that discovers customer needs and provides the products and services demanded certainly has a better chance for success than an enterprise that ignores such changes.

Information Gathering and Future Forecasting To collect data on the various factors is, to say the least, a tedious task. A study of 1,211 executives, all readers of the *Harvard Business Review,* gives some insights on how companies collect information about their competitors. The sources used most frequently include company sales persons, published information, and personal and professional contacts with competitors and customers. Less frequently used sources include formal market research, brokers, wholesalers and other intermediaries, analyses of processes and products of competitors, and suppliers. The least utilized sources include employees of competitors, advertising agencies, and consultants.[6]

Since there are many factors that need to be analyzed, the executives must be selective and concentrate on those factors that are critical for the success of the enterprise. Furthermore, it is not enough for the strategist to assess only the present environment. Planning for the future, and strategic planning in particular, is very much concerned with the more distant future. Thus managers must anticipate the future and forecast changes in the environment that will crucially affect the enterprise.

The Internal Environment: Weaknesses and Strengths

The demands of the external environment on the organization must be matched with the resources of the firm. Internal strengths and weaknesses vary greatly for different enterprises; they may, however, conveniently be categorized into:

1 Management and organization structure and climate
2 Operations
3 Finance
4 Other factors important for a particular organization

Management and Organization   This category includes not only managerial talent but also the labor force as a whole. It also encompasses labor relations; personnel policies; the appraisal, selection, training, and development of employees; and the reward system. The planning and control system as well as the organization structure and climate are equally important for the success of the organization.

The managerial style is an important determinant for the corporate strategy. When William Spoor brought the new goal-oriented management style to Pillsbury, he had to proceed gradually to give the experienced managers time for adjusting to the new approach. Also, the new organization had to be adapted to the capabilities of people.[7] IBM's success may be due in part to the organization structure. In order to be responsive to the market, IBM changed in the 1970s from a functional to a product orientation. A more recent example of restructuring the organization as a part of the strategy is Xerox Corporation, the giant in the copier market, which now faces major competition from Japanese firms. To cope with the competition and to implement the strategy of providing the office of the future, Xerox has undertaken a major restructuring with greater decentralization in order to be more responsive to the needs of customers.

Operations   Operations must be carefully analyzed in terms of research and development capabilities and the adequacy and productivity of the manufacturing facilities available to meet the expected growth and other objectives of the firm. Similarly, marketing must be assessed in terms of product distribution channels, brand name protection, competitive pricing, appropriate customer identification, service, and company image. Consider Texas Instruments, which in the middle of the 1970s used the strategy of high-volume production to obtain a leadership position in the market. Thus, the company's goal was to produce a $20 digital watch, a price so low that the competitors, such as Fairchild Cameras, Hughes Aircraft Company, and National Semiconductor, were caught unaware. But the high-volume production also required changes in marketing and distribution channels.

Finance   A careful evaluation of the company's strengths and weaknesses also must be made in the areas of capital structure, financing, profitability, taxes, financial planning, and the accounting system. Many financial ratios are available for making analyses. But financial management not only requires focusing on the past and the present situation, it also demands short- and long-term financial planning congruent with the firm's objectives and strategy.

Other Factors   The focus here is on the obvious factors on which the strengths and weaknesses of the organization must be evaluated. Other factors, however, such as patents, inventions, and the firm's image may be peculiar to an enterprise or may be prominent during a particular time period.

The *process* of analyzing the strengths and weaknesses varies from company to company. It may gradually evolve over several years or it may begin with a retreat of top executives. Shortly after he assumed the leadership at General Mills, James McFarland took thirty-five of his top managers for a three-day retreat. After reaching consensus on the broad financial goals, managers were assigned to groups of six to eight people. Each group then was asked to answer the question: "What is a great company?" from the perspectives of the shareholders, suppliers, employees, the public, and society. The next day, the groups discussed the firm's strengths and weaknesses relative to the ideal model. The final day was spent in discussing ways to overcome the firm's weaknesses and to find ways to make it a great company. The general consensus thus reached resulted in the acquisition-divestiture strategy at General Mills.[8]

Strategic Alternatives

The foregoing analysis of environmental opportunities and threats and the company's strengths and weaknesses encourages the creative process of developing alternatives. As any experienced manager knows, in almost all situations, alternative courses of action are available.

One strategy is to *specialize* or *concentrate*. Thus, a company may utilize its energy and strengths to pursue a single purpose or it may restrict its efforts to only a few aims. For example, American Motors for many years used its limited resources primarily for the production of small cars, rather than competing directly with General Motors, Ford, or Chrysler, who had a complete product line ranging from relatively small models to large, luxurious cars.

Other alternative strategies are backward and forward integration. In *backward integration* a company may acquire suppliers to ensure a steady flow of materials. In *forward integration* the attempt is to secure outlets for products or services and to reach toward the ultimate user of the product.

Another strategy focuses on *diversification* by moving into new and profitable markets. This may result in greater growth than would be possible without diversification. A company may diversify through external acquisitions or by a strategy of internal diversification. Tenneco, Inc., one of the largest conglomerates, grew at the beginning by acquiring about 100 companies. This conglomerate company, like many others, also acquired firms that were sometimes difficult to integrate with the established operations. More recently, facilitated by the profits from oil and chemicals, the company has diversified by using its existing technical internal strengths. Many of the ventures are in the high-risk, but possible big payout areas such as the offshore nuclear power business and ocean mining. The Tenneco example shows that a company may diversify through external acquisitions as well as by using internal strengths and special competence.

Whatever the strategy, diversification requires the commitment and involvement of top management. At General Mills and Xerox the diversification began with analytical studies and goal setting at the top to determine the general directions of these firms. Diversification requires the allocation of resources, and negotiations at the top level are necessary to build the support for the general direction the company is going to take.

Still another strategy would be to focus on *innovation*—new products and new services. Thus, a company vulnerable to obsolescence may look for new ideas whose time has arrived. Polaroid, a company known for innovation, developed through tremendous research and development efforts the successful SX70 instant picture camera, a truly innovative product. But, as exemplified by the same company, investing in innovation is also risky. Polaroid may have persisted too long and invested too much in promoting Polavision, the instant movie system.

A company may adopt a "no change" strategy and decide to do nothing. Instead of innovation or expansion, a firm may continue to follow the tried and proven path, utilizing existing products and services and letting others make possible mistakes in innovation.

A company may also select an *international* strategy, repeating the approach that was successful in its home country and extending its operations from there to different parts of the world. Companies with global strategies include Unilever, Colgate-Palmolive, Singer, Nestle, and IBM, to mention a few.

Still another strategic alternative is for an enterprise to decide on *liquidation,* which may require terminating an unprofitable product line or service. If the company is a one-product firm, this may mean dissolving the company—an especially difficult strategic decision.

In some cases the extreme decision of liquidation may not be necessary. Instead, a *retrenchment* strategy may be more appropriate. To be sure, this is often only a temporary measure and may involve reducing operating expenses or restricting the scope of the operation. Still, such a strategy may be a viable alternative to liquidation.

Finally, there is the alternative of engaging in *joint ventures,* which may take different forms. For instance, corporations may join with foreign firms to overcome political and cultural barriers. Another example of a joint venture is the Alaskan Pipeline, which was a project even too big for one of the financially strong oil companies. Still another kind of joint venture occurs when two or more firms pool their resources and establish a new company, which then is jointly owned.

The strategies discussed above provide an overview of possible approaches. Within these categories, of course, many variations are possible. In reality, enterprises often pursue a *combination* of these strategies. What has become clear is that evaluating and choosing a strategy, the next topic of discussion, is not a simple task.

Evaluation and Choice of Strategies

The strategic manager has to evaluate a multiplicity of possible strategies. Clearly, such a manager has to take into consideration both external realities and internal capabilities. Unfortunately, environments are not static but are *dynamic* and subject to constant change. Thus, the strategist has to make predictions of changes about the future.

In making strategic choices, opportunities must be evaluated in the light of *risks.* There may indeed be profit opportunities for a new product, but the company may not be able to afford the risks involved in the new venture. At other times, however, a firm cannot afford not taking a calculated risk.

Timing is another critical element in the strategic decision. Although early action may at times be desirable (e.g., to be the first in the market), a firm may not be able to take the risk associated with it. On the other hand, a company may have to enter a new field because its survival depends upon it.

Companies do not operate in a vacuum, of course. A new strategic action is usually met with a reaction from one or more *competitors.* This, in turn, requires counteractions. Clearly, strategic choices are made in a dynamic environment, which requires executives with a tolerance for ambiguity to cope with the many uncertainties.

Consistency Testing

During all stages of strategy formulation, the steps have to be examined for consistency with the enterprise profile, the present and projected environment, and the resources of the firm. In addition, the goals of the claimants to the organization have to be considered since the choice of strategy is not only based on a rational analysis of the facts, but also on personal values and personal goals, especially those of the chief executive officer, an important claimant to the enterprise, as pointed out above.

Alternative strategies are then tested for congruency with other medium- and short-range plans that, in turn, may require adjustments of the master strategy. Similarly, the feasibility of implementing the plans also needs to be examined. For example, the organization structure, as well as the availability and suitability of human resources, should be considered before strategic choices are made.

As shown in the model in Figure 2-1, consistency testing is necessary at the various steps in the strategic planning process.

Contingency Plans

Because the future cannot be predicted with great accuracy, contingency plans will have to be prepared, based on different premises. To be sure, not all possible contingencies can be taken into account, but those crucial to the survival and success of a firm—such as a cutoff or reduction of oil from foreign sources—should provide premises for alternative plans. For example, one large chemical company is known for not relying on a single corporate plan; instead the firm has several contingency plans based on different scenarios. But even smaller firms do well to develop alternative plans based on different assumptions about the future, such as whether the interest rate will be high or low, gross national product will increase or decrease, and whether or not new competitors will enter the market.

Strategic Planning and Incrementalism

Strategies are not the result of a meeting or even a series of meetings of top managers. Instead, strategies usually emerge gradually in a process in which incremental steps are taken. In a study of major corporations it was found that most effective strategy formulation builds on formal planning, but also includes power-behavioral aspects such as dealing with multiple objectives, the politics of decision making, negotiation in the formulation of the strategy, making decisions that are "good enough" (that is, they satisfice) rather than being optimal, forming alliances among managers, and the practice of "muddling through." Based on the analysis of strategic processes, one author suggests a "logical incrementalism" that includes the elements of the formal planning system and the power-behavioral approach.[9] Strategies that evolve incrementally are based on a series of decisions interacting toward the major goal or goals of the enterprise. It is a purposeful and conscientious effort by executives, requiring the improvement of information on which decisions are based and dealing with political realities and power enclaves within and outside the organization.

Even under pressure, managers frequently do not make strategic decisions on the spur of the moment, but gradually adjust their strategies in a way that leaves other options open. General Motors, for example, only gradually changed the car line in response to the oil crisis. A gradual change rather than an abrupt change in course provides for increasing commitment among top executives for the new direction. It also gains time for searching for other alternative courses of action and opportunities. Furthermore, it allows time for planning studies, which often precede the formulation of a strategy. These studies may project the future environment in which the strategy is carried out. These studies, then, usually become the premises guiding the planning process.[10]

STRATEGIC PLANNING IN ACTION

A strategic planning model is useful because it shows the important elements and their relationships to the process. In real life, however, strategy formulation is not a simple step-by-step process, rather, it evolves in increments over a long time. An illustration may show how a strategy could evolve. Let us say a farm machinery company with a successful operation in the United States is concerned about its future. The president, with a few top executives and a consultant, begins wrestling with questions such as: "Where do we want to be in seven years?" "What should the company look like at that time?" As a result of these and similar questions, a small executive group may identify the following:

1 The company should be number one domestically in terms of size, while maintaining a solid financial position.

2 It should be a major international firm.

3 It should show a balanced growth in domestic and international operations.

4 It should be staffed by a strong management, professionals, and workforce.

5 The company image should convey quality products, reliable service, and concern for its employees.

6 The company should have decentralized operation while maintaining centralized control.

With these tentative guidelines set, the president then may ask the executive committee to discuss the proposed thrust and to identify the strengths and weaknesses of the company. With the help of a consultant, opportunities and threats in the external environment are identified, trends are projected, and a consensus is reached on broad corporate goals.

Based on these discussions, it may be determined that the company has to restructure the organization, hire eighty managers and other professionals, train the existing team of managers to assume general management responsibility, and improve the profitability of certain product lines.

But, more detailed information is needed. Therefore, the president authorizes two studies, one in the home country and another one in Europe, the target for the next international expansion. Also, more managers within the firm get involved in the strategic process. The executive committee is informed about the general direction of the company and is asked to critique the proposals, to agree on eight broad corporate goals, and to obtain their consensus. Some managers and professionals are also asked to develop some specific goals. The total process up to this point may take a year or even more.

As consensus is building on the broad direction of the company at the top, more people get involved in the process. In a meeting of thirty-five high-level managers, the president explains the eight areas of major thrust and the broad goals. These managers then have an opportunity to discuss these goals, refine them, and reach a general consensus. Then these managers are asked to state in writing within three months how they contribute to the broad goals of the company and to submit their own objectives, programs, and budgets, all in line with the major thrust of the company. The total process is time consuming and may take as long as three to four years. At one point the link can be made between strategic planning and the more specific MBO process of setting objectives, developing action plans, implementing the plans, control of organizational performance, as well as appraisal of individual results.

IMPLICATIONS FOR MANAGERIAL PRODUCTIVITY

It is now generally realized that the overemphasis on short-term results may be damaging to the long-term profitability of the enterprise.[11] Thus, some traditional, short-term MBO programs may have inadvertently contributed to the current productivity crisis. Too much attention may be given to quarterly earnings and each year's earnings are expected to exceed those of the preceding year. Managers' performance is judged by measures covering a short time frame and their compensation is based on these results, rather than on their investment in and concern for the long-term success of the company.

In contrast, Japanese managers are not driven to the same extent by short-term earnings and the price of the companies' stock. Those managers have more freedom to make investments that result in the long-term health of the company.[12] Fortunately, some United States companies have recognized the undesirable side effects of short-term decisions. For example, Texas Instruments evaluates and rewards managers for short-term results *and* investment in the future.[13] Still, far too few companies have followed this example. Therefore, the inclusion of strategic planning in the MBO model is an urgent reminder that real productivity requires taking a long-term view.[14]

This chapter, then, provides an overview of the strategy formulation process that begins with the identification of the various organizational inputs that help in the preparation of the enterprise profile. The opportunities and threats of the present and future external environment are analyzed and matched with the company's resources. Based on this analysis, alternative strategies, tactics, and other actions are considered and choices are made from among those alternatives. During each stage of the strategy formulation process, attention must be given to the consistency of the various parts. Finally, since organizations operate in a dynamic environment, contingency plans must be prepared to cope with these changes.

NOTES

1 For the criteria used in evaluating strategic planning, see S. Tilles, "How to Evaluate Corporate Strategy," *Harvard Business Review* (July-August, 1963); C. R. Christensen, K. R. Andrews, and J. L. Bower, *Business Policy—Text and Cases,* 4th ed. (Homewood, Ill.: Richard D. Irwin, 1978); J. B. Quinn, *Strategies for Change—Logical Incrementalism* (Homewood, Ill.: Richard D. Irwin, 1980), chap. 5.

2 H. Koontz, C. O'Donnell, and H. Weihrich, *Management,* 8th ed. (New York: McGraw-Hill, 1984), p. 665. For additional meanings, see R. Evered, "The Strategic Decision Process," in D. Hellriegel and J. W. Slocum, Jr., eds., *Management in the World Today* (Reading, Mass.: Addison Wesley, 1975).

3 For an excellent discussion of the various approaches to forecasting, see S. Makridakis and S. C. Wheelwright, "Forecasting: Issues and Challenges for Marketing Management," *Journal of Marketing* (October 1977) in H. Koontz, C. O'Donnell and H. Weihrich, *Management: A Book of Readings,* 5th ed. (New York: McGraw-Hill, 1980).

4 C. M. Watson, "Counter-Competition Abroad to Protect Home Markets," *Harvard Business Review,* vol. 60, no. 1 (January-February, 1982), pp. 40–42.
5 "Marshall Field: Seeking New Markets in the South and West," *Business Week* (March 23, 1981), pp. 125, 129.
6 J. Wall, "What the Competition is Doing: Your Need to Know," *Harvard Business Review* (November-December, 1974).
7 Quinn, op. cit., chap. 2.
8 Ibid.
9 Ibid
10 G. A. Steiner, *Top Management Planning* (New York: Macmillan, 1969).
11 See, for example, "Management's Drag on Productivity," *Business Week* (Dec. 3, 1979) and W. G. Ouchi, *Theory Z* (Reading, Mass.: Addison-Wesley, 1981).
12 Ibid.
13 Texas Instruments has used this approach for a long time. See G. A. Dove, "Objectives, Strategies, and Tactics in a System," *The Conference Board Record* (New York: The Conference Board, 1970).
14 At TRW, for example, top-level managers determine the mission, objectives, strategies, plans, and programs, Moreover, productivity improvement efforts are integrated with strategic planning, realizing the long-term implications of current decisions. See W. A. Ruch and W. B. Werther, Jr., "Productivity Strategies at TRW," *National Productivity Review,* Spring 1983, pp. 109–125. For a macroanalysis of the productivity issue see B. J. Reilly and J. P. Fuhr, Jr., "Productivity: An Economic and Management Analysis with a Direction Towards a New Synthesis," *The Academy of Management Review,* vol. 8, no. 1 (January 1983), pp. 108–117.

CHAPTER 3

MAKING STRATEGIC PLANNING EFFECTIVE THROUGH THE TOWS MATRIX

The previous chapter gave an overview of the strategic planning process. It became clear that the formulation of a strategy requires the analysis of the situation and the linking of the organization's capabilities with its environment. This chapter elaborates on strategic planning by proposing a conceptual framework and giving practical hints on how to identify and analyze the threats (T) and opportunities (O) in the external environment and how to assess the organization's weaknesses (W) and strengths (S). The matrix that will be introduced is called TOWS, or situational, analysis. Although the sets of variables in the matrix are not new,* matching them in a systematic fashion is new. Many writers on strategic planning suggest that a firm uses its strengths to take advantage of opportunities, but they ignore other important relationships, such as the challenge of overcoming weaknesses in the enterprise to exploit opportunities. After all, a weakness is the absence of strength and to overcome an existing weakness, corporate development may become a distinct strategy for the company. The TOWS Matrix "forces"

---

*The author was first introduced to the analysis of threats/opportunities in the external environment and the weaknesses/strengths of the firm in a seminar conducted by George S. Steiner at UCLA in the late 1960s.

practicing managers to analyze the situation of their organization and to develop strategies, tactics, and actions for the effective and efficient attainment of organizational objectives.

This chapter begins with a review of matrixes used in strategic planning. Then the TOWS Matrix is introduced and discussed in detail. Finally, the TOWS Matrix is applied in the analysis of the strategy of Volkswagen and Winnebago Industries.

A MODEL FOR THE ANALYSIS OF THE SITUATION

It is common to hear the admonition that managers must identify the company's strengths and weaknesses as well as the opportunities and threats in the external environment. But managers receive little help with how to combine these factors and to develop distinct strategies based upon their combinations. To systematize these choices, the TOWS Matrix is proposed. But before describing the matrix, one should be aware of other "tools" that have been used effectively in strategy formulation.

Today, strategy designers have been aided by a number of matrixes showing the relationships of critical variables. For example, the Boston Consulting Group (BCG) developed the *Business Portfolio Matrix,* which shows the linkages between the business growth rate and the relative competitive position of the enterprise (identified by the market share). Market standing, for example, is evaluated in light of business growth rate and the relative competitive position of the firm. The growth-share matrix by the BCG is shown in a simplified version in Figure 3-1.[1]

The businesses in the "question mark" quadrant usually require a cash investment so that they may become "stars," which are businesses that are in the high growth/strong competitive position quadrant. These businesses have opportunities for growth and profit. The "cash cows" with a strong competitive position and a low growth rate are usually well established in the market and have a low-cost position. Consequently, they provide the needed cash for the enterprise. Finally, the "dogs" are those businesses with a low growth rate and a weak relative market position; they are usually not profitable. While this portfolio approach is popular, it is not without its critics. They contest that it is too simplistic and that the growth rate criterion has been considered insufficient for the evaluation of the industry's attractiveness. Similarly, the market share as a yardstick for estimating the competitive position may be inadequate.[2]

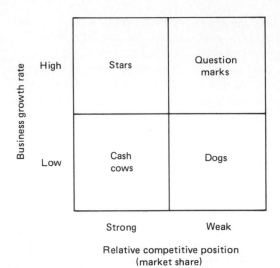

FIGURE 3-1
Business portfolio matrix. (Copyright © 1970 The Boston Consulting Group. All
rights reserved. Published by permission.)

Another useful matrix for developing a firm's strategy is General
Electric's *Business Screen.* Basically, the GE matrix consists of two
sets of variables: business strengths and industry attractiveness.
Each variable is divided into low, medium, and high ratings, resulting
in a nine-cell grid. Business strengths, for example, evaluates size,
growth, share, position, profitability, margins, and technology position, to mention a few of the items. Industry attractiveness, on the
other hand, is judged in terms of size, market growth, market
diversity, competitive structure, industry profitability, and so on. But
Charles W. Hofer and Dan Schendel suggest that the GE Business
Screen does not give adequate attention to new industries that are
beginning to grow. Consequently, they suggest a matrix in which the
"competitive position" and their "stage of product/market evolution"
are plotted.[3] Both matrixes, however, appear to give insufficient
attention to the threats and constraints in the external environment.

The TOWS Matrix described in this chapter has a wider scope and
has different emphases than the ones mentioned above. This matrix
does not replace either the Business Portfolio Matrix, the GE
Business Screen, or the matrix by Hofer and Schendel, but it is
proposed as a conceptual framework for a systematic analysis that

facilitates matching the external threats and opportunities with the internal weaknesses and strengths of the organization.

The TOWS Matrix: A Conceptual Model

The process of strategy formulation, shown In Figure 2-1 in the previous chapter, is now surrounding the TOWS Matrix in Figure 3-2. Preparation of the enterprise profile, Step 1, deals with some basic questions pertaining to the internal and external environments. Steps 2 and 3, on the other hand, concern primarily the present and future situation in respect to the external environment. Step 4, the audit of strengths and weaknesses, focuses on the internal resources of the enterprise. Steps 5 and 6 are the activities necessary to develop strategies, tactics, and more specific actions in order to achieve the enterprise's purpose and overall objectives. During this process attention must be given to consistency of these decisions with the other steps in the strategy formulation process. Finally, since an organization operates in a dynamic environment, contingency plans must be prepared (Step 7).

There are different ways of analyzing the situation. One is to begin with the identification of important problems. A second approach is to start with determining the purpose and objectives of the firm. A third way is to focus on opportunities. The question may be raised whether one should start with the analysis of the external environment or with the firm's internal resources. There is no single answer. Indeed, one may deal concurrently with the two sets of factors: the external and the internal environments. It is important, therefore, to remember that the process followed here is just one of several options.

The External Environment   Within the suggested framework, the analysis starts with the external environment. Specifically, the listing of external threats (T) may be of immediate importance to the firm as some of these threats (such as the lack of available energy) may seriously threaten the operation of the firm. These threats should be listed in box "T" in Figure 3-2. Similarly, opportunities should be shown in box "O."

Threats and opportunities may be found in different areas, but it is advisable to look carefully for the more common ones that may be categorized as economic, social, political, and demographic factors, products and services, technology, markets, and, of course, compe-

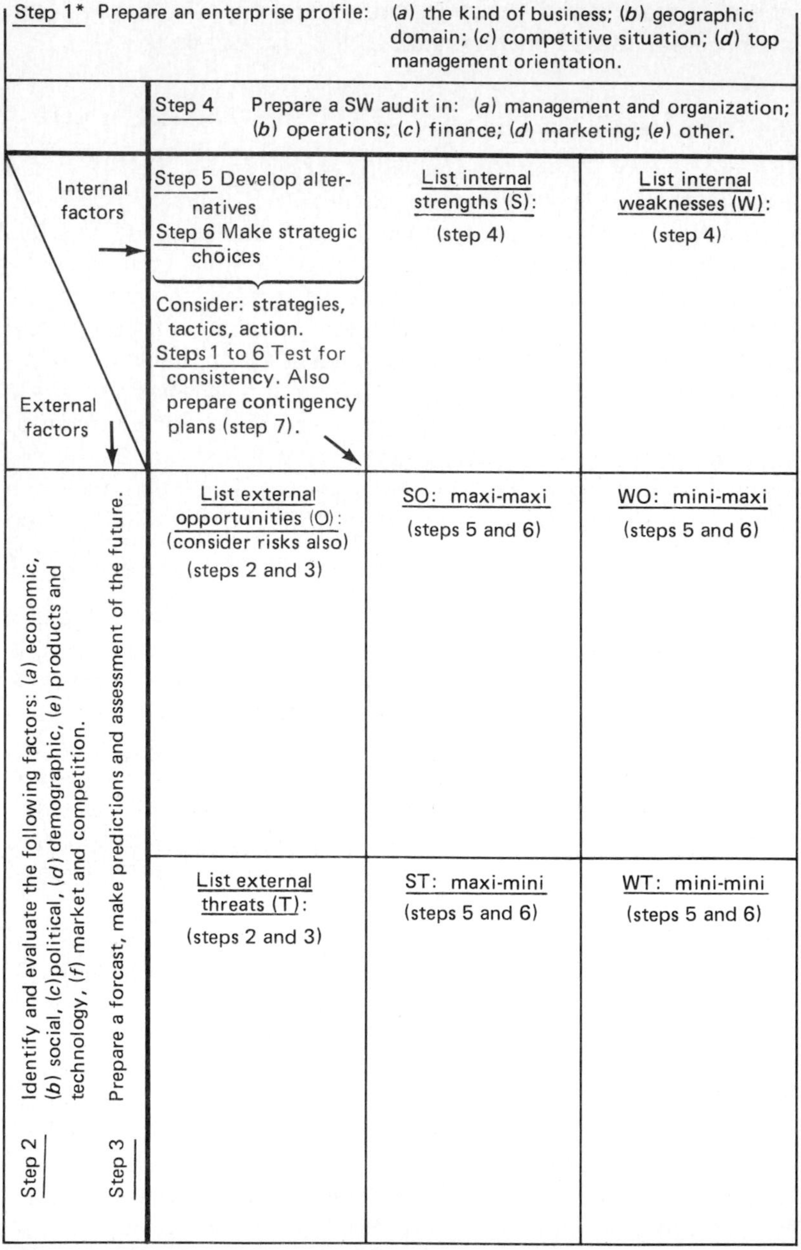

Step 1* Prepare an enterprise profile: (a) the kind of business; (b) geographic domain; (c) competitive situation; (d) top management orientation.

	Step 4 Prepare a SW audit in: (a) management and organization; (b) operations; (c) finance; (d) marketing; (e) other.		
Internal factors	Step 5 Develop alternatives Step 6 Make strategic choices Consider: strategies, tactics, action. Steps 1 to 6 Test for consistency. Also prepare contingency plans (step 7).	List internal strengths (S): (step 4)	List internal weaknesses (W): (step 4)
External factors			
Identify and evaluate the following factors: (a) economic, (b) social, (c) political, (d) demographic, (e) products and technology, (f) market and competition. Prepare a forcast, make predictions and assessment of the future.	List external opportunities (O): (consider risks also) (steps 2 and 3)	SO: maxi-maxi (steps 5 and 6)	WO: mini-maxi (steps 5 and 6)
Step 2 Step 3	List external threats (T): (steps 2 and 3)	ST: maxi-mini (steps 5 and 6)	WT: mini-mini (steps 5 and 6)

*The steps are suggestive and may vary.

FIGURE 3-2
Process of corporate strategy and the TOWS Matrix.

tition. The analysis of these factors must not only pertain to the present but also, even more important, to the future environment.

The Internal Environment The firm's internal environment is assessed for its strengths (S) and weaknesses (W), and then listed in the respective spaces in Figure 3-2. These factors may be found in management and organization, operations, finance, marketing, and in other areas. Since they were discussed in the previous chapter, they will not be repeated here.

Strategies, Tactics, and Actions The TOWS Matrix, Figure 3-2, indicates four conceptually distinct alternative strategies, tactics, and actions. In practice, of course, some of the strategies overlap or they may be pursued concurrently and in concert. But for the purpose of discussion the focus is on the interactions of four sets of variables. The primary concern here is strategies, but this analysis could also be applied to the development of tactics necessary to implement the strategies, and to more specific actions supportive of tactics.

1 *The WT Strategy* (mini-mini). In general, the aim of the WT strategy is to minimize both weaknesses and threats. A company faced with external threats and internal weaknesses may indeed be in a precarious position. In fact, such a firm may have to fight for its survival or may even have to choose liquidation. Some of the traditional industries, such as tires and steel, often have to adopt WT strategies. The Firestone tire company, for example, has plants that are outdated and show a low productivity. Externally, the firm is threatened by a declining market with reduced demand for tires, partly caused by radial tires that have a relatively long tire life. To cope with this threat, Firestone seems to have a strategy of liquidating investments in the "old" business and investing the proceeds in industries with better prospects. Moreover, the firm seems to focus its efforts on tires for heavy trucks. The WT strategy may also take other directions. For example, a firm may prefer a merger, or may cut back its operations, with the intent of either overcoming its weaknesses or hoping that the threat will diminish over time (too often wishful thinking). Whatever strategy is selected, the WT position is one that any firm will try to avoid.

2 *The WO Strategy* (mini-maxi). The second strategy attempts to minimize the weaknesses and to maximize the opportunities. A company may identify opportunities in the external environment but

have organizational weaknesses that prevent the firm from taking advantage of market demands. For example, an auto accessory company with a great demand for electronic devices to control the amount and timing of fuel injection in a combustion engine may lack the technology required for producing these microprocessors. One possible strategy would be to acquire this technology through cooperation with a firm having competency in this field. An alternative tactic would be to hire and train people with the required technical capabilities. Of course, the firm also has the choice of doing nothing, thus leaving the opportunity to competitors.

3 *The ST Strategy* (maxi-mini). This strategy is based on the strengths of the organization that can deal with threats in the environment. The aim is to maximize the former while minimizing the latter. This, however, does not mean that a strong company can meet threats in the external environment head-on, as General Motors (GM) realized. In the 1960s, mighty GM recognized the potential threat posed by Ralph Nader, who exposed the safety hazards of the Corvair automobile. As will be remembered, the direct confrontation with Mr. Nader caused GM more problems than expected. In retrospect, the initial GM response from strength was probably inappropriate. The lesson to be learned is that strengths must sometimes be used with great restraint and discretion.

4 *The SO Strategy* (maxi-maxi). Any company would like to be in a position where it can maximize both strengths and opportunities. Such an enterprise can lead from strengths, utilizing resources to take advantage of the market for its products and services. For example, Mercedes Benz, with the technical know-how and the quality image, can take advantage of the external demand for luxury cars by an increasingly affluent public. Successful enterprises, even if they temporarily use one of the three previously mentioned strategies, will attempt to get into a situation where they can work from strengths to take advantage of opportunities. If they have weaknesses, they will strive to overcome them, making them strengths. If they face threats, they will cope with them so that they can focus on opportunities.

Time Dimension and the TOWS Matrix

So far, the factors displayed in the TOWS Matrix pertain to the analysis at a particular point in time. External and internal environments are dynamic; some factors change a great deal over time while others change very little. Because of the dynamics in the environment, the strategy designer must prepare several TOWS Matrixes at different points in time, as shown in Figure 3-3. Thus, one may start with a TOWS analysis of the past, continue with an analysis of the present, and, perhaps most important, focus on different time periods in the future.

APPLICATION OF THE TOWS MATRIX TO VOLKSWAGEN

The foregoing discussion of the conceptual framework for strategic planning can be illustrated by an example. Volkswagen (VW) was chosen because it demonstrates how a successful company experienced great difficulties in the early 1970s, but then developed a strategy that resulted in an excellent market position in the late 1970s. In the 1980s, however, VW experienced considerable difficulties, especially in the U.S. market. The TOWS Matrix shown in Figure 3-4 will focus on the crucial period from late 1973 to early 1975, when important strategic decisions were made. The external threats and opportunities pertain mostly to the situation VW faced in the United States, but a similar situation prevailed in Europe at that time.

The External and Internal Environments

In a situational analysis as conceptualized above, one would first list and analyze the threats and opportunities in the external environment and the weaknesses and strengths of the enterprise before developing alternative strategies and tactics. However, in this illustration, to be concise, the situation and the related actions, shown in Figure 3-4, are combined.

Strategies and Tactics

Strategies, as discussed earlier, pertain to major courses of action for the achievement of the enterprise mission and comprehensive objectives. Tactics, on the other hand, refer to action plans by which strategies are executed. In practice, and even conceptually, these distinctions are often blurred.

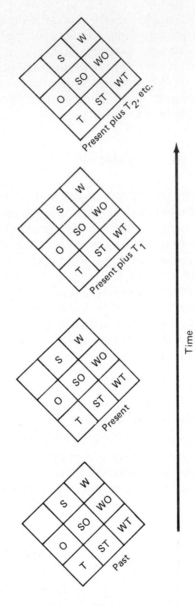

FIGURE 3-3
Making the TOWS Matrix dynamic.

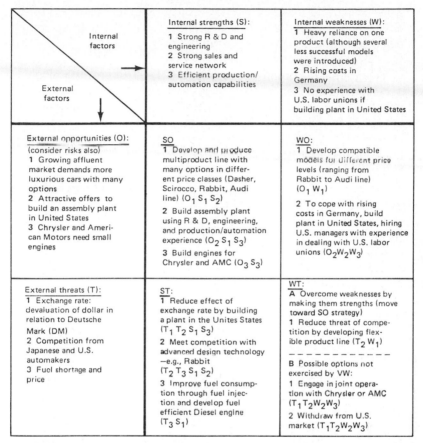

Internal factors ⟋ External factors	Internal strengths (S): 1 Strong R & D and engineering 2 Strong sales and service network 3 Efficient production/automation capabilities	Internal weaknesses (W): 1 Heavy reliance on one product (although several less successful models were introduced) 2 Rising costs in Germany 3 No experience with U.S. labor unions if building plant in United States
External opportunities (O): (consider risks also) 1 Growing affluent market demands more luxurious cars with many options 2 Attractive offers to build an assembly plant in United States 3 Chrysler and American Motors need small engines	SO 1 Develop and produce multiproduct line with many options in different price classes (Dasher, Scirocco, Rabbit, Audi line) $(O_1 S_1 S_2)$ 2 Build assembly plant using R & D, engineering, and production/automation experience $(O_2 S_1 S_3)$ 3 Build engines for Chrysler and AMC $(O_3 S_3)$	WO: 1 Develop compatible models for different price levels (ranging from Rabbit to Audi line) $(O_1 W_1)$ 2 To cope with rising costs in Germany, build plant in United States, hiring U.S. managers with experience in dealing with U.S. labor unions $(O_2 W_2 W_3)$
External threats (T): 1 Exchange rate: devaluation of dollar in relation to Deutsche Mark (DM) 2 Competition from Japanese and U.S. automakers 3 Fuel shortage and price	ST: 1 Reduce effect of exchange rate by building a plant in the Unites States $(T_1 T_2 S_1 S_3)$ 2 Meet competition with advanced design technology —e.g., Rabbit $(T_2 T_3 S_1 S_2)$ 3 Improve fuel consumption through fuel injection and develop fuel efficient Diesel engine $(T_3 S_1)$	WT: A Overcome weaknesses by making them strengths (move toward SO strategy) 1 Reduce threat of competition by developing flexible product line $(T_2 W_1)$ — — — — — — — — — — — B Possible options not exercised by VW: 1 Engage in joint operation with Chrysler or AMC $(T_1 T_2 W_2 W_3)$ 2 Withdraw from U.S. market $(T_1 T_2 W_2 W_3)$

FIGURE 3-4
Application of the TOWS Matrix to Volkswagen from late 1973 to early 1975.

Weaknesses and Threats (WT)   A company with great weaknesses often has to resort to a survival strategy. VW could have seriously considered the option of a joint operation with Chrysler or American Motors. Another alternative would have been to withdraw from the American market altogether. Although in difficulties, VW did *not* have to resort to a survival strategy because the company still had many strengths. Consequently, a more appropriate strategy was to attempt to overcome the weaknesses and develop them into strengths. In other words, the direction was toward the strength-opportunity position (SO) in the matrix shown as Figure 3-4.

Specifically, the strategy was to reduce the competitive threat by developing a more flexible new product line that would accommodate the needs and desires of the car-buying public.

Weaknesses and Opportunities (WO)   The growing affluence of customers resulted in "trading up" to more luxurious cars. Yet, VW had essentially followed a one-model policy that presented a problem when the design of the Beetle became obsolete. A new model line had to be introduced to reach a wider spectrum of buyers. In order to minimize the additional costs of a multiproduct line, the building block principle was employed in the design of the new cars. This allowed VW to use the same parts for different models ranging from the relatively low-priced Rabbit to the higher-priced Audi.

Another weakness at VW was the rising costs in Germany. For example, in 1973 wages and salaries rose 19 percent over the previous year. Similarly, increased fuel costs made the shipping of cars to the United States more costly. This situation favored setting up an assembly plant in the United States. However, this also created some problems for VW because it had no experience in dealing with American organized labor. To overcome this weakness, VW's tactic was to recruit managers from Detroit who were capable of establishing good union relations.

Strengths and Threats (ST)   One of the greatest threats to VW was the continuing appreciation of the Deutsche Mark against the dollar. For example, between October 1972 and November 1973, the mark appreciated 35 percent. This meant higher prices for the buyer. The result, of course, was a less competitive posture. Japanese and American automakers obtained an increasingly larger share of the small-car market. To reduce the threats of competition and the effects of the unfavorable exchange rate, VW was forced to build an assembly plant in the United States.

Another strategy for meeting competitive pressures was to build on VW's strengths by developing a car based on advanced-design technology. The result of this effort was the Rabbit, a model with features later adopted by many other car manufacturers.

The oil crisis in 1973–1974 caused not only a fuel shortage, but also price rises, a trend that continued for some time. To meet this threat, VW used its technological capabilities not only to improve its engines (through the use of fuel injection, for example), but also to develop the very fuel-efficient Diesel engine. This tactic, which was congruent with its general strategy, helped improve the firm's market position.

Strengths and Opportunities (SO)   In general, successful firms build on their strengths to take advantage of opportunities. VW is no exception. Throughout this discussion VW's strengths in research, development engineering, and its experience in production technology became evident. These strengths, under the leadership of the president, Rudolph Leiding, enabled the company to develop a product line that met market demands for an economical car (the Rabbit, successor to the Beetle), as well as the tastes for more luxurious cars with many available options (the Scirocco and Audi lines).

Eventually the same company's strengths enabled VW to plan and build the assembly facility in New Stanton, Pennsylvania. Thus, VW could benefit from substantial concessions granted by the state government to attract VW which, in turn, provided many employment opportunities.

In another tactical move, VW manufactured and sold small engines to Chrysler and American Motors. These companies urgently needed small engines for installation in their own cars and revenues from these sales improved the financial position of VW.

Let us now see how the TOWS Matrix can be applied in the analysis of the situation and the development of strategic actions at Winnebago.

APPLICATION OF THE TOWS MATRIX TO WINNEBAGO INDUSTRIES, INC.

Winnebago, the largest manufacturer of recreational vehicles (RVs), produced a full line of such vehicles, but emphasized traditional motor homes. The company, located in Forest City, Iowa, operated a large, modern, and efficient plant.[4]

The External and Internal Environments

The threats and opportunities that existed in the early 1970s in the external environment are condensed into the table shown as Figure 3-5. In the past, the company had prospered by the high demand for RVs. However, serious threats from competitors as well as the gasoline shortage had a great impact on the firm.

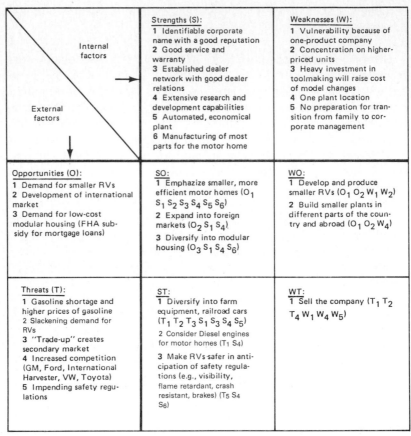

Internal factors / External factors	Strengths (S):	Weaknesses (W):
	1 Identifiable corporate name with a good reputation 2 Good service and warranty 3 Established dealer network with good dealer relations 4 Extensive research and development capabilities 5 Automated, economical plant 6 Manufacturing of most parts for the motor home	1 Vulnerability because of one-product company 2 Concentration on higher-priced units 3 Heavy investment in toolmaking will raise cost of model changes 4 One plant location 5 No preparation for transition from family to corporate management
Opportunities (O): 1 Demand for smaller RVs 2 Development of international market 3 Demand for low-cost modular housing (FHA subsidy for mortgage loans)	SO: 1 Emphasize smaller, more efficient motor homes (O_1 S_1 S_2 S_3 S_4 S_5 S_6) 2 Expand into foreign markets (O_2 S_1 S_4) 3 Diversify into modular housing (O_3 S_1 S_4 S_6)	WO: 1 Develop and produce smaller RVs (O_1 O_2 W_1 W_2) 2 Build smaller plants in different parts of the country and abroad (O_1 O_2 W_4)
Threats (T): 1 Gasoline shortage and higher prices of gasoline 2 Slackening demand for RVs 3 "Trade-up" creates secondary market 4 Increased competition (GM, Ford, International Harvester, VW, Toyota) 5 Impending safety regulations	ST: 1 Diversify into farm equipment, railroad cars (T_1 T_2 T_3 S_1 S_3 S_4 S_5) 2 Consider Diesel engines for motor homes (T_1 S_4) 3 Make RVs safer in anticipation of safety regulations (e.g., visibility, flame retardant, crash resistant, brakes) (T_5 S_4 S_6)	WT: 1 Sell the company (T_1 T_2 T_4 W_1 W_4 W_5)

FIGURE 3-5
Application of the TOWS Matrix to Winnebago in the early 1970s.

While Winnebago had considerable strengths, heavy reliance on essentially one product made the company vulnerable to the external threats.

Strategies and Tactics

Based on the analysis of the situation, several alternative strategies and tactics were available to Winnebago.

Weaknesses and Threats (WT)   The factors in the external environment, particularly the gasoline shortage, the high fuel prices, the slackening in demand for recreational vehicles, as well as the increased competition constituted serious threats to the enterprise. When these threats are seen in relation to the weaknesses, an alternative would have been to sell the company. But this strategic choice would probably have been unacceptable to the family-dominated management group.

Weaknesses and Opportunities (WO)   Customers in the United States and abroad demanded smaller RVs. But one of the weaknesses of the firm was the heavy reliance on relatively larger and higher-priced units. Consequently, the development and manufacture of smaller vehicles could take advantage of the demand for small RVs in a market segment neglected in the past by the firm. Furthermore, smaller plants could be built in various parts of the country, thus alleviating the comparatively high transportation costs for the smaller RVs from the factory to the dealers.

Strengths and Threats (ST)   To cope with the threats in the external environment, the company could use its strengths. Specifically, diversifying into farm equipment and railroad cars could alleviate problems caused by the custom of "trading up." Similarly, the use of Diesel engines in motor homes could reduce fuel consumption of these vehicles. Impending safety regulations were expected to make more demands on RV manufacturers. Rather than reacting to these regulations, Winnebago could use its extensive research and development capabilities to develop safer vehicles.

Strengths and Opportunities (SO)   Winnebago needed to use its strengths to take advantage of the opportunities. The good reputation of the firm, its service network, its research and development, as well as the manufacturing facilities, could be used effectively to produce smaller RVs. Similarly, most of these strengths could facilitate the expansion into the international market. Finally, the firm's capabilities could be used to diversify into modular housing. But the company had little or no knowledge of the housing market and some difficulties had to be anticipated.

In the analysis of the situation so far, the focus has been on strategy formulation in two product-oriented businesses, Volkswagen and Winnebago, but does strategic planning also apply to other kinds of organizations?

WHO NEEDS STRATEGIC PLANNING?

For a long time strategic planning meant making plans in light of the actions or potential actions of an adversary. In fact, it is the *military* that has had long experience with strategic planning.

In the business world, strategic planning has been used extensively by firms that have as an output a physical *product.* The concern is about the deployment of resources to make the kind of product the customers want at a price they are willing to pay. Companies also have to decide whether they want to be a product leader or follow the lead of innovative competitors.

But to focus only on businesses that make a distinct product leaves out the important sector of the *service* industry. Examples of service businesses are consulting, law, computer service firms, airlines, banks, and theaters. Dan R. E. Thomas drew attention to the fact that strategic management for such enterprises is significantly different from companies that make a physical product.[5]

Clearly, to describe services is abstract and more difficult than to show and demonstrate a product. There are two kinds of services: One is equipment-based (for example, automatic car washes) while the other is people-based (for example, consulting). A few illustrations of the latter will indicate some implications for strategic planning. It may be extremely difficult to evaluate the quality of services of a consulting firm. Consequently, a client tends to employ the services of a large consulting firm with an established reputation. Unfortunately, this makes it extremely difficult for a small consulting firm without such an image to enter the market. Another example pertains to pricing in the service industry. Product-oriented firms usually aim to reduce the cost and price of a product to increase their market share. In the service industry, however, a low price may be perceived as and associated with providing poorer quality of professional services.

Does this suggest that strategic management does not apply to the service industry? Certainly not. What is needed, however, is a change in the thinking pattern away from product-oriented management to the application of techniques and language peculiar to service-oriented businesses.

Of all the different kinds of organizations, Western *governments* probably make the least use of strategic planning. For example, little systematic planning was done to prepare for the oil shortage. There is a tendency to respond to problems rather than to anticipate them and prepare contingency plans. Many large businesses now make a situational analysis and establish goals that give the enterprise direction. Why shouldn't the same managerial concept be applied by our government?

IMPLICATIONS FOR MANAGERIAL PRODUCTIVITY

In the past, productivity improvements focused on the lower levels of the organization, on workers, because their outputs lend themselves for relatively easy measurement within a short timeframe. But what is easy does not necessarily lead to optimal results. In fact, greater productivity gains may be gained by making the right strategic decisions that give direction to lower-level objectives. Doing the wrong things efficiently is worse than doing nothing at all.

The aim of this chapter was to provide a framework for systematically matching the environmental threats and opportunities with the company's weaknesses and especially its strengths through the TOWS Matrix. The scanning of the external and internal environments helps to identify four distinct strategies and tactics. The mini-mini strategy attempts to minimize both weaknesses and threats. The mini-maxi strategy aims at minimizing weaknesses but maximizing opportunities. The maxi-mini strategy takes advantage of the organization's strengths to cope with external threats. Finally, the maxi-maxi strategy utilizes the organization's strengths to take advantage of opportunities. How the TOWS Matrix can be applied in analyzing the situation and developing strategies is illustrated by Volkswagen and Winnebago. The TOWS Matrix helps to analyze the situation at one point in time. But, the environment is dynamic, which necessitates making several TOWS analyses for different time periods. There is little doubt that strategic management will gain greater prominence in the future. Any organization—whether military, product-oriented, service-oriented, or even governmental—must use a rational approach of anticipating, responding to, and even altering the future environment to become and remain productive.

NOTES

1 B. D. Henderson, "The Product Portfolio," in *Perspectives* (Boston Consulting Group, 1970); B. D. Henderson, "The Experience Curve Revisited" (Boston Consulting Group, undated); B. Hedley, "Strategy and the 'Business Portfolio'," *Long Range Planning,* February 1977.

2 C. W. Hofer and D. Schendel, *Strategy Formulation: Analytical Concepts* (St. Paul: West, 1978); "Oh Where, Oh Where Has My Little Dog Gone? or My Cash Cow? or My Star?" *Fortune,* Nov. 2, 1981.

3 Hofer and Schendel, op. cit.

4 H. E. R. Uyterhoeven, R. W. Ackerman, and J. W. Rosenblum, *Strategy and Organization* (Homewood, Illinois: Richard D. Irwin, 1977).

5 D. R. E. Thomas, "Strategy Is Different in Service Business," *Harvard Business Review,* July-August, 1978.

4

ORGANIZATIONAL PRODUCTIVITY REQUIRES AN INTEGRATED HIERARCHY AND NETWORK OF AIMS

The previous chapter dealt with strategic planning. Although the determination of the overall aims of the organization is an integral part of strategic planning, we reserved the discussion of aims for this chapter. The term *aims* is used to refer to ends toward which activities are directed. Thus, aims range from the general purpose of the organization to specific objectives. Actually there are different views whether the overall aims of the enterprise should be established before the assessment of the external and internal environments of the organization (as discussed in Chapters 2 and 3). In his book on strategy formulation, William F. Glueck shows a model in which the aims come before strategy formulation.[1] At the same time, he realizes that objectives are affected by the external and internal environments as well as the values of top executives. In their model on the structure and process of planning, George A. Steiner and John B. Miner recognize that the expectations of stockholders, the current situation, and external opportunities and threats, as well as the company's strengths and weaknesses become the basis for the aims of the enterprise.[2] These aims also influence the assessment of the internal factors as well as the expectations of stockholders. It becomes clear that there is a close interaction between the strategic planning process discussed in the previous two chapters and the hierarchy and network of aims, the focus of this chapter.

Most people would take the position that clear and well-integrated objectives help direct activities effectively and efficiently toward the ends and thus improve organizational productivity. Yet, measuring organizational productivity is a difficult task that will be discussed first before the focus shifts to the nature and importance of the hierarchy of aims.

THE PROBLEM OF MEASURING ORGANIZATIONAL PRODUCTIVITY

Most literature on productivity deals either with measurement on the macrolevel, comparing different economies or industries, or with microproductivity measures with an emphasis on the individual worker. Productivity measurements on the organizational level are very scarce and have improved little. Organizational productivity is the ratio between total outputs and total inputs. William A. Ruch and James C. Hershauer, who did considerable work on productivity, pointed out that organizations may measure their productivity over time, but comparing firms with each other, especially if the firms are in different industries, is of questionable value.[3] Comparisons of companies or even organizational units within the firm are often made with the assumption that all face the identical environments. But there are economic, social, legal, and political differences (especially in multinational corporations) that make productivity comparisons difficult. To focus exclusively on what is relatively easy to measure—the productivity of production workers, for example—is to look at only one factor, which, in turn, may lead to suboptimization of the system. We should therefore keep in mind when reading this chapter that it is difficult to measure precisely organizational productivity.

THE NATURE AND IMPORTANCE OF
THE HIERARCHY OF AIMS*

Every part of an organization and each individual in it should contribute toward its purpose. Objectives are the ends toward which other plans and group efforts are directed. In order to select the appropriate means, it is essential that the ends are clear. Moreover, the aims have to be structured in some orderly way, starting with the broad purpose and mission at the apex of the organizational hierarchy and continuing to set objectives further down to each member of the enterprise.

Characteristics of Aims

To test the validity of objectives, Charles H. Granger suggests that the objectives are a guide to action, are explicit enough to lead to action, are used for measuring and controlling effectiveness, are stated with recognition of external and internal constraints, and are linked so that the more specific objectives contribute to the broader aims.[4] Although all objectives should contribute to the broad overall purpose of the enterprise, it is not always necessary to begin with the broad design. Objectives should make people reach, but at the same time, they should be realistic. Moreover, they should lead to a creative search for alternative means, and objectives should be reevaluated from time to time to test if they are still valid in light of changed circumstances. Finally, objectives should be communicated so that all persons understand how their work contributes to the overall aims of the enterprise and interrelate with each other.

The Cascade Approach

Professor Anthony P. Raia at UCLA, who conducted one of the earliest studies of an MBO program in the Purex Corporation, implies a hierarchy of aims in his "cascade" approach.[5] The process of determining aims begins with the purpose of the enterprise, and continues with long-range goals and strategic plans, which, in turn, are the basis for short-term performance objectives. This process

*Adapted from Heinz Weihrich, "A Hierarchy and Network of Aims." Used by permission of the publisher from *Management Review,* January 1982. Copyright © AMACOM, a division of American Management Association, New York. All rights reserved.

continues with the setting of derivative objectives for each organizational unit and down to the individual. Thus, the objectives cascade down the organizational hierarchy.

The Ends-Means Chain

The hierarchy of aims implies that each objective should support the next higher-level objectives in an organization. Conversely, each upper-level objective is the guide for setting objectives at the lower level. But one may also view this hierarchical structure as an ends-means chain. In other words, to achieve a goal (which is an end) activities have to be carried out (means). These activities, or means, require subobjectives (ends) that, in turn, necessitate other activities (means).[6] This process may proceed as follows.

After a feasibility, or situational study, general objectives are set. Then the means necessary to achieve the objectives are developed, evaluated, and selected. These means, then, are translated into subobjectives that require activities of achieving them. At least conceptually, this process continues throughout the organization down to the level where additional factoring is not necessary. This process is illustrated in Figure 4-1.

The ends and means structure forms a hierarchy of aims, which are topped by the socioeconomic purpose, the mission of the enterprise, and the overall corporate objectives. These become important inputs for the strategic plans that in turn require the setting of tactical and operational objectives. Although not shown in Figure 4-1, such objectives and plans may be developed in large organizations for divisions, departments, and sections. As one proceeds down the organizational hierarchy, goals usually become more specific, as the following example illustrates.

Top management	End:	To obtain a return on investment of 18 percent by the end of the fiscal year.
Vice president of marketing	Means:	Efforts to increase the market share.
	End:	To obtain a market share of widgets of 15 percent by the end of the current fiscal year without additional costs.
Sales manager	Means:	To develop a strategy for increasing sales.
	End:	To sell 10,000 units of widgets in the western and southern regions by the end of the fiscal year without additional costs.

Regional sales manager	Means:	To penetrate the sales territory by enlarging the sales force.
	Ends:	To hire three qualified salespersons by the end of June at a base salary not to exceed $35,000.
		To sell 5,000 units of widgets by the end of the fiscal year without additional costs.
		To increase the market share from 14 to 15 percent of product X by the end of the fiscal year and stay within the budget.
Salesperson	Means:	To contact all old and come new customers.
	End:	To sell 700 units of product X by the end of the fiscal year without additional costs.

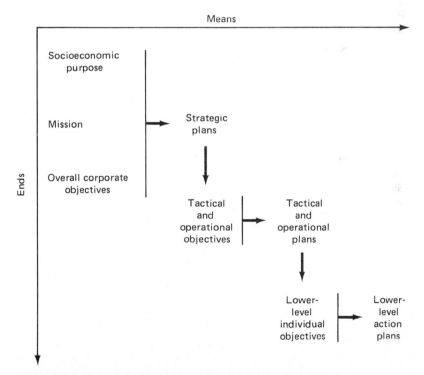

*Although not shown, at each step provisions must be made for feedback.
FIGURE 4-1
Ends-means analysis.

In order to achieve the overall aims, additional objectives for other product lines may have to be set and additional actions may be necessary. Furthermore, objectives congruent with the overall plan have to be set for other functional departments. For example, the vice president of production, the production manager, the first-line supervisors, and the production workers all should identify their contributions necessary to achieve the overall aims of the enterprise. The goal structure and the organization structure have basic relationships. At the top of the hierarchy of aims, the purpose and mission are stated broadly and often encompass complex programs. Similarly, at upper levels of the organization, authority is usually broadly defined. At lower organizational levels, on the other hand, both objectives and authority are usually more specific and limited.

A MODEL OF THE HIERARCHY OF AIMS

Organizations exist to achieve a purpose or a mission. The broad aims are broken down into overall corporate objectives, division, department, and unit objectives.

The Socioeconomic Purpose

At the zenith of the hierarchy of aims (Figure 4-2) is the socioeconomic purpose.[7] Business organizations, for example, receive their charter from society to produce and distribute goods and to provide services at a profit. However, to make the total system work, society, through its governments, places constraints on enterprises. These constraints include laws pertaining to pollution, discrimination in unemployment practices, and so on.

It is generally taken for granted that business firms are relatively free to pursue their aims. But it is conceivable that the charter given to business may be revoked by society. For example, during the oil crisis in the early 1970s, oil companies were perceived—rightly or wrongly—by the public as taking advantage of the situation by charging what were thought to be exorbitant prices for gasoline. Consequently, the possibility of nationalizing the oil companies was discussed. The point is simply this: In our society free enterprises have a socioeconomic purpose, which is to contribute to the welfare of the nation while at the same time work toward their own aims.

1 Socioeconomic purpose

2 Mission (or organizational purpose)

3 Overall objectives of the organization
(long-range, strategic)

4 More specific overall objectives

5 Division objectives

6 Department and unit objectives

7 Individual objectives
a performance
b personal development objectives

FIGURE 4-2
Hierarchy of aims.

Mission of the Organization

The mission statement, also sometimes called organizational purpose, gives the enterprise the overall direction. It is the basis for determining long-range objectives, strategies, and operational plans. The mission statement is the answer to fundamental questions—previously mentioned in Chapter 2—such as:

"What is our business?"
"Who are our customers?"
"What do our customers want?"
"What should our business be?"

An example of a mission statement is one promulgated by General Electric (GE) in the early 1950s. It began:

To carry on a diversified, growing, and profitable worldwide manufacturing business in electrical apparatus, appliances and supplies. . . .[8]

Several other statements were added to complete the mission for this large, diversified company. Today, many years after this statement was first issued, we can look back and see that the mission (also called corporate purpose) provided direction for the years that followed. General Electric certainly is diversified, it has been growing, and it has worldwide manufacturing facilities.

The corporate purpose of Westinghouse Electric emphasized growth in profits, sales, high turnover investment, sharing of the fruits of increasing productivity among stockholders, the beneficial aspects of their products and services to society, responsiveness to and satisfaction of customers, a dynamic product line, high ethical standards, and an internal environment that results in high job satisfaction of employees.[9] Looking at the mission statements (or corporate purpose) by General Electric and Westinghouse, it becomes clear that they do set the tone for their businesses.

Another influence on the mission of an enterprise is the values of top managers. George W. England found that successful managers do value pragmatism and achievement.[10] These managers also have a dynamic orientation. On the other hand, less successful managers may hold values that favor static or passive states. It is likely that top management's orientation influences the decision in what kind of business the firm will be. Opportunities in the production and distribution of alcoholic beverages may not be pursued because of the chief executive officer's attitude toward the consumption of alcohol. Values are also often reflected in written philosophies or creeds of the enterprise, which may be expressed as the purpose of the firm and the ethical values guiding the operation. Union Carbide prides itself as being "the discovery company." RCA is "the most trusted name in electronics."

Typically, these creeds, purposes, or mission statements are vague and highly abstract. But they do set the tone, express a philosophy, and provide general direction. The mission statement, however, must be translated into more specific objectives to become operational.

Overall Objectives in Key Result Areas

The overall objectives of an organization can be either long range and strategic, or they can be specific with a long-, medium-, or relatively short-term orientation. An example of a long-range strategic objective is "to increase the market share of microprocessors from 4 percent to 6 percent over the next five years." An example of a short-term strategic objective (with long-range implications) would be "to complete the merger with another company within the next twelve months." Specific overall objectives usually need to be set in all key result areas (KRAs); these are areas where performance is vital for the health and long-term survival of the enterprise.[11]

1 *Markets.* This is a natural KRA because it is the customer who is the reason for the existence of the enterprise whether it be a business, a university, or a nonprofit organization. Market standing, for example, must be evaluated in light of the business growth rate and the relative competitive position of the firm.

2 *Products and services.* The KRA for products and services is closely related to the previous one. The organization's task is to provide something of value to the customer. The objective in this KRA may be for current or new products and services. But they may also concern the withdrawal of products or services from the market because of technical obsolescence or for other reasons.

3 *Innovation and research.* Innovation and research may be needed to achieve the objectives in the marketing KRA. However, it is often difficult to predict and measure the impact of innovation, which is usually costly and risky, as illustrated by Ford's Edsel car. A great deal of capital was spent in the development of the car, which did not get the market acceptance that market research had indicated. But not innovating can be equally disastrous for other companies. While each enterprise must determine the appropriate outlays for innovation, it must be remembered that even successful products and services will eventually become obsolete and provisions must be made for their obsolescence.

4 *Productivity.* There probably is no other topic that receives as much attention today as productivity. It is one of management's most important tasks to *increase* productivity. Yet, it is also management's most difficult task to establish criteria for measuring productivity because of the great variety of contributing factors. We usually focus on quantitative factors that lend themselves to relatively easy measurement. Yet, some of the greatest contributions to productivity may be difficult to measure, such as determining the future course of the enterprise through strategic planning.

5 *Financial and physical resources.* To achieve objectives, financial and physical resources are needed. Financial objectives may be related to the capital structure, collection of receivables, and the like. Physical resources are needed, for example, to achieve the marketing objectives. Thus, a company must make provisions for adequate plants, offices, machines, and tools. Other required resources vary with the types of business.

6 *Human resource management.* Perceptive managers regard people as the most important asset of an enterprise. It is, therefore, essential to plan for obtaining, developing, and using effectively the human resources necessary for the success of the enterprise. The development efforts must not only be concerned about individual growth, but must also be expanded to encompass organization development (OD), which is a systematic approach to analyzing and developing the total organization or a major division. Organizational development, which will be discussed in a later chapter, may focus on the organization structure, team building, or conflict resolution.

7 *Social responsiveness.* Enterprises do not exist in a vacuum; they are a part of society. Consequently, they must be concerned about the public interest and engage in actions that consider both the welfare of the public and their own interests.

8 *Surplus value.* The goal of any enterprise should be the accomplishment of an objective or mission with the least inputs of material, as well as human and other resources. It may also mean to achieve the highest level of an objective with the resources available. For business organization the surplus is profit. The term *surplus* is used in this discussion rather than profit because it applies not only to businesses, but also to nonprofit organizations, governments, and universities.

Although the listed KRAs may be applicable for most business organizations, they must not be blindly copied. Instead, it is necessary to analyze the operation and determine what is really critical for the success of a specific enterprise. After the identification of KRAs, objectives are set in each area. Table 4-1 illustrates how this can be done. Objectives are expressed as performance standards that can be measured. Verifiable objectives should be expressed, if possible, in terms of quantity, quality, time, and costs. Costs, it should be noted, may not have to be stated in dollars, but may be expressed in working hours. The market objective in Table 4-1 states the quantity and time—criteria always necessary for measurement. This objective, as written, has the limitation of not indicating the costs involved for increasing the market share. But at times it may not be possible, or it may be time-consuming, to make realistic cost estimates. The second objective in Table 4-1 (products and services) again states quantity and time, and if necessary could state the quality of the product and the costs involved. Thus, the objectives could have been stated as follows: "To introduce five new products in the 'widget' line by December 31, with a scrap rate not to exceed 0.5 percent at an additional cost not to exceed 1,000 working hours."

The objectives shown in Table 4-1 are illustrations only. As seen, they can be Improved. Still, the objectives, although not perfect, are measurable and indicate at least *what* should be achieved and *when*. The next section discusses additional, and more specific, areas in which productivity criteria can be set.

TABLE 4-1
ILLUSTRATION OF OBJECTIVES IN KEY RESULT AREAS

Area	Objective
Markets	To increase the market share of product X to 3 percent (currently 2 percent) by June 30.
Products and Services	To introduce five new products in the "widget" line by December 31.
Innovation and Research	To develop an electronically controlled fuel injection system for a six-cylinder engine by May 31, at a cost not to exceed $1.5 million.
Productivity	To increase the output of product "Y" by 4% without an increase in costs or reduction of current quality level by December 31.
Financial and physical resources	To increase working capital by $1 million by December 31.
Human resource management	To implement Phase I and II of the MBO program in the Aircraft Division at a cost not to exceed 500 working hours of the personnel in the organization development department by December 31.
Social responsiveness	To hire and train 500 members of minorities by December 31 of this year at a cost not to exceed 400 working hours.
Surplus value	To have a return on investment of 20 percent for the fiscal year ending June 30.

Organizational Productivity Indicators

Productivity consists of both effectiveness and efficiency. Many objectives are stated in terms of outputs only, without due consideration given to the inputs, that is, resources. There is no universal set of criteria applicable for all organizations, but the following examples, if adapted to the specific situation, may be a useful guide.[12] A business firm may use productivity measurements such as sales per number of employees or labor costs; number of units produced divided by the cost of producing them; number of units sold divided by sales costs; sales per payroll dollar; profit per employee; absentee rate; employees leaving voluntarily divided by the labor force; percent of job offers accepted (recruitment); savings achieved through computer application compared with investment in computers. In research and development, productivity indicators may be the dollar value of a proposal won (assuming a normal profit margin) divided by the dollars spent to obtain the proposal, or profits divided by R & D dollar spent.

These ratios should be supplemented by statements indicating *when* the performance is to be achieved (time dimension) and the quality of the outputs. Care must also be taken that the productivity standards do not become counterproductive. For example, in the 1960s the French automaker Renault had a considerable share of the imported auto market. But apparently not enough attention was given to building a quality dealership network with sufficient service facilities. Thus, high sales figures (outputs) were obtained with relatively little inputs (investment in building a dealer network). The productivity ratio probably was excellent—at least in the short run. In contrast the Japanese car manufacturers entered the United States market only after considerable market studies and a careful planning of their dealer network (inputs). Although their productivity index may not have been very favorable at the beginning, success came later. The point is that productivity indexes must be carefully selected and the short- as well as the long-term effect must be considered. Productivity ratios must not be obtained at the expense of quality.

The Network of Aims

So far the hierarchical nature of objectives has been emphasized. Certainly the vertical integration of objectives is important to ensure that each organizational unit contributes to the department or division at the next higher level. But horizontal consistency of goals is as important as vertical consistency. It makes little sense for production to overachieve its output goals of a product the sales department cannot sell. Unfortunately, the interdependency of objectives often leads to conflicts. For example, the objective of a credit manager to reduce bad debts by restricting credit may conflict with the objective of increasing sales that may require more liberal credit terms. Obviously, the objectives of the credit and sales managers must be balanced to keep bad debts at a reasonable level without a disastrous impact on sales. It is the very nature of systems thinking that it should recognize the interdependency and network nature of objectives that should form a mutually supportive network of aims with vertical and horizontal integration as shown in Figure 4-3.

Approaches to Setting Objectives

The discussion of ends-means analysis and the hierarchy of aims may give the impression that the process of objective setting should follow the organizational hierarchy, namely from the top to the lowest level of the organization. But this is not necessarily the case. The hierarchy of aims merely emphasizes the point that all objectives, of

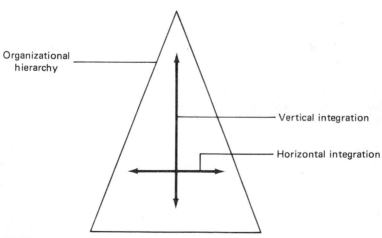

FIGURE 4-3
Vertical and horizontal integration of objectives.

all organizational units, and of all personnel (managers, staff, and workers) should contribute to the overall aim of the organization. The process of determining the objectives can be both top-down as well as bottom-up, where subordinates initiate the setting of objectives for their position.

Proponents of the top-down approach suggest that the total organization needs direction through corporate objectives provided by the chief executive officer (perhaps in conjunction with the board of directors). Proponents of the bottom-up approach, on the other hand, argue that top management does not really know the potential of the organization until the information comes from lower levels to the top in the form of objectives. Besides, it is proposed, participation in goal setting elicits commitment that eventually results in higher overall performance than if the objectives were set by top management. This school of thought proposes that team building and participative decision making come first and overall organizational goals are the natural result of this process.

The president of a large savings and loan association that achieved excellent results with the bottom-up approach maintains that he would not have dared to set the objectives at a level as high as his subordinates proposed. Similarly, the general manager of one of the largest automobile dealerships in the United States asked subordinate managers to set their own goals. They responded by setting goals 40 percent higher than the general manager thought possible. Perhaps even more important, these goals were not only achieved, but also they were surpassed. Managers felt a sense of "goal ownership" because the goals were not those of the superior, but their own—and they went out of their way to achieve them.

Although the bottom-up approach to goal setting worked in these two organizations, it does not ensure equal success in other situations.

Top-Down or Bottom-Up Depends on the Situation

The practicing manager, of course, wants to know whether the top-down or the bottom-up approach should be used. The answer to this question, unfortunately, is not simple. It depends on various factors such as the managerial philosophy, the organizational climate, the task requirements, the size of the organization, the willingness of top management to participate in the process, and the purpose of the program. For example, it is unrealistic to expect that an organization with a history of autocratic management will change overnight to a participative bottom-up goal-setting approach. On the other hand, an organization not willing to subscribe to the MBO philosophy which allows at least some participation as well as self-control will not gain the benefits of MBO. In fact, in enterprises with top-down autocratic management, MBO is most likely to fail because it will be opposed by organizational members who see it as an encroachment on their managerial discretion. Later chapters, especially Chapters 6 and 10, will deal with behavioral aspects of goal-oriented programs that emphasize the motivational aspects of the bottom-up approach.

The foregoing discussion of the hierarchy of aims is especially pertinent to a comprehensive goal-oriented program that may involve the whole organization and include strategic planning. But there are other, more limited approaches. A goal-oriented program may be used to carry out a specific project by a team consisting of professionals and specialists. In such a situation a bottom-up approach may be quite appropriate, with team members recommending objectives to upper management. Other programs may have as their primary purpose the growth and professional development of their managers. Again, bottom-up goal setting may be appropriate with individuals setting their developmental objectives largely by themselves.

These few examples illustrate that the decision whether to emphasize the top-down or the bottom-up approach must be based on the analysis of the situation. There is no single approach and any simple recommendation would be misleading.

Setting Strategic and Overall Objectives

Closely related to the previous discussion is the question whether strategic and overall objectives should be set in broad or specific terms. At times it is not advisable to set specific goals because they may become the rallying point for those opposing the intended strategic direction. Also, once specific goals are stated, it is rather difficult to change them without confusing managers throughout the organization. Announcing the goals too early in the strategic planning process may preclude thinking about alternative goals and courses of action. Since strategic planning is done in the light of competitors, specific overall objectives can alert them about the intended direction of the firm. Finally, conflicts may be reduced and cohesion enhanced by stating broad goals at the beginning but making them more specific when consensus is reached on the direction of the organization.

But there are also situations when it might be advantageous to state overall goals in specific terms. For example, a firm being almost exclusively dependent on government contracts may state that 60 percent of its business will be in the private sector within five years. At times, specific objectives such as a return on net assets within a time period may provide a challenge to find ways to achieve this aim. General Motors set an initial goal of reducing the weight of a specified model by 400 pounds. Johnson and Johnson set a goal of $1 billion in sales with a 15 percent aftertax return on investment within a specific time.[13] Whether strategic or overall objectives should be set initially in broad or specific terms depends on the situation.

Clear organizational aims provide a variety of benefits. If they are understood and shared by organizational members, they promote morale. They also help to identify problems and areas for improvement. In a well-managed fire department the organization members felt they had no problems. However, during organizational development workshops and goal-setting exercises it became evident that many opportunities for making the department more productive had been overlooked. Problem solving and improvement objectives are often the most beneficial outcomes of goal-oriented management.

Strategic and overall goals of the organization are seldom set in one meeting or even a few meetings. Instead, it is an incremental process that can take several years. Goals have to be set, evaluated, and re-evaluated in light of changes within the organization and in the external environment because certain events cannot be foreseen.

GETTING ACTION INTO OBJECTIVES*

Each member of an organization should contribute to the overall objectives of the enterprise. The efforts of managers can be made more productive by clarifying individual contributions and responsibilities through the application of the key result area (KRA) matrix shown in Figure 4-4.

Top management, with the collaboration of key executives, identi-

*Parts of this discussion have been adapted from H. Weihrich, "Getting Action Into MBO," *Journal of Systems Management,* vol. 28, no. 11 (November 1977), pp. 10–13. Used with permission.

Key result areas \ Management position	President	Research and development	Engineering	Production	Quality control	Marketing and sales	Finance	Personnel	Other	Other
1 Markets	✓	✓	✓	✓	X	✓	X	✓		
2 Products and services	✓	✓	✓	✓	✓	✓	X	X		
3 Innovation and research	X	✓	✓	✓	X	✓	X	X		
4 Productivity	✓	✓	✓	✓	✓	✓	✓	✓		
5 Financial and physical resources	✓	X	X	✓	X	✓	✓	X		
6 Human resource management										
7 Social responsiveness										
8 Surplus value										

*A check mark (✓) means that the person in the respective position does make a major contribution to, or has a major responsibility for, the key result area. An "X" indicates that the person does *not* make a major contribution to the key result area. You may want to complete this table for your organization.

FIGURE 4-4
Relating key results to managers' responsibilities.

fies the KRAs, or the objectives, in these areas. Each manager states whether he or she contributes to the respective KRA or has a major responsibility related to the KRA. Contributions are marked by a check (√) in Figure 4-4. Each checkmark indicates a major contribution to any of the KRAs and requires the setting of objectives in these areas. For example, the objective for the personnel manager, who makes a major contribution to the KRA of human resource management, may be: "To develop and teach five three-day courses on capital budgeting for 150 managers with at least 90 percent of the managers passing a specified test. The courses are to be completed by March 31, requiring not more than 500 working hours of the management development department."

The KRAs in the matrix Figure 4-4 are only described by words or phrases, but the chief executive officer (CEO) may want to elaborate on what he or she wants to accomplish. Two approaches can be taken for specifying contributions to the KRAs. First, the CEO may state in general terms what the organization is expected to accomplish. Then the other members of the management team may be asked to indicate in what way they can contribute to the KRAs. These intentions are communicated to other managers who have a need to know. Then, through the bottom-up approach, specific overall objectives can be set in the KRAs, based on the inputs from lower-level managers. In other words, the CEO gives broad direction and provides the framework, but the setting of specific objectives is primarily a bottom-up approach.

With the second approach to using the matrix, the CEO develops rather specific objectives in the KRAs, using inputs from other managers. Examples of such objectives are shown in Table 4-1. These objectives are communicated to managers at lower levels of the organization who then set their objectives congruent with the objectives of the next higher organizational unit. This is primarily a top-down approach—with rather specific objectives at the outset— followed by bottom-up communication of objectives to the top level in the organizational hierarchy. The CEO reviews the objectives obtained from lower levels and makes necessary changes in the overall objectives.

Which approach should be used? The first one, which starts with general KRAs at the top followed by specific objectives through the bottom-up approach? Or the second approach, which emphasizes top-down goal setting, starting with rather specific objectives? The answer is that it depends on the inclination of the CEO and the situation. But generally it has to be a two-way process: top-down and bottom-up. The difference lies in the degree of emphasis of one or the other. Most organizations probably prefer to elicit active participation of lower-level managers to obtain their commitment and to provide an environment in which managers, as a group, contribute to the overall aims of the enterprise.

IMPLICATIONS FOR MANAGERIAL PRODUCTIVITY

Objectives are the end points toward which activities should be directed. Clear objectives, then, should provide direction for individuals, groups, and organizations. Moreover, objectives are the criteria against which organizational productivity can be measured. Not only is the concern for the achievement of objectives, but the aim is to do so with the least amount of undesirable consequences, costs, or other inputs.[14] It will be remembered that productivity indicators should include both. In an organization with an effective structure of the hierarchy and network of aims, and a good coordination of these aims, undesirable consequences can be held to a minimum. Objectives can be viewed as an ends-means chain, as a hierarchy of aims, and a network of objectives with vertical and horizontal integration.

In this chapter we focused on the macro aspect of objectives related to the structure and integration of aims. We de-emphasized the micro features of goal setting for individuals, a topic discussed in the next chapter.

NOTES

1 W. F. Glueck, *Business Policy and Strategic Management,* 3d ed. (New York: McGraw-Hill, 1980).

2 G. A. Steiner and J. B. Miner, *Management Policy and Strategy,* 2d. ed (New York: Macmillan, 1982).

3 W. A. Ruch and J. C. Hershauer, *Factors Affecting Worker Productivity* (Tempe, Arizona: Bureau of Business and Economic Research, Arizona State University, 1974). For a more recent discussion of organizational effectiveness see G. H. Gaertner and S. Ramnarayan, "Organizational Effectiveness: An Alternative Perspective," *The Academy of Management Review,* vol. 8, no. 1 (January 1983), pp. 97–107.

4 C. H. Granger, "The Hierarchy of Objectives," *Harvard Business Review,* vol. 42, no. 3 (May-June 1964), pp. 63–74.

5 A. P. Raia, *Managing by Objectives* (Glenview, Ill.: Scott, Foresman and Company, 1974).

6 J. G. March and H. A. Simon, *Organizations* (New York: John Wiley & Sons, 1958), pp. 190–191. For a more recent discussion of the relationships between means and ends see J. F. Fredrickson, "Strategic Process Research: Questions and Recommendations," *The Academy of Management Review,* vol. 8, no. 4 (October 1983), pp. 565–575.

7 G. A. Steiner, *Top Management Planning* (London and Toronto: Collier-Macmillan Canada, Ltd., 1969).

8 R. J. Cordiner, *New Frontiers for Professional Managers* (New York: McGraw-Hill, 1956), pp. 119–120.

9 Westinghouse Electric Corporation, *Guide to Business Planning* (Pittsburgh, 1969), p. 1.

10 G. W. England, "Personal Value Systems of Managers and Administrators," *Academy of Management Proceedings* (August 1973).

11 P. F. Drucker, *The Practice of Management* (New York: Harper & Brothers, Publishers, 1954). Key result areas should not only be identified for the total organization, but also for divisions, departments, and sections.

12 *R & D Productivity—Investigation of Ways to Evaluate and Improve Productivity in Technology-Based Organizations,* 2d ed. (Culver City, Calif.: Hughes Aircraft Company, 1978).

13 J. B. Quinn, *Strategies for Change—Logical Incrementalism* (Homewood, Ill.: Richard E. Irwin, Inc., 1980).

14 The city of San Diego provides an interesting example of a comprehensive effort to productivity improvement ranging from total program management (TPM) to specific processes such as paperwork simplification. See "The City of San Diego—Organization Effectiveness Program," published by the City of San Diego, February 1983.

CHAPTER 5

IMPROVING INDIVIDUAL AND GROUP PRODUCTIVITY BY SETTING OBJECTIVES AND PLANNING FOR ACTION

This chapter examines individual and group productivity in goal setting and the development of action plans. Considerable literature and research exist on the aspect of setting objectives, partly because it can make individuals and organizations more effective.[1] This does not mean, however, that other parts of the managerial process contribute less to productivity. It simply is more difficult to gather solid research evidence of the impact of, let us say, strategic planning on productivity. Besides clarifying the ends, we must also determine the activities that are necessary to achieve the objectives, group and coordinate the activities, and delegate sufficient authority to achieve the goals. Action plans, then, provide systematic means to find new and productive ways to achieve results.

THE NATURE AND IMPORTANCE OF SETTING OBJECTIVES*

Setting of objectives is not an easy task. But, a conscientious effort to clarify the aims can greatly benefit the organization as well as the individual.[2] The potential advantages of MBO and goal setting are:

*Adapted from H. Weihrich, "How to Set Goals That Work for Your Company—and Improve the Bottom Line!" By permission of the publisher. *Management Review*, February 1982. Copyright © AMACOM, a division of American Management Association, New York. All rights reserved.

• Clarity of direction of the enterprise and for individuals contributing to the aims of the enterprise, the division, the department, and the section.

• An improved understanding of the role of individuals, their accountability, and what is expected of them.

• Improved vertical and horizontal integration of goals and activities.

• Better communication, not only between the superior and subordinate, but also throughout the organization.

• Commitment to objectives and results through genuine participation in the managerial process.

• Improved motivation and better utilization of individuals' potentials through self-direction and self-control without loss of accountability.

• Better planning and control.

In short, MBO, if properly implemented and practiced, results in better managing.

Since setting objectives can be rather difficult in practice, we will deal in detail with the setting of verifiable objectives. Verifiability means that, at the end of the time period, one must be able to measure whether or not the objectives have been achieved. If this cannot be done, objectives are not verifiable.

An effective comprehensive program usually has many of the following characteristics:

1 Managers and nonmanagers at all organizational levels set objectives.

2 Superior and subordinates jointly agree on what should be accomplished at a specific time in the future; these statements then become the individual manager's objectives.

3 In the case of complex and important objectives, action plans are developed that identify the activities and organizational efforts necessary to achieve the objectives.

4 These plans are implemented by providing an environment in which individuals, working together in groups, are motivated and committed toward the achievement of objectives.

5 Performance—individual and organizational—and results are measured against previously set objectives.

6 Objectives are set again for the future, and the process is repeated.

Some managers argue that these characteristics of the MBO approach are nothing more than good management. Agreed. Yet, few managers or companies use this approach systematically and vigorously.

Setting Individual Objectives

Individual goal setting has benefitted from the attention by researchers for some time. A considerable amount of research has been done under laboratory conditions.[3] In studies at the University of Maryland it was found that asking subjects to strive for specific objectives resulted in higher performance than simply asking subjects to do their best.[4] Moreover, high levels of intentions were associated with high levels of performance.[5] These and similar studies, many published in psychological journals, gave impetus for further research on the effects of MBO in companies. Thus it was found that:

1 There were relationships between difficult goals and positive attitudes toward MBO.

2 An increase in goal clarity, importance, and relevance was related to a positive position toward MBO by subordinates and improved relations with their superior.

3 When goal priorities were established, there were also more positive attitudes toward MBO by subordinates and improved relations with their boss.[6]

There are also indications that in an industrial setting, productivity was high when it was considered a means to achieve personal objectives under the assumption that the need of the individual was sufficiently high, the goal relatively salient, and the path free from barriers.[7] One of the first extensive field studies on an MBO program, supplemented by a follow-up study, indicated "a significant upward movement in the overall average level of goals."[8] Furthermore, an improvement in the attainment of goals and a continuing increase in productivity was noted, which, however, tapered off by the time the follow-up study was made. At any rate, management perceived the program as being advantageous for planning and control, despite the fact that the approach was not without its problems.

Another study examined the effects of MBO on performance and satisfaction in a governmental organization.[9] The findings in the state human services showed that after the implementation of MBO, a combined measure for quantity of performance and two quality measures improved; so did satisfaction with supervision. However, satisfaction with work did not improve. In all, MBO was beneficial and the study suggests that a goal-oriented program may be effectively implemented in a public sector organization.

The Process of Setting Objectives for Individuals

There are different processes for setting objectives within the organization, depending, to some extent, on the degree the top-down or bottom-up approach is used in developing the hierarchy and network of aims. In one approach, the MBO cycle starts with the organization's common goals, followed by a review, and if necessary, a revision of the organization structure before the superior and subordinate jointly set their objectives.[10] Another approach suggests that subordinates write a "manager's letter" to their superior.[11] To begin with, it is important that the objectives of all managers are defined in terms of their contribution to the larger organization unit to which they belong. Moreover, managers should be actively involved in the development of objectives of the higher organization unit to which they contribute. This furthers the understanding of the ultimate organizational goal, clarifies what is expected of the managers, and identifies the criteria on which subordinates are going to be evaluated and how they are to be judged. Managers should write a letter twice a year to their superior, stating how they see the objectives of their superior, as well as their own objectives. Then the subordinate managers list their performance standards as they see them, develop action plans to achieve the objectives, identify obstacles hindering their performance, and suggest ways in which their superior can help them. Finally, the manager outlines the action plan for achieving next year's goals. The "manager's letter" is a simple but powerful device to identify inconsistencies, to clarify expectations, and to improve communication.

Let us look more closely at the process of setting objectives. Once goals for the enterprise and the organizational unit have been clarified, the tedious task of setting objectives for individuals begins. Consider these steps:

1 One can start by asking "Why does the job exist?" "What is the unique contribution of this position?" "What authority and responsibility is associated with this job?" The answers to these questions lead to a statement of the job's purpose. (Companies that compile job descriptions will find them useful here.)

2 The next step is to identify individual key-result areas (IKRAs) or key tasks (both terms can be used). It's not unusual to learn that these may cover only 20 percent of the job but account for 80 percent of the results.

3 The relative importance of the IKRAs must be determined. Similarly, key tasks must be prioritized.

4 To set realistic objectives, internal and external environments must be forecast. For example, will gross national product (GNP) increase 5 percent or will the economy move toward recession? This forecast, then, becomes the premise underlying certain key objectives and plans.

5 Objectives must be set for individual key-result areas or key tasks. These objectives may be categorized as regular performance objectives, improvement or creative objectives, and professional development objectives.[12] How the achievements are to be measured should also be stated.

6 Action plans for achieving complex and critical objectives must be developed. This may result in modification of previously set objectives.

7 Objectives and action plans have to be integrated vertically and horizontally so that they are congruent with the aims of other managers. This may require meetings and negotiations with superiors, subordinates, and peers on the same or similar organizational level.

8 Because all plans are made in light of uncertainties, contingency plans must be prepared. Specifically, plans may be developed on assumptions different from, say, the one cited in item four above.

9 Unless performance is reviewed in a timely manner, the program will fail. First, a *comprehensive* formal review should be conducted, usually once or twice annually. Second, *progress* reviews (periodic and intermittent) should be scheduled from time to time to ensure progress toward the objective and to identify problems that may inhibit performance. Third, *informal monitoring* is needed to ensure prompt attention to deviations from plans. If any do occur, the supervisor and subordinate should take action immediately, without waiting for the next comprehensive or progress review.

The MBO process is not completed with the performance review. Building on the benefits of past experience, the participants repeat the entire process, beginning with a brief review of the job and key tasks. New objectives are set, and a new countdown—steps one through nine—is initiated.

Differentiation of Objectives Many companies do not use MBO throughout the organization. Still, objectives may be set on a department level or for individuals without a formal company program. In any case, great benefits can be gained by distinguishing different kinds of objectives.

In his pathsetting book *Management by Objectives* (1965) and his later book *MBO II,* George S. Odiorne, identified four categories of goals pertaining to: (1) routine activities, (2) emergency actions, (3) innovative and creative projects, and (4) personal growth and development.[13]

Setting goals for *routine activities* has the advantage of crystalizing the things that the subordinate must do, or should do, on a regular basis. These kinds of objectives also serve as the basis for distributing duties and work among subordinates. These responsibilities may be a part of the job description. Measurement of routine performance is often done by focusing on exceptions or unexpected deviation from standards.

Setting goals for *emergency situations* is far more difficult, because changes in the environment leading to an emergency or unexpected event are hard to foresee. Some examples in this category are the need for investigating an accident, finding a substitute for an ill employee, or entertaining an unexpected visitor.

Often the greatest benefits from MBO can be obtained by setting *innovative* and *creative goals.* Objectives maintaining the status quo are not enough. Instead, managers should be encouraged to make their job a more interesting one by using new techniques, new technology, or simply rearranging the work to achieve greater productivity. In one of the seminars I conducted in Jamaica, at first the fire chief insisted that his operation could not be improved. After some discussion it became clear that the time that elapsed between the sounding of the fire alarm and the fire truck's leaving the building was of crucial importance. After some creative thinking, the chief found a relatively simple solution to reduce substantially the response time by placing the fire protective clothing on the fire truck rather than having it stored in a different location. By creatively thinking about the critical factors that stand in the way of improved performance, alternative ways can be found to make people and organizations productive.

The final set of objectives relates to *personal growth and development.* People want to benefit from a program such as MBO. Since their potential is usually underutilized, they welcome the opportunity to gain greater job knowledge and to prepare themselves for the future. We will see in later chapters that professional development and career planning can be effectively integrated with a goal-oriented management system.

One Manager's Objectives   There is no universal format for stating objectives. Most companies develop their own forms, ranging from a simple statement of objectives to a complex form calling for many details. The form shown in Figure 5-1 will fit most positions, though In this instance it has been set up to illustrate how objectives can be set for a branch manager of a construction firm.

Note how the individual KRAs, or key tasks (column 1), have been categorized and ranked (column 2). The relative importance can also be indicated by an A-B-C ranking or by assignment of percentage weights.

The statements of objectives (column 3) may be too cryptic or otherwise unclear in some instances, for example, "To obtain six new *profitable* industrial contracts by 5/1 in the amount of . . ." could have spelled out exactly what profits were expected. In this instance, the manager had other objectives listed elsewhere that specified the profitability of the operations. Since the setting of verifiable objectives is one of the most difficult tasks, additional guidance is needed.

Guidelines for Goal Setting   Setting objectives appears deceptively simple. But when one actually sits down to write them, many difficulties are usually encountered. Goals are too often stated in generalities, with little operational usefulness. Objectives such as "to improve communication" or "to maximize profit" are platitudes with little value for the operating manager. The checklist (Table 5-1) provides guidelines that spotlight commonly encountered difficulties. (The numbered paragraphs below correspond to the checklist questions.)

1 Objectives should cover the job's main features. Key tasks can usually be derived from the job description, though not all tasks can, or should, be translated into objectives. In most situations, however, a few key activities account for a majority of results. Thus it is important to focus on the few crucial activities that generate results.

2 The number of objectives should be manageable; often MBO neophytes list 20 or 30 objectives, not realizing how difficult it is to

Agreement on Objectives

Name: J. Miller   Job title: Branch manager   Date: 1-3   Initial: J.M.   Next progress report: 4-1

Superior: O. Smith   Job title: District manager   Date: 1-3   Initial: O.S.   Next performance review 12-28

Purpose of the position: To manage the operation of the XYZ Company in the Western Region in an effective and efficient manner.

Individual KRA* key tasks	Importance	Objectives/standards/expected results	How measured	Progress review (date + results)	Performance review (date + results)	Comment/action/improvement
Productivity	2	To increase labor productivity of journeymen by 10% (or 100% std) by 4-1.	Productivity report	4-1. Labor productivity increased 8%.	12-28. The objective of 10% increase was achieved 2 months late (5-31).	It is necessary to involve union leaders to further the increase productivity.
Markets	1	To obtain 6 new profitable industrial contracts by 5-1 in the amount of $2 million.	List of contracts	7-1. Obtained 5 contracts of $1.8 million.	12-28. Construction in area was 30% below projection. In light of this, performance was good.	Not achieved because construction decreased 30% in the area.
Material	3	To decrease material inventory by 30% compared with the present level by 10-1.	Inventory report	10-1. Decrease in inventory 20%.	12-28. Performance not adequate.	Inventory control system must be modernized. Contract consultant to redesign system.
Human resource development	4	To develop and teach a seminar on scheduling and work planning for 20 foremen by 10-30. 70% of participants should pass test.	Standardized test	10-1. Seminar ready for presentation.	12-28. 80% of participants (20) passed the test.	Was very successful. Do similar seminar on electrical codes.
*KRA = key result areas	Rank, ABC, %	Develop action plan, if necessary	Control information	Short, frequent reviews	Comprehensive review	Improvement and development plan

FIGURE 5-1
Managerial objectives.

TABLE 5-1 CHECKLIST FOR MANAGERIAL OBJECTIVES

1 Do the objectives cover the main features of my job?   □*
2 Is the list of objectives too long? If so, can I combine some objectives?   □
3 Are the objectives verifiable; that is, do I know at the end of the period
   whether or not they have been achieved?   □
4 Do the objectives indicate   □
   (a) quantity? (how much, or what)   □
   (b) quality? (how well, or specific characteristics)   □
   (c) time? (when)   □
   (d) cost? (at what cost)   □
5 Are the objectives challenging yet reasonable?   □
6 Are priorities assigned to the objectives? (ranking, weighting, etc.)   □
7 Does the set of objectives also include
   (a) improvement objectives?   □
   (b) personal development objectives?   □
8 Are the objectives coordinated with other managers and organizational
   units? Are the objectives consistent with the objectives of my superior, my
   department, the company?   □
9 Have I communicated the objectives to all who need to be informed?   □
10 Are the short-term objectives consistent with long-term aims?   □
11 Are the assumptions underlying the objectives clearly identified?   □
12 Are the objectives expressed clearly and in writing?   □
13 Do the objectives provide for timely feedback so that I can take any
   necessary corrective steps?   □
14 Are the resources and authority sufficient for achieving the objectives?   □
15 Have I given the individuals who are expected to accomplish objectives a
   chance to suggest their objectives?   □
16 Do my subordinates have control over aspects of the work for which they
   are assigned responsibility?   □
17 Are the right objectives selected? Can they induce dysfunctional behavior?   □

*Mark "+" if the objectives meet the criteria; mark "−" if the objectives do not meet the criteria.

Source: Adapted from H. Koontz, C. O'Donnell, and H. Weihrich, Management, 8th ed. New York: McGraw Hill, 1984. Used with permission.

keep track of so many goals. Some management advisors believe that a manager cannot pursue more than two to five objectives effectively because too many objectives may not sufficiently highlight the really important ones. We have learned, however, that a manager can combine minor goals and state them as one major objective. At any rate, the exact number of objectives depends on the position of the MBO participant, his or her specific tasks, and the degree to which a manager can assign tasks to subordinates.

3 Perhaps the most difficult—and crucial—aspect of setting

objectives is stating them in verifiable terms so that at the end of a period the manager and supervisor can determine whether or not objectives have been achieved or to what degree they have been accomplished. Terms such as "maximize," "minimize," "as soon as possible," and "adequate" indicate nonverifiability. An economist can discuss with authority theories regarding "profit maximization." However, a chief executive officer or board of directors doesn't want to know that a manager has "maximized" the unit's profits, but that he/she has attained the 15 percent (or whatever) gain that was set as a goal at the previous planning session.

Some managers distinguish between quantitative and qualitative objectives. A quantitative objective would be to produce 100 widgets per month at a certain cost. An example of a qualitative objective would be to "install a computerized control system in the production department by December 31 at a cost not to exceed $100,000." The latter objective shows how an activity can be translated into a verifiable objective.

I prefer not to distinguish between quantitative and qualitative objectives because it can be difficult to do so. Moreover, many objectives are stated not only in terms of quantity but also in terms of quality—by which we mean the property or characteristic of the output or result. Thus we talk here about the quality of output, not of qualitative objectives, which are mostly activities stated in the form of verifiable objectives.

4 Verifiable objectives should state quantity, quality, time, and cost. At the minimum, they should indicate the quantity in answer to the "how much" question and state the time by which the results are to be achieved. Quality may be important when, for example, the life and welfare of people depend on the product or service. On the other hand, a return-on-investment objective of 12 percent by the year-end may not require an explicit statement about quality. In summary, then, the quality of a product, service, or result should be stated when it is crucial and feasible.

More of something is not necessarily better. We may not want to increase the quantity of the objective but desire to achieve the same result at a lower cost. The cost aspect of objectives is crucial at a time when we are concerned about productivity which, in a simplified form, can be stated as output divided by input, or $P = O/I$. This means we may (1) increase output with the same input, (2) decrease input and obtain the same level of output, or (3) change both input and output in a way that produces a more favorable ratio.

5 Objectives should be challenging, yet reasonable, and require some effort for their achievement. The belief that unrealistically high objectives will motivate subordinates is erroneous. Nonachievable objectives are often demotivating to many people. Also, unrealistic goals may lead managers to engage in unethical or illegal actions because of fear or their concern of not achieving the goals.[14]

6 Priorities should be assigned to objectives on the basis of their relative importance. Figure 5-1 shows that the priorities of objectives can be indicated by (1) ranking them, (2) assigning ABC categories to them, and (3) assigning porcentage weights. But there is another alternative. George L. Morrisey, who wrote extensively on the various aspects of goal setting, suggests three groupings: the "got-to-do's" are the objectives that must be achieved; the "ought-to-do's" are the objectives necessary for improved performance, but their nonachievement is not catastrophic; and the "nice-to-do's" are those objectives that are desirable but could be postponed or eliminated.[15]

7 Objectives should not relate only to routine operations. Indeed, the greatest benefits of MBO may be gained by focusing on improvement and creative objectives designed to change and improve traditional ways of doing things. Innovative approaches initiated by top management are usually most visible. Lee Iacocca changed Chrysler's direction in a rather dramatic way. The new line of cars was a major departure from the past. Similarly, the problems of S. S. Kresge in the 1960s were creatively translated into opportunities through the K Mart stores. But opportunities for improvement can be found at all levels of the organization. However, top management must set the tone through example; it also must be tolerant toward those managers that take calculated risks and fail from time to time. Moreover, objectives should also include personal and professional development accomplishments.

8 Objectives must be coordinated with other managers and organizational units, since few positions are independent of others and an organization is an interdependent system in terms of activities and goals.

9 Objectives, to be operational, should be communicated to all who need to know. For example, an objective to increase sales certainly requires communication with production.

10 Short-term objectives should be consistent with long-range aims. In the past, most MBO programs emphasized short-term results, which were at times achieved at the expense of the enterprise's long-term health. Japan's high level of productivity may, in part, be attributable to the managerial system that favors decisions benefitting the company in the long run.

11 Assumptions underlying major objectives should be clearly stated. Because the future cannot be predicted accurately, the wise manager will make contingency plans based on different sets of assumptions.[16] Moreover, managers may hesitate in making commitments to specific goals because of the uncertainties in the environment. To overcome the legitimate concern of managers, objectives can be stated in terms of ranges. For example, an objective may be an increase in sales in the next fiscal year ranging from 11 to 15 percent, depending on the economic situation. A more precise approach is to make three estimates: an optimistic one, a realistic one, and a pessimistic one. For example, the optimistic objective may be an increase in sales of 15 percent if real GNP is to increase 5 percent and if the product acceptance is somewhat better than estimated. The realistic objective is an increase in sales of 14 percent based on the assumption that GNP will increase by 5 percent and that no new competitor will enter the market. The pessimistic objective may be an increase in sales of 11 percent with a real GNP increase of 3 percent and the entrance of a competitor in the latter half of the fiscal year. Making three estimates encourages managers to think seriously about the future conditions of the environment and at the same time alleviates some of the anxieties in making commitments through verifiable goals.

12 Objectives should be expressed clearly in writing, stating them in terms of quantity, time, and, if feasible, quality and costs. Some managers have their objectives clearly in mind; however, most benefit by recording them. This not only helps to clarify objectives but also creates a document that can be distributed to individuals with a need to know.

13 Opportunities for timely feedback should be provided. Prompt feedback facilitates actions to correct deviations from plans before they become major problems.

14 The setting of objectives should be accompanied by examination of resources and the authority needed to achieve the goals. A manager should have access to appropriate financial, human, and physical resources and the authority commensurate with his or her responsibility.

15 In general, objectives should be set by the managers who will carry out the activities to achieve their results. MBO emphasizes, whenever appropriate, participation in setting goals, since participation elicits commitment to aims. On the other hand, goals imposed by superiors on subordinates are often resisted. Experience has shown that, in the proper organizational environment, objectives set by individuals themselves are often higher than those set by their superiors.

16 Individuals should have control over those job requirements for which they are held accountable. Few things cause more frustration than being held responsible for tasks beyond the individual's control. Yet, most positions in modern organizations are interdependent with activities in other organizational units. The ideal situation of equality of authority, responsibility, and accountability can seldom be obtained. Consequently, the network of aims may have to include group goals, which may in turn require team building, involving managers whose tasks are highly interdependent.

17 Care must be taken to select the right objectives and to avoid those that may produce dysfunctional behavior. Objectives must focus on goals that encourage managerial behavior that benefits the organization. Pursuit of wrong objectives wastes resources and is counterproductive. For example: "To reduce the number of warranty claims by 10 percent by December 31" appears to be a good objective. But if sales increase by 50 percent in the same period, reducing warranty claims as stated may be impossible.

Another caution: Objectives frequently cause undesirable behavior that may be detrimental in the long run. Taking the above example, the objective of reducing warranty claims could motivate field engineers to reject customer complaints outright, rather than handle them objectively. The resulting loss of customer goodwill would be detrimental.

Consider also that by selecting one goal others may have to be foregone. For example, limited resources may preclude an organization from pursuing several attractive investments concurrently. Similarly, a choice may have to be made between goals that are in conflict. Thus, layoffs may require choosing between cutting costs and improving profitability on the one hand, and the desirability of providing employment stability for the workforce on the other hand.

Some Additional Considerations   Professor Babcock of the University of San Francisco suggests that there are environments in which it is not feasible, nor desirable, to set verifiable objectives. In some situations the future conditions are too unpredictable for accurate planning and goal setting. These environments can be characterized as either reactive or novel (no prior experience). In a reactive environment the task is to perform as the condition arises. The goal of the fire department may be to extinguish forest fires effectively and efficiently. A verifiable objective to put out a specific number of fires would be inappropriate. Yet, the fire department personnel could still set objectives for maintaining and improving their firefighting capabilities. In my work with the Phoenix fire department, for example, we set objectives for reducing the occurences of fire by disposing of dry and flammable material in back alleys and other high-risk areas. Furthermore, fire inspections were increased in public places. It is true that the cause-effect relationship between the improvement efforts and the reduction of fires cannot be clearly determined. The important point is that the fire chief and his team began thinking creatively about their role, which was not only to extinguish fires, but also to prevent them by setting improvement objectives.

There are also environments too unpredictable for setting verifiable goals. In such a case the goal may be general (not necessarily verifiable) and as the person works toward the aim, information about the task and experience is gathered that facilitates setting measurable criteria in the future. There are also situations where it is too expensive to collect the data for goal verification or where no records are kept for control. But with the introduction of relatively low-cost computers the task of collecting data has become less expensive. At any rate, the benefits of a control system must outweigh the costs. Another area where objectives may be difficult to set is for those whose primary task is to give advice: staff personnel.

Objectives for Staff Positions

A frequently heard complaint is that MBO may be difficult to apply to staff positions. There are some differences between line and staff applications, but MBO can be used.[17] Some managers find it difficult to set verifiable objectives for staff positions because staff activities may focus on development of programs. However, MBO can be applied by stating objectives in terms of activities. For example: The objective of a systems analyst may be "To install a computerized control system in the warranty department by March 31, involving 300 work hours and a downtime of the system not to exceed 5 percent during the first two months of operation." This objective states *what* has to be done, *when* it will be done, the *costs* in terms of work hours (the labor cost could also be stated in dollars), and *quality* in terms of downtime.

The accountability of staff is always an issue. One could argue that the systems engineer cannot be held solely responsible for the downtime because it is also the operator's responsibility to keep the computer in working order. Some would say that responsibilities should be further specified for the systems designer and the operator. But one could also argue that staff should be made responsible for results, and line and staff must jointly share responsibility and credit for achieving objectives. Whatever position is taken, dual responsibility cannot be completely avoided in organizations with interlocking tasks. Most managers depend on the contribution of others. Similarly, managers also contribute to other organizational units.

ACTION PLANNING[18]

Objectives are a starting point in the managerial process. The action plan is concerned with *what* key functions, tasks, and activities must be carried out to achieve the objectives. Moreover, it has to be decided *how* to reach the objectives most effectively and efficiently because in almost all situations alternative courses of action can be taken. Since timing is critical in the management process, it has to be decided *when* things must be done. Finally, unless it is stated *who* is going to do the tasks, they will not get done.

Opinions differ on whether action plans are needed to supplement objectives. While excessive paperwork is an easy way to elicit resistance to a program, no plans for achieving objectives can also lead to failure. I recommend the use of action plans when critical or complex objectives are involved. For example, when the objectives of one department are greatly dependent on those of another, action planning helps to identify the contribution of each. But there are other reasons for suggesting the preparation of action plans. If objectives are set for the first time and their level is unclear, an action plan helps to identify the tasks necessary to achieve the aims and thus arrive at realistic objectives. In another situation the risk of failure may be so high that a detailed plan for achieving the objectives may increase the chance of accomplishing the intended results.

Benefits of Action Plans

Action plans not only facilitate the setting of objectives, they may result in other *benefits* as well. First, they force the manager to look for and test several alternatives available to achieve the objectives. Second, the necessary activities are identified and can be grouped in the most effective and efficient manner based on the available human and material resources. Third, responsibilities are determined and authority is delegated congruent with the responsibilities. Fourth, during the action planning process, potential problems are uncovered and steps can be taken to prevent their occurrence. Fifth, resource requirements and costs are estimated and allocated to the objectives. Sixth, time schedules are established that facilitate realistic time frames for objectives and plans.

The Action-Planning Process

During goal setting it may become evident that for some objectives a simple statement of what is to be accomplished is not sufficient. Consequently, an action plan has to be developed. The following eight steps facilitate this process:

1 Identify the end results. This is really a part of the goal-setting process. It is restated here to emphasize that activities must contribute to the achievement of objectives.

2 Determine important functions, tasks, and activities necessary to achieve the end results. If the list of activities is too long, it would be useful to group the activities.

3 Provide for vertical and horizontal integration of the tasks of groups and individuals.

4 Identify the key tasks and activities for individual positions.

5 Define the roles, authority, and responsibility for each individual position.

6 Schedule the time needed for major activities and coordinate them into a time network. Adjust, if necessary, the objectives.

7 Determine the adequacy of human, financial, and other resources necessary to achieve the objectives and to carry out the activities.

8 Review the action plans and see if they are congruent with the objectives.

These steps provide a useful framework, but it must be understood that they do not always follow the above sequential order. For example, when setting objectives, it may be necessary to determine the time dimensions of critical events. One may first make a tentative time schedule before finalizing the objective. Therefore, the steps cannot be followed rigidly, but rather, they must be applied with flexibility to fit the particular situation.

IMPLICATIONS FOR MANAGERIAL PRODUCTIVITY

In the past, productivity improvements focused on the tasks of workers. It is, of course, relatively easy to measure the output of mass-produced items that can be counted and the quality that can be evaluated. But, it is suggested that the greatest potential for improvement for the total organization is in management. To be sure, measuring inputs and managerial outputs is more difficult than counting the products coming off the assembly line. The setting of verifiable objectives is one way of making managers more productive, as studies have indicated. Traditional MBO programs emphasized outputs only, but real productivity consists of both inputs (for example, resources used and costs) as well as outputs.

Setting of objectives, the key to measuring productivity, is a demanding task. Yet, if it is done well, it can be rewarding. The managerial objectives form illustrates how individual key result areas, or key tasks, can be translated into verifiable objectives against which productivity can be measured. But objectives are not of equal importance; they must be prioritized. These objectives, then, become the basis for the progress and the comprehensive performance reviews, the correction of undesirable deviations from plans, and the improvement of managerial performance. Since the setting of objectives is a difficult task, the checklist and guidelines introduced in this chapter focus on problem areas and suggest how to overcome these difficulties.

Clear objectives are essential for directing the efforts of managers toward these ends, but it is also necessary to develop systematically the means to achieve those ends. Thus, in action planning we identify the necessary functions, tasks, and activities and coordinate them vertically and horizontally. Furthermore, these plans show how much time it takes to carry out the activities and who is responsible for which actions.

In summary, then, objectives clarify the ends, and action plans systematize the means for achieving them. Both aspects of this managerial process are required for improving managerial and organizational productivity.

NOTES

1 Goal setting is the most widely discussed and researched aspect of MBO, as the following sources indicate: J. M. Ivancevich, "Effects of Goal Setting on Performance and Job Satisfaction," *Journal of Applied Psychology,* vol. 61, no. 5 (October 1976), pp. 613–621; J. M. Ivancevich, J. T. McMahon, J. W. Streidle, and A. D. Szilagyi, "Goal Setting: The Tenneco Approach to Personal Development and Management Effectiveness," *Organizational Dynamics,* vol. 6, no. 3 (Winter 1978), pp. 58–80; G. P. Latham and G. A. Yukl, "A Review of Research on the Application of Goal Setting in Organizations," *Academy of Management Journal,* vol. 18, no. 4 (December 1975), pp. 824–825; M. L. McConkie, "A Clarification of the Goal Setting and Appraisal Process in MBO," *Academy of Management Review,* vol. 4, no. 1 (January 1979), pp. 29–40; G. S. Odiorne, "How to Succeed in MBO Goal Setting," *Personnel Journal,* vol. 57, no. 8 (August 1978), pp. 427–429, 451; A. P. Raia, "Goal Setting and Self-Control," *Journal of Management Studies,* vol. 2, no. 1 (1965), pp. 34–53; B. K. Scanlan, "Participation in Objective Setting," *The Personnel Administrator,* vol. 14, no. 2 (February 1969), pp. 1–12; H. L. Tosi, Jr. and C. J. Carroll, "Setting Goals in Management by Objectives," *California Management Review,* vol. 7, no. 2 (Winter 1970), pp. 70–78; D. D. Umstot, T. R. Mitchell, and C. H. Bell, Jr., "Goal Setting and Job Enrichment: An Integrated Approach to Job Design," *Academy of Management Review,* vol. 3, no. 4 (October 1978), pp. 867–879.

2 For research studies on the benefits of MBO, see S. J. Carroll, Jr. and H. L. Tosi, Jr., *Management by Objectives—Applications and Research* (New York: MacMillan, 1973), chap. 2; H. Weihrich, "Management by Objectives: Does It Really Work?" *University of Michigan Business Review,* vol. 28, no. 4 (July 1976), pp. 27–31; J. M. Ivancevich, J. T. McMahon, J. W. Streidl, and A. D. Szilagyi, Jr., op. cit.

3 See, for example, E. A. Locke, "The Relationship of Intentions to Level of Performance," *Journal of Applied Psychology,* vol. 50, no. 1 (February 1966), pp. 60–66, and E. A. Locke, "A Closer Look at Level of Aspiration as a Training Procedure," *Journal of Applied Psychology,* vol. 50, no. 5 (October 1966), pp. 417–420.

4 E. A. Locke and J. F. Bryan, "Performance Goals as Determinants of Level of Performance and Boredom," *Journal of Applied Psychology,* vol. 51, no. 2 (April 1967), pp. 120–130.

5 Locke, "The Relationship of Intentions to Level of Performance."

6 S. J. Carroll, Jr. and H. L. Tosi, Jr., "Goal Characteristics and Personality Factors in a Management-by-Objectives Program," *Administrative Science Quarterly,* vol. 15, no. 3 (September 1970), pp. 295–305; and Carroll and Tosi, *Management by Objectives.*

7 B. A. Georgopoulos, G. M. Mahoney, and N. W. Jones, Jr., "A Path-Goal Approach to Productivity," *Journal of Applied Psychology,* vol. 41, no. 6 (December 1957), pp. 345–353.

8 A. P. Raia, "A Second Look at Management Goals and Controls," *California Management Review,* vol. 8, no. 4 (Summer 1966), pp. 49–58.

9 K. R. Thompson, F. Luthans, and W. D. Terpening, "The Effects of MBO on Performance and Satisfaction in a Public Sector Organization," *Journal of Management,* vol. 7, no. 1 (1981), pp. 53–68.

10 G. S. Odiorne, *MBO II—A System of Managerial Leadership for the 80s* (Belmont, Calif.: Fearon Pitman, 1979).

11 P. F. Drucker, *Management—Tasks, Responsibilities, Practices* (New York: Harper & Row, 1973, 1974). It is interesting to note that the manager's letter became the basis for Douglas McGregor's classic article, "An Uneasy Look at Performance Appraisal," *Harvard Business Review,* vol. 35, no. 3 (May-June, 1957), pp. 88–94.

12 The different kinds of objectives are discussed by Odiorne, *MBO II,* chaps. 11–14.

13 This discussion is largely based on G. S. Odiorne, *Management By Objectives* (New York: Pitman, 1965) and *MBO II,* op. cit.

14 "Overdriven Execs," *The Wall Street Journal,* Nov. 8, 1979.

15 G. L. Morrisey, *Management By Objectives and Results* (Reading, Mass.: Addison-Wesley, 1970), p. 49.

16 Forecasting and establishing planning premises is ignored by many practitioners and writers. But it is emphasized by Harold Koontz, *Appraising Managers as Managers* (New York: McGraw-Hill, 1971), chap. 3.

17 See H. Weihrich and S. N. Tingey, "Management by Objectives—Does It Apply to Staff?" *Industrial Management, vol. 18, no. 1 (January-February 1976), pp. 24–29.*

18 This section is based, in part, on H. Weihrich, "Getting Action Into MBO," *Journal of Systems Management,* vol. 28, no. 11 (November 1977), pp. 10–13. Used with permission.

CHAPTER 6

IMPLEMENTING ACTION PLANS AND PROGRAMS

Plans and programs have to be implemented. This requires creating and maintaining an environment conducive to the efficient achievement of organizational and individual objectives. To create the environment for making people productive, we must understand the nature of people and their leadership styles. Furthermore, people play psychological games that inhibit managerial productivity. In this chapter, then, we will first deal with assumptions about the nature of people. Then we will use the managerial grid to analyze the effect of leadership styles on the MBO process. Finally, we will identify productive and nonproductive transactions, as well as psychological games in order to improve managerial productivity by applying concepts of transactional analysis (TA). This chapter deals primarily with the human aspects on the micro level; that is, the focus is on individuals and small groups. Additional human considerations for implementing MBO on the macro level (concerning, for example, the organizational climate) are discussed in Chapter 10 on organizational development.

ASSUMPTIONS ABOUT PEOPLE*

Our lives are greatly influenced by our concepts about the nature of people. These assumptions will influence the way we manage. We want to explore in this chapter how these sets of assumptions may influence the way the essential steps in MBO are carried out. These steps are, you may recall:

1 Setting objectives
2 Developing action plans
3 Implementing the action plans and programs
4 Controlling organizational performance and appraising individual results

The MBO philosophy is based, in part, on the notion of self-control, self-direction, and professional growth, which, in turn, must start with the very basic question of how managers see themselves in relation to others. This requires some thoughts on the perception of human nature. Douglas McGregor identified two sets of assumptions—two theoretical constructs—about the nature of people. He called one Theory X and the other Theory Y.[1]

Expressed in a simplified manner, Theory X assumptions include the following: (1) People don't like to work and will, if possible, avoid it; (2) people have to be forced and directed to work; and (3) people dislike responsibility.

On the other hand, Theory Y assumptions include, among others, the following: (1) People are not by nature passive and like to work; (2) people work best by directing their own efforts toward objectives of the organization; and (3) people want to assume responsibility.

That these two sets of assumptions are fundamentally different needs little elaboration. Clearly, Theory X is pessimistic, static, and rigid. Control is primarily external, that is, imposed by the superior. In contrast, Theory Y is optimistic, dynamic, and flexible with an emphasis on self-control and the integration of individual and organizational needs. There is little doubt that each set of assumptions will affect the way an organization implements MBO. Table 6-1 summarizes the conjected behavior that relates the two theories with the steps in the MBO process. At the outset it should be stated that

*Adapted from H. Weihrich, "MBO: Theory X and Theory Y," *Personnel Administrator,* vol. 22, no. 2 (February 1977), pp. 54–57. Used with permission from The American Society for Personnel Administration, 606 North Washington Street, Alexandria, VA 22314.

TABLE 6-1

MBO: THEORY X AND THEORY Y—A NEW PERSPECTIVE

	Theory X—People dislike work; people must be forced to work; people do not willingly assume responsibility.	Theory Y—People like to work; people work best under self-direction; people like to assume responsibility.
1 Setting objectives	Autocratic approach. Superior sets objectives. Little participation by subordinates. Low commitment to objectives by subordinates. Few alternative objectives considered. Rigid organization. Little coordination.	Subordinate sets own objectives. Superior as a coach. Objectives as a challenge. Contribution to higher levels. Organizational objectives are coordinated. Personal development objectives included. Integration of individual and organizational objectives. Flexible and adaptable organization.
2 Developing action plans	Superior determines tasks. Few alternatives explored. Superior sets time frame. Problems with uncertain tasks. Low creativity. Superior defines responsibilities.	Subordinates develop action plans. Many alternatives are explored. Coordination may be a problem. Teamwork emphasized. People seek responsibility and are accountable for results.
3 Implementation	Rigid, mechanistic program. Paperwork and policy manuals emphasized. Little coaching. People resist MBO. Philosophy of MBO not taught.	MBO flexible and adaptable. Active participation. Possibly pilot program. People are prepared for MBO. MBO philosophy taught. Opportunity for growth. Integration of organizational demands and individual needs. Team approach.
4 Control and appraisal	External, rigid controls. Superior as a judge. Inappropriate standards may be pursued. Team performance may suffer. Low trust. Focus on past. Minimum feedback and information. Little self-control and self-development.	Utilizing human potential and creativity. Internalized self-control. Commitment to performance. Frequent review of standards. Superior as a helper. Considerable trust. Necessary information available. Focus on future opportunities and improvement. Feed-forward control. Self-development. Problem-solving attitude.

McGregor was very concerned that Theory X and Theory Y might be misinterpreted. I share this concern. The following remarks, therefore, are designed to facilitate understanding and keep the discussion in its proper perspective.

First, Theory X and Theory Y assumptions are just that; they are assumptions only. They are not prescriptions, nor managerial strategies. Rather, these assumptions must be tested against organizational realities. Second, Theory X and Y do not imply hard and soft management. The hard approach may produce resistance and antagonism. The soft approach may result in laissez faire management and is certainly not congruent with Theory Y. Instead, effective managers recognize the dignity, capabilities, but also limitations, of people and adjust their behavior as demanded by the particular situation. Third, in this chapter the possible effects of two different sets of assumptions (Theory X and Theory Y) on the fundamental steps of MBO are proposed. It should be noted that this is a tentative view that awaits validation of data-based research. Fourth, this discussion is not a case for consensus management, nor is it an argument against the use of authority. But authority is seen as only *one* of the many ways a manager exerts leadership. Fifth, different tasks and situations require a variety of approaches to management. At times, authority may be the best way to get quick action.

The MBO Process: Theories X and Y

In the MBO process, activities are directed toward the achievement of objectives. This requires that the superior and subordinate agree about what is to be accomplished. Action plans are then developed and implemented. Performance—organizational and individual—is measured against objectives, as shown later in Chapter 7. This process will take different dimensions, depending on how managers view the nature of human beings.

Step 1: Setting Objectives   Setting objectives is one of the most difficult steps in the MBO process. It requires effective interactions between the superior and subordinate. It also necessitates coordination of objectives of different organizational units. Obviously, production objectives must be synchronized with those of the sales department. The discussion that follows will illustrate setting of objectives based on Theory X and Theory Y assumptions.

Theory X   The superior, assuming that people, especially subordinates, dislike work and consequently must be forced to work, tends to take a directive, authoritarian role in the goal-setting process. The boss will set the objectives for subordinates with little opportunity for their participation. Therefore, subordinates are not committed to the achievement of objectives and will often consider them as being imposed, unrealistic, and inappropriate. The organizational atmosphere, then, is not conducive to exploring alternative objectives, and the organization becomes relatively rigid and not adaptive to environmental changes. In addition, insufficient efforts are made to coordinate objectives with those of other organizational units.

Theory Y   This theory is based on the assumptions that people want to work, exercise self-direction, and like to assume responsibility. In an organization with managers adhering to these assumptions, the setting of objectives is quite different. After thinking about their jobs, subordinates set objectives for themselves and the superior assumes the role of a coach. Objectives are challenging, yet realistic, and contribute to those of their superiors. Furthermore, objectives of the various organizational units are coordinated with each other. The objectives not only pertain to performance measures but also include personal development. As a result, there are many opportunities for self-realization; organizational demands and individual needs are basically congruent. Because of their active involvement in the process, people are committed toward the achievement of their own objectives and those of the company. Also, the internal and external environments of the organization are continuously scanned for new opportunities. This kind of organization, therefore, is characterized by flexibility and adaptability to the changing environment.

Step 2: Action Planning   In order to achieve objectives, functions and activities have to be carried out. An action plan may be required, especially for critical and complex objectives, because in most situations alternative courses of action are feasible. Not only are the necessary activities identified, but also the method to achieve results most effectively and efficiently is determined. Moreover, a timeframe for completion of the various tasks is essential for concerted action. Finally, responsibilities for carrying out the tasks and activities are defined.

Theory X   As in the goal-setting process, the superior plays a decisive role in determining functions, tasks, and activities. Probably only a limited number of alternative courses of action will be examined and only minor contributions will be made by subordinates. Timing of activities is considered the primary task of the superior. If the manager is competent and has the inclination for planning, and if the tasks are repetitive or well defined, such a plan may work reasonably well. However, problems often occur if plans involve new and vaguely defined activities that require participation of peers and subordinates in this process. Also, this organizational climate is not conducive to creative evaluation of different alternatives. Responsibilities for subordinates are usually defined by the superior who does not give sufficient opportunities to subordinates to utilize their creativity and potential.

Theory Y Subordinates have more possibilities for developing action plans to achieve their objectives. Many alternative courses of action will be examined before a decision is made. Because of the great variety of plans, care must be given to their coordination. On the other hand, the prevailing team spirit is conducive to integration of the efforts of individuals and different organizational units so that activities are channeled toward the common aims of the organization. People seek, rather than avoid, responsibility and feel accountable for results.

Step 3: Implementation of Action Plans and Programs   MBO focuses on action and results. Depending on the assumptions about the nature of people, the implementation of MBO will vary widely.

Theory X Because of the limited view of people, the implementation of MBO is rather rigid and less capable of adapting to the specific organizational situation. The program, usually conceived by top management, may be mechanistic. In fact, the emphasis is too often on filling out forms, rather than on getting results. There is little coaching of participants in MBO; rather, policy manuals may describe the program. In this climate, people are distrustful of the new programs because they do not know how it will affect them. The result is an overt or covert resistance to these "newfangled" ideas. Participants in the MBO program are not prepared for this new way of managing, which is based on the philosophy of self-control and trust in the basic nature of people.

Theory Y MBO, based on Theory Y assumptions, is flexible and able to adapt to the needs of the particular organization. Because of the trust in people, organizational members are allowed to participate actively in developing and implementing the program. Based on this experience, large organizations may decide to use MBO first in a pilot program in order to perfect it before it is implemented on a companywide basis. People are provided with necessary information and are prepared for the required organizational change. Understanding of what MBO really is reduces anxiety and resistance to change. The philosophy of MBO is taught. Considerable responsibility is given to subordinates that provides them with opportunities for self-development; individuals learn and grow professionally. The result is that there is a high degree of congruence of individual aspirations and organizational aims, which in part, is promoted by a team approach to management.

Step 4: Controlling and Appraising Control and appraisal involves setting standards, measuring performance, and—if necessary—correcting undesirable deviations. Control, in this context, refers to the organizational performance, and appraisal emphasizes individual performance. Because similar phenomena are included in both, they will be discussed together, but with an emphasis on appraisal.

Theory X With Theory X assumptions, appraisal and control is rather rigid and externally imposed, with little opportunity for self-control. The superior takes an active role in the appraisal, acting as a judge in evaluating the performance of subordinates. There is a tendency to pursue even inappropriate standards set by the superior because subordinates may be expected to follow orders rather than to get involved in setting their own standards. Consequently, there is little commitment to achieve results. Individual performance may be emphasized even when it is detrimental to group performance. The appraisal meeting is marked by low trust between the superior and subordinate, with the focus on the past rather than the future. But the past cannot be changed; the future can. In this atmosphere, the subordinate receives little honest feedback about his or her performance, and only minimum information about the direction of the organization is given. With Theory X assumptions actuating the appraisal meeting, there is little opportunity for self-control or self-development.

Theory Y This set of assumptions is, in contrast to the above, conducive to the utilization of a person's potential and creativity.

Control is internal and is primarily self-control. The subordinates, setting their own standards, are committed toward their achievement. Although standards should not be changed lightly, they are adjusted if environmental changes demand it. It is absurd to pursue standards that are obsolete or inappropriate in light of changing realities. The superior assumes the role of a helper who assists subordinates to achieve their standards that, of course, are congruent with the team's objectives.

The appraisal meeting is characterized by trust with optimum information available to subordinates. The superior and subordinate not only look at past performance, but also focus on future opportunities and improvements. The accent is on feedforward control (see Chapter 7) that prevents deviations before they occur. Consequently, self-development—utilizing the strengths of individuals and overcoming their weaknesses—is the prevailing attitude, emphasizing problem solving instead of fault finding.

In summary, managerial productivity depends on the effective implementation of action plans and programs, which is influenced by the assumptions we make about the nature of people. But not only assumptions influence managerial behavior. The leadership style itself has a great impact on the way the basic MBO steps are carried out.

MBO AND THE MANAGERIAL GRID*

The managerial grid, developed by Robert Blake and Jane Mouton, has been widely used for developing managers in the United States and abroad.[2] The question naturally arises whether the grid can facilitate the implementation of MBO. In the next few pages we will explore how the essential steps in MBO may be carried out by using different managerial styles.

Blake and Mouton suggest that the concern for people and the concern for production are not mutually exclusive, rather they are complementary. The production manager, therefore, will have a great concern for production as well as for people. Unfortunately, few managers measure up to this ideal model, as will be seen in the discussion below. Yet every manager has a discernible style. It is assumed that managers, identifying their style and its implications, are proceeding toward improving not only themselves, but also the organization. The tool that facilitates this process is the managerial grid.

The grid is simply a chart with two 9-point scales ranging from 1 to 9. The horizontal scale represents concern for production; the

*Adapted from H. Weihrich, "Effective Management by Objectives through the Grid," *Manage,* vol. 28, no. 5 (September/October 1976), pp. 8–11,30. Used with permission.

vertical scale pertains to concern for people. Scale value 1 is a low concern (for production or people) and 9 represents a high concern. In theory, then, there are 81 possible positions. However, we will focus only on four extreme positions to illustrate their probable relationships with the MBO process.

The Essential Steps in MBO and the Grid Positions

The essential steps in the MBO process, as will be recalled, are: (1) setting objectives, (2) developing action plans, (3) implementing the plans and programs, and (4) controlling organizational performance and appraising individual results.

Task Management (9,1)   Managers with a high concern for the task (scale value 9) and a low concern for people (scale value 1) would most likely set objectives and develop the action plans for subordinates without letting them participate in these tasks. In fact, these managers would see authority as the only means of determining the goals and plans of those reporting to them. Because of this lack of participation, problems in coordination may surface. In the implementation phase, human aspects are largely ignored, resulting in considerable resistance to the program which may rely on a manual with strict procedures. Managers using this managerial style will rather closely control the performance of the department and subordinates, providing little opportunity for self-appraisal and self-control.

Country Club Management (1, 9)   Managers with a low concern for production and a high concern for people emphasize harmonious relationships with subordinates. While personal objectives may be set, production goals are largely ignored. Furthermore, hardly any efforts are made to identify, analyze, and choose courses of action in a systematic way. Such managers do not exert the necessary leadership to direct the activities of subordinates toward organizational goals. The appraisal, although conducted in a friendly atmosphere, is not taken very seriously. Consequently, subordinates do not feel accountable for results.

Impoverished Management (1, 1)   With a minimum concern for production and people, things do not get done. No goals are set, no direction is provided, no communication exists, no action plans are developed. Organizational and individual performance cannot be measured without organizational and individual goals. In fact, one could argue that a manager using this style does not manage at all.

Team Management (9, 9)   Managers adopting the managerial style with high concern for production and people are the true managers. It is the aim of grid training to bring managers closer to this model. Managers set challenging, yet attainable, objectives and develop action plans that are coordinated with the efforts of other organizational units. In fact, there is a great deal of commitment to objectives, frequent and open communication with other people, and concerted action toward common goals. But the high concern for people does not result in neglect of monitoring. Control standards are established at critical points and performance is analyzed with the intention of finding the causes of undesirable deviations, not finding fault. In appraisal, the problem-solving attitude prevails. In this positive atmosphere, the superior is seen as a helper rather than a judge.

In summary, managerial styles have a considerable effect on the way the steps in MBO are carried out. Productive managers, according to Blake and Mouton, have a high concern for production as well as people. The managerial grid is a means to determine one's managerial style, which, in turn, is a first step for changing one's way of managing. Another way managers can strengthen their authentic behavior is through the application of concepts derived from transactional analysis.

PSYCHOLOGICAL GAMES MANAGERS PLAY*

Superiors and subordinates, teachers and students, adults and children, in short, everybody plays psychological games. Yet, games can be destructive; they consume valuable time, they waste psychological energy, they concentrate on self-gain, they create bad feelings, they cause organizational warfare; and, above all, they prevent individuals from being authentic.

Games also inhibit the managerial process. In the organizational environment games tend to:

- Inhibit the setting of challenging objectives
- Impede sound decision making

*Adapted from H. Weihrich, "Games Organizational People Play," *Management International Review*, vol. 18, no. 4 (1978), pp. 33–40. Used with permission.

- Restrain effective problem solving
- Hinder the proper functioning of the organization
- Hamper staffing decisions and selections based on qualifications for the job
  - Result in incorrect appraisal of managers and nonmanagers
  - Prevent people from being motivated and contributing to organizational aims
    - Result in ineffective leadership
    - Obstruct honest communication
    - Make control systems ineffective

When we recognize the destructive aspects of psychological games, we must find a way to stop or prevent them. One way is to apply transactional analysis (TA) to identify and forestall the games.

TA, fortunately, is a tool that is easy to learn. It uses a language that is relatively free of professional jargon; it facilitates communication; it increases personal effectiveness; and it helps to solve organizational and personal problems. But TA alone cannot solve all managerial problems. It is not a panacea. Rather, it must be integrated with other managerial processes such as MBO as it is discussed throughout this book. However, many who write about MBO ignore the intricate interrelationships between people, even though it is the people in the organization that make MBO work. The purpose of this section is to show how TA can be used to analyze human transactions and psychological games. Even more important, we will learn how to improve transactions and how to prevent games, which, in turn, facilitates the implementation of MBO.

An Introduction to Transactional Analysis (TA)

When Eric Berne introduced and popularized TA, it was primarily a method of psychotherapy;[3] later, however, the general value of TA was recognized. More recently, it has also been used to improve communication in organizations. Nevertheless, very little has been written showing how TA can be linked directly to the managerial process. Although TA considers both the emotional and intellectual aspects of understanding human behavior, the emphasis is on the rational and analytical process. Moreover, the focus is on observable behavior rather than on the inner psyche. While managers usually cannot deal with the latter, they can learn to observe, interpret, and modify their own behavior and that of others.

To say that TA deals with the interactions of people is probably insufficient for the practicing manager. Therefore, the more appropriate and useful approach for analyzing psychological games is to discuss TA theory within the framework of (1) structural analysis with the focus on the individual, (2) the analysis of transactions between people, and (3) the way time is structured.

Structural Analysis Every person, according to TA theory, has three ego states: the Parent, the Adult, and the Child. These terms have nothing to do with the actual age of a person; rather they refer to ego states. They are therofore capitalized as shown in this diagram:

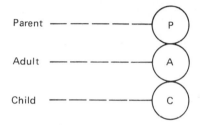

FIGURE 6-1
The ego states.

It should be noted that each ego state is a distinct source of behavior. Usually, one does not constantly remain in a particular ego state, rather one switches occasionally during the course of communication. Let us examine the three ego states more closely.

The *Parent* ego state is derived from a set of brain recordings of unquestioned events from *external* sources, especially during a person's early life. It also represents the attitudes and behavior associated with these influences. The Parent ego state may be inferred from words and phrases such as: always, never, do as I say, let me help you, and so on. However, one should not only listen to words and phrases, but also note the way they are said and the tone of voice which, if coming from the Parent ego state, may sound condescending or punitive, but may also express support and sympathy. Other clues indicating the particular ego state as a source of behavior are gestures, postures, and facial expressions. The combination of these clues—if they are complementary—gives an indication of a person's ego state as a source of his or her behavior.

The *Adult* ego state is the rational part of our personality. It is characterized by objectivity, problem solving, and decisions based on reality. Words and phrases that are indicative of this ego state are: what, why, when, how, where, who, what are other alternatives, what are the facts, and so on.

The third ego state, the *Child*, contains mental recordings of *internal* events and pertains to the emotional part of our personality. Verbal clues may include: wow! can't, I want, help me, and so on. The Child ego state may be exhibited through illogical and stubborn behavior, as well as through laughter, happiness, and creativity.

Is one ego state better than the others? No! All three are important for a well-rounded personality. But problems usually occur when an ego state unsuitable for a particular situation determines behavior. It is, therefore, the Adult that must decide which ego state is effective for various transactions, the next topic in our discussion.

Transactions   Ego states do not exist in isolation; rather, they interact with those of other persons. Basically, there are three kinds of transactions: complementary, crossed, and ulterior. A *complementary* transaction occurs when the transactional stimulus gets the predicted transactional response. For example, the superior may say: "John, this is the last time I will warn you about being late" (Parent injunction). The subordinate may respond: "Yes, sir, it will never happen again." This complementary (or parallel) transaction can be diagrammed as follows:

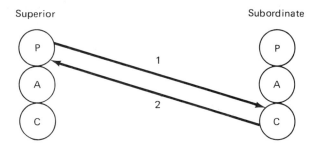

FIGURE 6-2
Complementary transaction.

A *crossed* transaction would have occurred if the subordinate had answered: "You mind your own business. Who do you think you are anyway?" This transaction can be shown as follows:

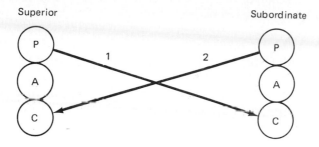

FIGURE 6-3
Crossed transaction.

It is clear, then, that crossed transactions usually terminate communication—and in this case probably employment also.

The third kind is the *ulterior* transaction, which has a hidden agenda. This transaction appears to be OK, but it has a double message. For example, the superior who says, "I will call up the customer for you" may, in fact, mean: "You are so stupid, you would spoil the sale." Correspondingly, a subordinate saying "Thank you" may mean "Yes, you are right, I am stupid; kick me."

Here the socially acceptable message appears to be Adult to Adult. But the disguised double message (indicated by the broken lines in the next diagram) is between the Parent and the Child ego states of the superior and subordinate, respectively. The diagram of this transaction looks like this:

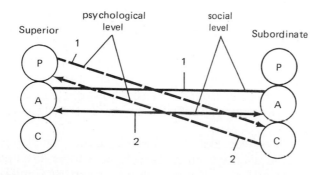

FIGURE 6-4
Ulterior transaction.

These transactions are the psychological games that consist of (a) a set of complementary transactions on the social level, (b) an ulterior transaction on the psychological level, and (c) a psychological payoff. Later, we will discuss other games organization people tend to play.

Time Structuring The last TA concept in this discussion pertains to the way time is structured. In a sense, time is a unique resource. It cannot be hoarded nor is it retrievable. Everything we do takes time. Despite the recognition of its obvious value, time is frequently used ineffectively. In fact, all too often it is wasted in playing games.

Basically, there are six ways time can be spent within the organization. First, there can be *withdrawal* from others, either physical or psychological. The second way to spend time is through *rituals*. These are socially accepted gestures, phrases, and responses such as "Hi, how are you?" The third way of using time is through *pastimes;* this can be simply making conversation, for example, about the weather or a favorite football team. The fourth way to structure time is through *activities;* this includes work. A fifth way to spend time is by engaging in *authentic communication* (called intimacy in TA). This involves sharing, trusting, and caring. Finally, time is structured by playing *psychological games*. Basically, games are dishonest; they involve a sequence of transactions that have a hidden motive. The next section will describe in greater detail some of the games organization people play.

Games Organization People Play

Organizations, by their very nature, require cooperative effort to reach common aims. Unfortunately, this interaction is often the occasion for psychological games. These games are played at all levels in the organization, in all departments, in all kinds of organizations—business and nonbusiness—and by all people, managers and nonmanagers. In our discussion, however, we will emphasize the delicate relationships between the manager and employees.

Why Don't You—Yes, But In this game, a very common one in organizations, the first player presents a problem and asks for advice from another player. However, when advice is given (Why don't you), it is discounted with "Yes, but," and superficial reasons why the suggestions will not work. This game may be played by superior and subordinate, managers and consultants, line and staff. For example, a staff person who tries to recommend changes to managers (Why don't you) may encounter many objections and reasons from line managers (Yes, but) stating why the suggestions will not work. The reasons, then, clearly show that staff is much too theoretical and cannot grasp the difficult situation of the line managers.

Similarly, a manager may appear to elicit suggestions from employees about improving productivity. The superior then discards the suggestions with "Yes, but." This, in turn, "proves" that subordinates are not OK and are incapable of making practical recommendations.

On the surface (the social level) these transactions appear to be on the Adult-Adult level, involving data collecting, fact finding, and problem solving. However, the psychological transactions are between the Parent and Child ego states. Before suggesting ways to stop games, let us look at some others played by organization people.

See What You Made Me Do; If It Weren't For You/Them These are two common games indulged in by players who try to blame others for their own problems in not achieving objectives. The players do not assume responsibility for their own actions, nor do they feel accountable for results.

A subordinate, for example, may blame his boss, claiming that the objectives were inappropriate. At other times he may follow blindly the boss's instructions. So, if something goes wrong, he can play the game of "See What You Made Me Do."

But games are not played solely between the superior and her subordinates. A manager may accuse other managers on the same organizational level of not cooperating, which results in poor performance of her department. Or she may blame the "unskilled and uneducated" work force for her failure (If It Weren't for Them). To be sure, there may be forces that are beyond a person's control, and one should not be held accountable for them. But too often employees play these blaming games instead of assuming responsibility for their actions. The perceptive superior who is familiar with TA will distinguish between valid reasons for deviations from plans and psychological games.

Blemish Blemish is a game played by nitpickers. A manager, for example, may look for mistakes of subordinates and be happy to find even minor ones. Major accomplishments by the employee, on the other hand, are overlooked. This approach is obviously demotivating for the subordinate. The employee knows that the superior will find at least one minor fault in whatever he or she does.

A clear statement of what is expected of subordinates is needed. Moreover, objectives should be ranked according to their importance. This way minor, unimportant, and inconsequential things do not distract from major accomplishments.

Now I've Got You   At times, a Blemish player may switch to the game "Now I've Got You." He sets up another person—let's say the subordinate—to fall into a trap and make a mistake.

For example, there is the superior who sets impossible objectives for his subordinates. When standards are not met, the superior feels justified in getting angry at the subordinate. A somewhat more sophisticated approach, but one with similar results, is when the manager compels employees to set objectives for themselves but does not provide the required resources for the accomplishment of the aims. The manager then waits until the subordinate fails.

It is clear that this creates a very unfavorable organizational environment. The employee knows that the boss is out to get him. Consequently, employees will not take risks—not even calculated ones. They will not take the initiative, and they will not attempt to develop better ways of doing things. Instead, they will play it safe and protect themselves by documenting their actions, thus using time in a nonproductive way.

These games are, of course, in sharp contrast to the MBO approach, in which the superior is seen as a helper, a resource person, and a coach. Furthermore, TA concepts help to uncover psychological games so that human energy can be channeled toward more productive behavior.

How to Stop Games

Games can be stopped. We can utilize TA as a tool to uncover games—our own and those of others—and stop them. The following recommendations based on TA concepts tend to discourage psychological games and promote the effective implementation of MBO.

First, one should recognize the *ego states* in oneself as well as in others. All ego states are important, but they should be used to fit the situation. Often the Adult state is, unfortunately, underutilized.

Second, *transactions* between individuals can decide whether organizations are productive or nonproductive. The Parent-Child transactions may be appropriate in some instances, but they too often hinder effective interaction and growth of individuals. In most modern organizations with a competent and highly educated labor force, Adult-Adult transactions need to receive more emphasis.

Third, *time,* the unique and valuable resource, *needs to be structured* effectively. It can be used up through pastimes and games, or it can be used effectively by focusing on results and authentic communication. Games inhibit the management process while authentic cooperation and ooordinated efforts bring results.

IMPLICATIONS FOR MANAGERIAL PRODUCTIVITY

One of the most important factors for improving productivity is the human factor in the implementation of MBO. This chapter focused on the assumptions we make about the basic nature of people, managerial styles, and psychological games.

Managerial behavior is greatly influenced by our assumptions. If we assume that people dislike work, that they must be forced to put forth effort, and that they will avoid responsibility, then action plans and programs are most likely to be implemented rigidly, based almost exclusively on authority and controlled by the superior. If, on the other hand, we believe that people like work, exercise self-direction, and seek responsibility, then MBO most likely will prove to be a humanistic, optimistic, and positive approach to managing. It will be flexible and adaptive to a changing environment.

Similarly, the managerial style does have a considerable, and probably decisive, effect on the way action plans and programs are implemented. A high concern for production with a low concern for people does not give sufficient attention to the important human aspects. On the other hand, a high concern for people with a neglect of production does not result in optimum performance. No concern for production or people results in minimum performance. To be productive, a high degree of concern for production as well as people is needed. In such an environment objectives are challenging, yet attainable; organizational demands and individual needs are integrated; tasks and activities are coordinated for optimum results; and the organization becomes an interlocking system with open communication and frequent, accurate feedback.

Finally, managers can become more productive through authentic behavior free of psychological games. Most of us spend a substantial part of our lives in organizations; unfortunately, not all of this time is used effectively. Rather, a great deal of time is wasted by playing games, which not only keep us from being successful, but also hinder the management process.

We have highlighted a number of common games and perhaps have even recognized some of our own. This insight is the first step in stopping these games. The tool of transactional analysis is now available to managers to improve communication and interpersonal relations; and to stop the games organization people play. Then both the people *and* the organization will be productive.

NOTES

1 D. McGregor, *The Human Side of Enterprise* (New York: McGraw-Hill, 1960). For an approach to goal setting that is similar to Theory Y, see R. L. Brock, "How to Maintain a Creative Environment in the Goal-Setting Process," 1982 *Proceedings, 10th Annual International MBO Conference* (Bowling Green: MBO Institute, 1983), pp. 25–30.
2 R. R. Blake and J. S. Mouton, *Building a Dynamic Corporation Through Grid Organization Development* (Reading, Mass.: Addison-Wesley, 1969) and R. R. Blake and J. S. Mouton, *The Versatile Manager* (Reading, Mass. Addison-Wesley, 1981).
3 E. Berne, *Games People Play* (New York: Grove Press, Inc.,1964).

7

MEASURING PERFORMANCE THROUGH ORGANIZATIONAL CONTROL AND INDIVIDUAL APPRAISAL

Measurement is a key to productivity. Decades ago, the concern was largely on productivity measurement at the worker level in the organization. The focus, for example, was on the units of output per hour. Today, it Is realized that productivity requires a more comprehensive view that includes the measurement of organizational and managerial performance, the topic of this chapter.

As will be recalled, the more detailed MBO process consists of (1) setting objectives, (2) planning for action, (3) implementing MBO and action plans, and (4) controlling of organizational performance and appraising individual contributions. This chapter focuses on the last step. It closes, in a sense, the loop that began with the setting of objectives, by measuring performance against these previously set criteria.

The first part of this chapter deals with aspects of control. In the context of this book, the emphasis is on the control of organizational performance. The second part, on the other hand, concerns appraising the contributions of individuals and the delicate interaction between superior and subordinates.

CONTROL OF ORGANIZATIONAL PERFORMANCE

The function of controlling is designed to assure that objectives and plans are achieved. The steps, shown in Figure 7–1, generally involve:

1 Setting of verifiable objectives that become standards
2 Carrying out the actions to achieve objectives; actual performance
3 Measuring organization performance against these criteria
4 Taking action to correct undesirable deviations from the standard

These steps for organizational control are similar to appraisal. In appraisal, as will be shown later, many other dimensions, such as the emphasis on self-control and self-direction, must be considered. But first some comments on the basic control process are in order.

The Control Process

The *setting of objectives,* discussed earlier, is essential for effective control. In fact, verifiable objectives become the *standards* against which performance is monitored. In order to facilitate measurement, verifiable objectives should state at least the quantity (how much) of the output or a desired situation and the time when performance should be achieved. In many instances the quality (how well) of performance is vital. The importance of quality in health care when human life is at stake is obvious. But also consider the importance of quality in the fast-food business where small differences in the heat of hamburgers have an impact on sales. At Burger King, owners found that the temperature of the hamburger should be precisely at certain degrees for best results in increasing sales per hour. In order to maintain the temperature, the company developed a sheet metal piece that collects the heat in the hamburger bin which, in turn, contributes to increased sales (output) with hardly any additional cost (input), thus increasing productivity.[1] Standards should, if possible, also indicate the costs involved—for example, resources needed—to achieve the standards. This draws attention to the recognition that whatever is done is done at a cost. Clearly, our concern for productivity requires attention to the inputs, such as the costs of resources.

After setting the standards, the actual *work is carried out.* It is important that the organizational situation is conducive for utilizing the potentials of people by creating an environment in which people

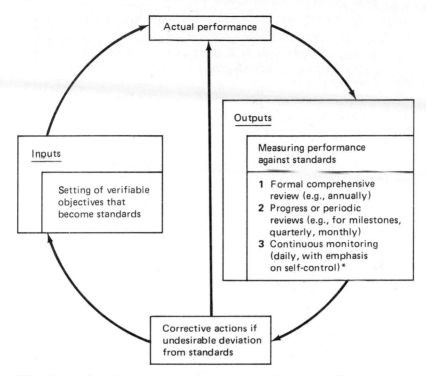

*The kinds of reviews are discussed later in this chapter. The author appreciates the suggestion for this model by a book reviewer who remains anonymous.

FIGURE 7-1
The control and appraisal process.

can contribute to the aims of the enterprise. The issues involved in establishing a favorable situation for productivity have been discussed in previous chapters.

Periodically, performance is *measured* against preestablished standards. If these standards are accurate, and stated in measurable terms as suggested in the discussion of verifiable objectives, measuring is relatively easy. Although performance is formally reviewed at specified times, the control process really involves a continuous monitoring of performance. One does not wait for the review date when it becomes obvious that corrective actions are needed.

Measuring of performance is not done for its own sake. Rather, it provides the signal for *corrective action.* In fact, it is crucial to arrange for steps that assure prompt corrective action. Often one thinks only of negative deviations from plans that need correction. But it is also important to note positive deviations that may require the resetting of objectives and redrawing of plans. For example, overachieved sales objectives may require changing production plans and schedules. After all, an organization has a network of interdependent goals and plans, deviations from plans—either positive or negative—in one department may require adjustments in other parts of the organization.

Control Tools and Methods

There are many tools available for controlling the operation of the organization. Since planning and controlling are closely related, the tools often serve both purposes. One of the most widely used control methods is budgeting. A budget is a plan expressed in numbers, often financial terms. For example, budgets may pertain to revenues, expenses, profits, cash, and balance sheet items. But, it is also possible to prepare budgets for material used in the process, for allocating space, and for budgeting time used for manufacturing a product. There are many financial control methods such as the balance sheet, income statement, cash flow, and funds statements. Information derived from these sources allows us to prepare different kinds of ratios such as the debt/net worth, the profit margin on sales, return on total assets, return on net worth, return on investment, and other financial criteria.

Other control methods may include observing whether or not performance is according to plans by making an internal audit for evaluation of the operation of the firm, by conducting special studies of selected aspects in an enterprise, such as analyzing procedures and the information system in terms of their effectiveness. There is even a way to control the human factors in the enterprise. This approach, pioneered at the Institute for Social Research at the University of Michigan, will be discussed in the chapter on organizational development. In all, these illustrations indicate that there are many tools and methods available for controlling the performance of an enterprise.

Future-Oriented Controls

Control systems rely mostly on feedback. After deviations are detected, corrective actions are taken. The time elapsing between detection of a deviation and corrective actions can be costly. The ideal system would be one which identifies deviations *before* they become major problems. Therefore, Harold Koontz and Robert W. Bradspies suggest what they call "feedforward control," which anticipates deviations.[2] This approach monitors inputs into the system and makes adjustments to the inputs before deviations in outputs occur. The concept of feedforward control can be illustrated by bicycle riders who want to maintain a constant speed by making an extra effort before the speed is reduced by an upcoming hill. They do not wait until the speed drops. Instead, they accelerate, or change to a lower gear, before they approach the incline. The same principle applies to business control. One does not wait until the company runs out of cash before finding sources to replenish the required cash fund.

To overcome the inherent problems in control systems that rely on feedback, Koontz and Bradspies suggest a number of guidelines, including the following:

1 Feedforward, to be effective, requires careful analysis, planning, and identification of input variables.

2 Feedforward needs to be dynamic in a sense that the system must be monitored for input variables and new influences affecting performance. Data on these variables have to be regularly collected and evaluated.

3 A model (a schematic drawing, for example) will assist in the identification of the variables and an understanding of their relationships.

4 Anticipated deviations require speedy actions so that major problems can be avoided. Indeed, it is the nature of prompt actions (not overreaction) that makes this system effective.

In all, then, future-directed control is more than a specific technique or even a specific approach. It is an orientation based on the idea that prevention is better than cure. Organizations, whether business, nonprofit, military or government, could benefit from this new approach that anticipates deviations and takes prompt actions to avoid costly problems.

How to Make Control Systems Productive

Besides future-oriented systems, there are other approaches for making controls productive. We will focus on some typical problems and on ways to overcome them.

Control is closely related to planning and setting objectives. Since a control system should measure the *right things,* it is important that the objectives set in the planning process are relevant to the purpose of the organization. This means that controls should measure performance in the key result areas. In other words, controls should highlight important developments, not trivia. Controls should also be *efficient,* pointing out deviations at a minimum cost, and the benefits should exceed the costs. This also requires that controls should be *simple* enough to be understood. Cumbersome controls are very likely to be resisted by managers.

Controls should also show deviations from standards in a *timely* manner so that corrective actions can be taken before they become major problems. But this does not necessarily call for real time information for all controls. In fact, short-term fluctuations in daily performance may distort trends. In retailing, for example, a sudden drop in sales may be due to bad weather rather than indicating a direction of falling sales that may trigger an unnecessary increase in the advertising budget. Also, short-term controls in research and development could encourage engineers to opt for mediocre designs. On the other hand, the best-engineered product coming to the market two years too late may be of little benefit to the company. Therefore, effective controls should have a time span that is appropriate for what is being measured.

Since no control system fits all organizations, it must be *tailored* to fit the organizational demands. While in some enterprises tight control may be necessary, other firms, such as those in research and development, usually have relatively broad controls. There is, of course, the concern that one could lose control. But clear standards that are understood and accepted relieve managers from the need of overcontrolling activities because accountability is achieved by measuring results. Controls should also be *flexible* and uniform standards may be inappropriate. Let us look at an example. It might appear that the performance standards for savings and loan branch managers doing similar tasks should be the same, but a short reflection shows the fallacy of this kind of thinking. Managers of branches located in a retirement community should have relatively high performance objectives for obtaining savings deposits, while branch managers operating in an area where new homes are built should have relatively high objectives in respect to real estate loans. Clearly, control systems and standards must be made to fit the situation and the organization.

Not everything can be measured. Therefore, controls should point out deviations from plans that are *crucial* for the success of the enterprise. Too many control points may divert the attention from those that are really important. Although we emphasized the importance of verifiable objectives, there is also a danger of *overemphasizing quantitative criteria,* while ignoring those that do not lend themselves to precise measurements. The company image may be difficult to measure, yet it may be a key success factor for the firm.

Deviations from standards may actually draw attention to *symptoms* of problems rather than show their causes. To note that there is a high employee turnover rate is not sufficient; a search for the underlying cause of the problem is required. So, determining deviations from standards is only the first step and must be followed by *corrective actions,* or, even more important, it should lead to steps to prevent deviations from occurring, as was suggested in the discussion of feedforward control. Finally, one must consider the impact of the control system on *human behavior.* For example, if the reward system is closely linked to selected performance measures, there is the tendency of managers to focus only on those measures that are rewarded and ignore other important activities and results that are not specifically reflected in performance standards.

APPRAISAL OF INDIVIDUAL PERFORMANCE

This part deals with performance appraisal that can be considered a kind of control. But the emphasis here is not on organizational performance, but on individual contributions, although the two aspects are, of course, closely related. Early appraisal approaches focused on personality traits such as initiative, creativity, alertness, stability, maturity, and many other attributes. But there is no agreement on which specific traits contribute to performance. Equally troublesome is the problem of measuring these traits. Moreover, different situations and tasks may require different traits, yet, the same appraisal form is used for evaluating people in diverse positions. In his famous article, "An Uneasy Look at Performance Appraisal," Douglas McGregor pointed at the weaknesses of traditional approaches that focused on personality traits.[3] But even today, this uneasiness can still be found. Some organizations have taken positive steps by focusing on results, departing from the traditional trait appraisals. But problems remain. Managers still resist judging the performance of subordinates. They still resist giving employees honest feedback about their performance. Even the results-oriented

MBO approach has its limitations. Later in this chapter we will discuss some of the critical issues and make suggestions to improve appraisal.

Purposes and Uses of Appraisal

Management by objectives has been used in various phases of the management process. A national survey showed that 19 percent of the 515 respondents felt that the purpose for using MBO in their organization was performance appraisal. This was the second most frequently mentioned purpose preceded only by planning, which was given as the main purpose of MBO by 34 percent of the respondents.[4]

Besides evaluating the performance of managers, there are other reasons for conducting an appraisal. Most people want to *know how well they are doing.* Yet even a cursory survey would reveal that most people do not have a clear idea of what the superior expects of them. You might try a simple do-it-yourself test by writing down what you think your boss expects of you. Then your superior should do the same by listing the criteria for evaluating your performance. A comparison between the two assessments usually shows that agreement is the exception rather than the rule.

Another purpose of performance appraisal is to identify *developmental* needs of managers. Yet, appraisal encounters often are conducted in an atmosphere that emphasizes judgment, not development. Specifically, most discussions focus on undesirable performance deviations, with little attention given to what can be done to prevent such deviations from occurring in the future.

Still another purpose of appraisal pertains to *salary* decisions. In fact, it is not uncommon to view the appraisal meeting as the occasion for justifying a salary increase, or the denial of it. In one company, for example, managers were told that salary increases for subordinates could not be granted and the appraisals should reflect this situation. Perhaps this is an extreme case of misuse of performance appraisal, but it may not be so uncommon as suspected. Even managers of goodwill may subconsciously rate subordinates low because not enough money is available for providing a reward congruent with a high rating of superior performance.

Another purpose, related to the foregoing discussion, is to use appraisal for *promotion* decisions. The trait appraisal proved to be inadequate for making sound decisions. Even the results-oriented approach has its limitations because performance may be influenced by extraneous factors that are not related to managerial ability. Thus, excellent performance may be due to the bankruptcy of a competitor, while poor performance may be caused by an unforeseen downturn of the economy.

An extensive study by The Conference Board shows that the *objectives* of appraisal on the basis of frequency are as follows:[5]

1 Management development
2 Performance appraisal
3 Performance improvement
4 Compensation
5 Potential identification
6 Feedback
7 Manpower planning
8 Communication

However, when respondents were asked how the companies *use* the appraisal, the ranking differs and shows the following results:

1 Performance feedback
2 Compensation administration
3 Promotion decisions
4 Identification of management development needs
5 Manpower planning
6 Validation of selection procedures

The differences between the stated objectives of appraisals and the way they are used may be an important reason for dissatisfaction with the appraisal indicated by some of the personnel managers participating in this study. It should also be noted that some of the objectives and uses of appraisals have a different orientation. In determining compensation, or often even in evaluating performance, superiors assume the role of a judge. In contrast, when the aim is to develop subordinates, managers need to act as a counselor, a helper, and a teacher.

The General Electric Studies

Some of the best-known studies on performance appraisals were done at the General Electric Company.[6] The findings of the initial study showed that (1) criticism has a negative impact on goal accomplishment, (2) praise has little effect, (3) specific goals improve performance, (4) critical appraisal results in defensive and inferior performance, (5) coaching should be done on a day-to-day basis rather than once a year, (6) joint objective setting, not criticism, increases performance, (7) meetings with the purpose of improving performance should not at the same time impact on the salary or promotion decision, and (8) subordinate's participation in setting objectives improves performance.

Based on the findings, General Electric developed a new appraisal program called Work Planning and Review, in short, WP&R. This new approach emphasizes frequent discussions of performance without summary ratings. Moreover, salary actions are discussed in separate meetings. Finally, problem solving and joint objective setting are emphasized. The experience at General Electric suggests that the two purposes of performance appraisal should be separated because if used as the basis for salary action the superior assumes the role of a judge, while in the attempt to motivate employees the manager takes the role of a coach. It is through recognizing the split roles in performance appraisal and by setting specific goals mutually agreed upon by the superior and the subordinate that productivity can be improved.

Work Planning and Review in Forestry Organizations

One frequently heard comment is that performance appraisal based on MBO concepts may work well in profit-oriented business organizations, but not in government. However, the example taken from forestry organizations shows that MBO appraisal can effectively be applied in public organizations.

Performance appraisal cannot be separated from planning because the objectives set during the planning phase become the standards against which performance is measured. It is, in general, rather difficult to contribute performance improvement directly to a specific managerial change. Yet, such an attempt was made in some forestry organizations that placed heavy emphasis on MBO and tracked the changes in productivity.[7] The results in the Oklahoma area, for example, are impressive. From the 1977 to 1980 fiscal year, seedlings produced increased 93 percent; tree planting was up 38 percent from fiscal year 1980 to 1981. Similar results were produced in North Carolina where tree planting increased by 81 percent from fiscal year 1979 to 1980. Although one might have to await the long-run results, one cannot overlook the performance changes. Some of the key success factors in this program were (1) the choosing of the term "work planning and performance review" for their approach rather than MBO, because some people had negative experiences with programs with the MBO label and would have resisted, (2) top management was actively involved in the program, and (3) team building was an important element in the introduction of the program.

Performance Appraisal in a Public Agency

Another example of a well-planned appraisal system can be found at the National Aeronautics and Space Administration (NASA).[8] This research and development organization has over 20,000 employees, about half of them scientists and engineers.

The appraisal and merit pay system was introduced systematically. Specifically, a task force was charged with the design of the performance appraisal system that was based on several premises. First, it should reflect the characteristics and demands of the NASA organization. Second, it should be flexible and dynamic rather than rigid and mechanistic. Third, it must be evident that headquarters and top management are behind the program. Fourth, the program must contribute to, not deter from, research and development. Finally, it should be relatively simple and should not become a burden to the practicing manager.

The key characteristic of the system that may have contributed to its success was an involvement of large segments of the work force in designing the program. Moreover, the advisers from headquarters helped to train managers so that the system was thoroughly understood by the participants. The program, based on MBO concepts, was first tested before it was implemented. There was also a linkage between the position description, the work to be performed, and the standards for measurement. Finally, and this is very important, the system was kept flexible so that it could be adjusted to the specific requirements of the organization.

The program itself consists of three phases. The first phase involves *performance planning,* with an emphasis on key result areas and key tasks (critical elements) as well as nonroutine objectives that are important for organizational success. Although the objectives are stated in specific terms, it is also realized that some objectives—and this is especially true in research—are difficult to quantify. In this stage attention may be given to managerial tasks such as planning, organizing, directing, and controlling, which had been the research focus in studies in different organizations several years earlier.[9]

The second phase of the NASA program focuses on *progress review.* The purpose is to identify problems and new requirements due to changes in the environment, evaluate progress toward the objectives, and provide feedback to subordinates.

The third and final phase of the program is the *comprehensive appraisal,* with the aim of assessing actual performance against plans and objectives through a discussion between the superior and subordinate. The superior's initial evaluation is reviewed by his or her superior at the next higher organizational level. Then the superior and subordinate discuss the appraisal in greater detail. The subordinate also has an opportunity to respond in writing to the appraisal and, if requested, has the appraisal reviewed by a higher-level manager. Finally, objectives are set for the next period.

This example shows that performance appraisal can be implemented in a public agency, but it also indicates that a great deal of effort is necessary to make it effective.

Different Views on Appraisal Issues

Despite the concern about effective appraisal and the considerable attention given to the topic, there is still a controversy surrounding key aspects. We will focus on eight critical issues.

1 *Means vs. ends*   Although past experience indicates that personality trait evaluations are rather ineffective, many appraisal forms used today still contain personality items. There are still those who think that traits contribute to the attainment of the ends and should therefore be evaluated. The opposite view is expressed by those who take the position that results and only results count. The means used to achieve the aims must, of course, be ethical, within the company policy, and within the law. Behavior, it is suggested, will adjust to achieve the ends.

Suggestion: Results are, of course, important, but managerial behavior should not be completely ignored. This is not an argument for the outdated trait approach, nor is it proposing any kind of behavior. Instead, the focus is on observable *managerial* behavior. Such an approach has been developed by Harold Koontz in his book *Appraising Managers as Managers.*[10] In this program, MBO appraisal is supplemented by an evaluation on how well managers carry out their key managerial activities. The program identifies seventy-three questions that reflect basic management principles and concepts. We cannot repeat all the questions, but the following will serve as illustrations. In planning, one question is: "Does the manager check plans periodically to see if they are still consistent with current expectations?" In organizing, a question is: "Does the manager delegate authority to subordinates in accordance with results expected of them?" The seventy-three questions are grouped into the managerial functions of planning, organizing, staffing, leading, and controlling. Each question is rated on a scale ranging from zero (being inadequate) to five (being superior). Although the program requires managers to make subjective judgments, it is an improvement over the appraisal of questionable traits. It is an attempt to assess the quality of managing and it serves as a tool for management development by pinpointing areas that need improvement.

2 *Subjective vs. objective evaluation*   There are those who still maintain that subjective rating of subordinates is sufficient. After all, it is argued, managerial performance is difficult to evaluate. On the other side of the argument are those who maintain that an appraisal must be completely objective and only numbers count; either a person achieves the previously set objective or not.

Suggestion: There is no doubt that the focus of the appraisal should be on results. But one must be careful to avoid the numbers game. Figures can be manipulated to suit the individual, and thus defeat the purpose of appraisal. Also, pursuing a limited number of verifiable criteria may ignore other, not formally stated, objectives, as one cannot and should not set objectives for all tasks. It is, therefore, not only important to look at the performance figures but also at the causes of positive or negative deviations from standards, although this may involve some subjective judgments.

3 *Judging vs. self-appraisal*   There is the view that managers have the authority vested in their position and therefore a manager should be the sole judge in assessing the performance of his or her subordinates. But many managers dislike being placed in the role of a judge, especially when they are asked to evaluate subordinates on personality characteristics. Similarly, employees feel uncomfortable being judged on factors that have questionable relationships to the task they are doing. The other view holds that people should be asked to appraise themselves. It is realized that some subordinates may be harsher on themselves than their superior would be. But other individuals may rate themselves unreasonably high, especially if the rating influences their salary.

Suggestion: The MBO philosophy places emphasis on self-control and self-direction. But this presupposes that verifiable objectives have been previously set (primarily by the subordinate in conjunction with the superior) against which performance can be measured. Indeed, if this is done well, appraising is relatively easy. There should be no surprises during the appraisal meeting. Subordinates know what they want to achieve and superiors know what contribution they can expect from their subordinates. Besides the comprehensive appraisal, periodic reviews and constant monitoring of performance can uncover deviations from standards. Generally, then, subordinates should have an opportunity to exercise self-control, but the superior still has the veto power in case of a controversy about the level of the objective that is the basis for performance appraisal.

4 *Assessing past performance vs. future development*   This issue is closely related to the one just discussed. Some managers see the purpose of appraisal primarily as assessing past performance. But others focus on the developmental aspects of appraisal as shown in the previously cited Conference Board study. This improvement orientation is toward the future.

Suggestion: With the emphasis on self-appraisal and responsible self-direction, the judgmental aspect in appraisal is considerably reduced. To be sure, one should learn from past mistakes, but then use these insights for translating them into developmental plans for the future. Clearly, appraisal can be an excellent opportunity to emphasize a person's strengths and to prepare action plans for overcoming weaknesses.

5 *Who shall do the rating?*   Different kinds of people can be involved in the appraisal. First, there is, of course, the immediate superior. A careful analysis of his or her ratings becomes, then, the basis for the discussion with subordinates. This approach is usually most acceptable in a tradition of top-down managing. Second, both the superior and subordinate are asked to rate the subordinate's performance independently. This usually provides a cross-check and uncovers differences in perception. Discrepancies so discovered can be openly discussed and misunderstandings clarified. Although this approach may require more time than the first approach, the feedback and the improvement in communication may be worthwhile. Third, the rating may be done by the subordinate only. The assumption is that when one of the purposes of appraisal is development, then self-development can best be achieved by the individuals themselves. The superior, naturally, can enter the discussion as a coach and helper. A fourth approach is to get peers and co-workers involved in the appraisal. This is obviously very time-consuming. Fifth, subordinates can also be asked to rate their superiors. Sixth, a committee can be used to do the appraisal. Seventh, people from the personnel department can participate in the appraisal. Finally, internal or external consultants may be asked for their appraisal inputs. Although having the above-mentioned third parties involved in the appraisal may provide some additional inputs, there are also clearly problems with these approaches.

Suggestion: There is no one best approach to appraisal; a combination may be used. In general, however, the immediate superior is in the best position to assess the contribution of their subordinates who, in congruence with MBO philosophy, exercise a great deal of self-control. In addition, it is suggested that the appraiser's superior review the appraisal. This double-check not only has the potential of increasing the validity and objectivity of the appraisal, but it also can be used for comparing several managers reporting to the same superior. Thus, the tendency of a manager's being too lenient or too strict may be uncovered. When performance is tied to a bonus plan, the appraisals of top managers may be reviewed by a bonus committee often consisting of outside members of the board of directors.

6 *Link between appraisal of performance and salary*   There are those who argue that performance against verifiable objectives should be the only criteria for granting salary increases. But others take the position that a person may perform well—or poorly—due to factors beyond his or her control, and salary decisions should be independent of performance.

Suggestion: There is probably no other item that is as controversial as the relationship between appraisal of performance and salary. It would, of course, be unfair to have a basic incongruency between performance and salary. Yet, if this link is made too soon, too closely, and is too rigidly implemented, undesirable consequences can be expected, as shown by the example of one large bank that introduced MBO in the organization. The program had top management support, with the person in charge of the program on the vice presidential level. Furthermore, considerable training was undertaken. Thus, important requirements for effective implementation of the program were present. There was also a close link between performance measured against preestablished objectives and the bonus plan. This, unfortunately, caused a great deal of dissatisfaction because many managers did not perceive the system as being fair for all. The basic idea of linking performance with the bonus plan was sound, but problems occurred because the link was made too early, before the objective-setting program could be perfected. One has to gain experience first before one knows what the appropriate standards are. Furthermore, the experience in this company showed that everyone likes to share in the success of the company through the accompanying bonus, but it is more difficult to forego the bonus during economically bad times. In this bank the link between MBO and the bonus plan was the reason for an enthusiastic acceptance of the results-based program. But this link was also the reason for problems that eventually led to the discontinuation of the program.

In conclusion, the various experiences with linking salary to performance are diverse. Clearly, there should be a correlation between performance and reward, but there is no easy solution to making this link effective. Wage administration is a complex task. The MBO approach facilitates the development of a fair reward system; but it is not a cure-all. Other factors must be taken into account, and rewards can take many forms.

7 *When to discuss salary* Another, related, issue is when salary should be discussed. Some say it should be done at the same time that the performance is evaluated. But others maintain that this discussion should be held at the anniversary employment date or at some other time.

Suggestion: If salary is discussed at the appraisal meeting, then it is quite common that the appraisee is only interested in whether or not a raise is forthcoming, and how much it is. Thus, too little attention is given to an objective assessment of deviations from plans. Furthermore, finding the reasons for deviations is also often neglected. Similarly, concern about managerial development and the setting of objectives for the ensuing period is overshadowed by monetary concerns. Therefore, and much can be said for this position, many experienced managers prefer to discuss salary issue at a meeting separate from the appraisal discussion.

8 *Frequency of Appraisals* There is general agreement that a formal appraisal should be conducted at least once a year. But others suggest that such discussions should take place more frequently. Also, some companies do all the reviews within a short period of time each year, while others schedule the appraisal throughout the year, often at the employment anniversary. A case could be made against a rigid schedule of annual performance reviews. Instead, it could be argued that performance should be reviewed, for example, after the completion of a particular project. This helps to assess the effectiveness of the handling of the project.

Suggestion: No universally applicable suggestion can be made about the timeframe for the *formal comprehensive review.* It de- pends on the nature of the task, past company practices, and other situational factors. Once, twice, or even three times may be appropriate for a particular organization or a person who is new in a job.

What is, important, however, is that the formal comprehensive reviews are supplemented by frequent *progress or periodic reviews.* These reviews can be short and relatively informal, but they help to identify problems or barriers that hinder effective performance. They also keep communication open between the superior and subordinates. Furthermore, priorities can be rearranged and objectives can be renegotiated if warranted by changed situations. It certainly is inappropriate to pursue obsolete or inappropriate objectives that were agreed upon in an environment of uncertainties.

Finally, there is the continuous *monitoring* of performance. This means that when performance deviates from plans, one does not even wait for the next periodic review. Instead, the superior and subordinate discuss the situation so that corrective actions can be taken at that time in order to prevent a small deviation from developing into a major problem.

IMPLICATIONS FOR MANAGERIAL PRODUCTIVITY

Productivity implies measurement, the focus of this chapter. Organizational control includes the steps of setting standards, measuring performance, and taking corrective actions. There are many different kinds of tools and methods available,[11] but perhaps the most desirable control is feedforward control that attempts to prevent deviations from occurring. This control approach requires planning and monitoring input variables for a system that is often schematically shown as a model. In short, feedforward control anticipates deviations and takes actions before major problems develop.

Effective controls measure the right things, are cost-efficient, simple, and timely. They are also tailored to fit the organization and its climate, are flexible, focus on critical deviations, and emphasize quantitative as well as qualitative criteria. Finally, effective controls search for the causes of undesirable deviations, lead to corrective actions, and recognize the impact of control standards on human behavior.

There is some disagreement on the purpose of appraisal. While some see the purpose of appraisal simply as a measurement of performance, others point at the uses for managerial development, salary administration, and promotion decisions. The study by the Conference Board found considerable differences between the objectives of appraisals and how they are actually used.

The recommendations based on the findings in the General Electric studies include frequent discussions of performance, emphasis on problem solving and joint objective setting, and separating the judging and helping roles of managers in performance appraisal. Performance appraisal based on MBO concepts not only works in business, but also on government organizations, as illustrated by forestry organizations and NASA.

Despite the attention given to appraisal, there are still many issues on which no complete agreement can be reached. These different views are highlighted in this chapter and suggestions are made to reconcile the various approaches.

NOTES

1 "How Three Companies Increased Their Productivity," *Fortune,* March 10, 1980.

2 H. Koontz and R. W. Bradspies, "Managing Through Feedforward Control—A Future-Directed View," *Business Horizons,* vol. 15, no. 3 (June 1972), pp. 25–36. Some authors use the term "steering control" instead of feedforward control.

3 D. McGregor, "An Uneasy Look at Performance Appraisal," *Harvard Business Review,* vol. 35, no. 3 (May-June 1957), pp. 88–94.

4 J. N. Kondrasuk, "MBO: Who's Using It and What They Think of It," 1981 *Proceedings, IX Annual Management by Objectives State of the Art Conference* (Bowling Green, Ohio, MBO Institute, 1981).

5 R. I. Lazer and W. S. Wikstrom, *Appraising Managerial Performance: Current Practices and Future Directions* (New York: The Conference Board, Inc., 1977).

6 H. H. Meyer, E. Kay, and J. R. P. French, Jr., "Split Roles in Performance Appraisal," *Harvard Business Review,* vol. 43, no. 1 (January-February 1965), pp. 123–129.

7 S. R. Atkinson, L. S. Beck, and B. A. Courtright, "How to Use MBO-Based Work Planning and Performance Reviews to Increase Productivity in a Public Agency," *1981 Proceedings, IX Annual Management by Objectives State of the Art Conference* (Washington, 1981), pp. 7–13.
8 This discussion has been based on M. Stein and W. A. Mecca, Jr., "Organization-Wide Management by Objectives (MBO) and Performance Appraisal in a Government Agency: The NASA Experience," *1980 Proceedings, VIII Annual Management by Objectives State of the Art Conference* (Dallas, Texas, 1980), pp. 22–27.
9 H. Weihrich, "An Uneasy Look at the MBO Jungle—Toward a Contingency Approach to MBO," *Management International Review,* vol. 16, no. 4 (1976), pp. 103–109.
10 H. Koontz, *Appraising Managers as Managers* (New York: McGraw-Hill, 1971). See also cassette recordings by H. Koontz and H. Weihrich, *Measuring Managers—A Double Barreled Approach* (New York: AMACOM, a division of American Management Association, 1981).
11 G. P. Latham and K. N. Wexley, *Increasing Productivity Through Performance Appraisal* (Reading, Mass.: Addison-Wesley, 1981); M. S. Sashkin, *Assessing Performance Appraisal* (San Diego: University Associates, 1981); and G. L. Morrisey, *Performance Appraisals in Business and Industry* (Reading, Mass.: Addison-Wesley, 1983).

CHAPTER 8

IMPROVING PRODUCTIVITY THROUGH HUMAN RESOURCE PLANNING AND MANAGERIAL DEVELOPMENT

The core activities in management by objectives are setting objectives, developing action plans, implementing plans, controlling, and appraising. Now many programs include strategic planning as an essential aspect of MBO. But there are other systems that need to be effectively integrated with the MBO process. This chapter deals with two such managerial systems: human resource planning and managerial development. First we focus on the need for planning primarily from the viewpoint of the organization. Later in this chapter we emphasize the need for integrating training and development into the managerial process. This theme is further developed in the next chapter on career management.

PRODUCTIVITY AND HUMAN RESOURCE MANAGEMENT

The national concern for productivity led to the National Productivity and Quality of Working Life Act that was passed by Congress in 1975. The purpose of the law was to make Americans aware of the advantages of increased productivity and to encourage joint actions by business, labor, government, and the public. This law also required that the National Center for Productivity and Quality of Working Life try to obtain commitment and help from each of these groups. In its report to the President and the Congress, the center pointed at the importance of developing human potentials of employees, employers, and managers. The application of capital and technology for productivity improvement depends on how effectively people use new methods and machines.[1] The center studied major sectors in the economy and found, for example, that in the apparel industry, which employs 1.3 million workers, one of the areas that needed attention for productivity improvement was recruitment, training, and retention. Based on the center's three years of experience, a number of measures were suggested that could be taken to improve productivity. One of these measures was improved manpower planning, which will be called human resource planning in this book. For our purpose, *human resource planning* is defined as determining the human resource need, comparing it with the people available, appraising people, and obtaining people from internal and external sources through recruitment, selection, placement, press, and promotion. *Human resource development,* which is discussed in the second part of this chapter, refers to conscious efforts in professional growth that may require changes in knowledge, skills, attitudes, and behavior to increase managerial productivity. In a broader sense, it also includes programs that help this process. This chapter, then, first focuses on human resource planning, followed by human resource development with the aim of improving managerial, and, in turn, organizational productivity.

Few managers would deny that people are critical for the productive functioning of an enterprise.[2] In fact, people are important inputs of the MBO model that was discussed in Chapter 1, and that is the framework for this book. It is true that productivity attributable to effective human resource management is rather difficult to measure, yet what really counts is not measurement, but results. For example, Japanese management is praised for its high productivity increases. Most people attribute the success to the effective use of human resources; yet, it would be difficult to prove this scientifically. Thus, we suggest that human resource planning and development will contribute to the long-run productivity of enterprises although, admittedly, it is difficult to satisfy those who demand scientific proof.

Today, many companies engage in some kind of human resource

planning, but many of these enterprises use a piecemeal approach to staffing, reacting largely in response to present demands. Only a few companies that use MBO integrate human resource planning and the MBO process. Moreover, of those companies that do some planning of human resources, few do it systematically. The program of the utility company, discussed here as an illustration, is probably not very common. This firm looked at its long-range plan, the existing organization, the number of managers required to fill the organizational roles, and the availability of managers. Based on these findings, the company engaged in recruitment, placement, promotion, training, and career development. To be sure, it may be somewhat easier to make such plans for a utility company with a relatively stable environment (although the environment is now also changing rapidly for this industry) than for a high-technology firm operating in a very dynamic and unpredictable environment. Still, the need for such planning is important for both kinds of organizations. Let us now introduce a conceptual human resource model that integrates the different aspects of human resource planning in a systematic manner.

THE HUMAN RESOURCE PLANNING PROCESS[3]

Human resource planning should not be considered in isolation; rather it should be an integral part of the MBO process as shown in Figure 8-1. Specifically, strategic and operational objectives and plans become the basis for the organization structure and action plans because the structure of the organization is derived from its strategy. The current and the expected organization structure in the future determine the organization's demand for managers. This demand is compared with the organization's supply of managers, its current work force. Based on this analysis, the variances are determined. If there is an oversupply of managers, the company will aim at reducing the work force. On the other hand, if there is additional demand for managers, the company will pursue a strategy to fill this need from internal and external sources, using a variety of approaches. Through performance appraisal, the organization obtains feedback about the competencies of its managers. Finally, human resource planning is situational, which means that internal factors of the company and the external environment are taken into account in the planning process. After this overview, let us now focus on the main variables in the model.

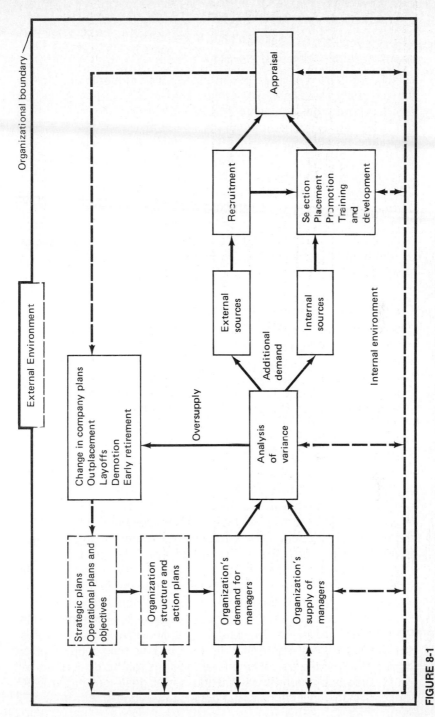

FIGURE 8-1
Human resource planning. [*Adapted from H. Koontz, C. O'Donnell, and H. Weihrich, Management, 8th ed. (New York: McGraw-Hill, 1984.)*]

Basis for Human Resource Planning

Effective human resource planning starts with strategic and operational planning (enclosed with broken lines in Figure 8-1). As will be recalled from previous chapters, external opportunities and threats are matched with internal capabilities. Objectives are set and alternative courses are developed, evaluated, and selected. To carry out these plans, an organizational structure is established. Specifically, to achieve the objectives, it is necessary to identify and group the necessary activities, as well as delegate authority to managers to carry out these activities. Furthermore, these groups of activities are coordinated horizontally and vertically through authority and informational relationships. The roles established in the organizational structure must be filled and maintained with competent people, which is the focus of human resource planning.

Organization's Demand for Managers

The number and quality of the managers required depends on expansion or contraction plans of the organization, the turnover rate, and the forecasted retirement rate of managers. Of course, the organization structure may also be changed by widening or narrowing the span of control and thereby decreasing or increasing the demand for managers.

Organization's Supply of Managers

Increasingly, companies use an inventory system to identify the supply of available managers. An inventory chart may depict an organizational chart keyed to the promotability of the manager. For example, a manager may be ready for promotion now, in a year, or in the more distant future. Others may have reached a stage where a future promotion is unlikely and still others may be identified as performing unsatisfactorily. Such an inventory chart may also indicate the number of years a person has been in the current position. Additional records may be kept about a person's specific experience, special skills and knowledge, formal education, publications, licenses, patents, languages, and salary data. Moreover, stating professional and career goals (further discussed in the next chapter) gives an indication of the person's needs, interests, and ambition. As will be recalled, we emphasized that the set of goals set in the MBO process should include personal development goals.

Variance Analysis: Oversupply and Additional Demand for Managers

If the variance analysis reveals an oversupply of managers, the company can pursue several alternative courses of action. The firm may adjust its strategic and operational plans to take advantage of the available managers. If this is not possible, the firm may resort to outplacement, which is an attempt to assist managers in finding and selecting other suitable employment outside the company.[4] Other alternatives are layoffs, demotions, or early retirement of personnel.

If, on the other hand, the demand for managers exceeds its supply (a common situation found in fast-growing companies), external and internal sources must be utilized. Through recruitment, managers or potential managers are attracted from outside the firm. This may be done through media advertising, computer services designed to match the needs of the organization with the competency of potential employees, college recruiting, internship, and the use of placement firms. But often companies do not find the required personnel outside or these firms have a policy of internal promotion.

A high demand for managers also requires a good *selection* system. There are different approaches to selection. It is recommended to start with job objectives that can be categorized into regular and routine, problem-solving, and innovative or change. The performance of the candidate for a position is then evaluated against these objectives.[5] In a situation of high demand for managers the emphasis is also on *placement,* which is similar to selection but the accent is on finding or designing a position congruent with the individual's strengths and weaknesses. Another human resource strategy is *promotion,* which usually involves moving a person to a position that demands advanced skills and more responsibilities than in the previous position. In a situation of great demand and limited supply of managers on the outside, companies have to give even more attention to training and developing their own managerial personnel. This topic will be discussed in greater detail later in this chapter. Finally, progress in achieving performance objectives and professional development is assessed in performance appraisal, as shown in the human resource planning model.

Situational Factors in Human Resource Planning

Figure 8-1 shows the human resource plan sequentially. In reality there is seldom a systematic progression beginning with strategic objectives and plans to appraisal. Yet, one must recognize the interrelatedness of the various aspects of human resource planning and the link to the MBO process. Furthermore, the various feedback loops in the model draw attention to the fact that each step in the process must only be undertaken if it is congruent with, or at least does not interfere with, other aspects of the process.

It is also important to recognize that situational factors in the *internal environment* affect human resource planning. For example, some companies have a policy of promotion from within that excludes competition from qualified candidates from the outside. In contrast, a policy of open competition encourages the search for the best-qualified person for a vacant position. Thus, candidates from within the firm or from the outside are considered. Human resource planning must also take into account the influences in the *external environment*. For example, the sociocultural environment and the educational background encourages people not to accept orders blindly. Instead they demand to participate in the decision-making process. Also, managers must recognize that the company is an integral part of society and that the public demands socially respon-sive actions and adherence to high ethical standards. Similarly, legal constraints require enterprises to adhere to the laws and regulations issued by the various governments. Finally, the recognition of the interdependency of various countries and the growth of multinational corporations affects human resource planning. It is not unusual for firms to have top management teams comprised of people with different nationalities. Having provided an overview of human re-source planning, we turn now to manager development and training.

TRAINING AND DEVELOPMENT

Productive organizations are led by competent managers. While some people still think that managers are born, the prevailing school of thought is that managers can be developed. This requires managerial training that aims at improving the knowledge, skills, attitudes, and performance through on-the-job training as well as internal and external programs that develop people on their current job and prepare them for future positions.[6]

Problems With Training and Development

Many companies make substantial efforts, at great costs, to develop their managers. Yet, they often do not get the results they expect, or worse, they are not even clear about the objectives of the training efforts. In many cases the underlying problem is a poorly coordinated training effort rather than a systematic approach to training and development. Let us highlight some of the typical problems.

First, training is often not related to the individual's objectives, nor the department's objectives, nor the organization's mission. One company with a generous educational reimbursement program received requests for many kinds of courses, such as "popular photography," that were offered at a local university extension. This topic may be interesting to explore as a hobby, but it usually has little connection to a person's professional objectives. Second, training programs are not tailored to the specific needs of the individual or the organization. In the 1960s, for example, sensitivity training was quite popular and companies felt a need to have their employees "exposed" to it without being really clear about the objectives of this program and the relationship to the specific needs of the firm. Not only can the wrong program be costly, but it can also be harmful to the firm by creating an environment for conflicts. Third, training and development of subordinates is not the primary responsibility of the training or personnel department. To be sure, such a department should assist managers in their training efforts, but the final responsibility for training rests with every manager and cannot be abdicated. Fourth, training and developing subordinates is certainly time-consuming. Managers are often not rewarded for their efforts, which may result in their neglecting this important managerial activity. Therefore, managers must be appraised of how well they carry out their responsibility of training subordinates. This is done in the "appraising-managers-as-managers" approach (see Chapter 7), which consists of seventy-three questions, three of them criteria for evaluating superiors in their training efforts:

Does the manager take steps to make certain that subordinates are given the opportunity to train for better positions, both in their present departments and elsewhere in the organization?

Does the manager utilize appropriate methods of training and developing subordinates?

Does the manager effectively practice coaching of subordinates as a means of training?[7]

Managers are then evaluated on these criteria on a five-point scale. This approach has the advantage that managers know that training is a part of their job and that they get recognized for their efforts.

They will then become more concerned about the professional growth of their subordinates. Another way of encouraging managers to develop subordinates is to follow General Motors' policy of only promoting those managers who have trained a person who can succeed them.

The Training and Development Process

Training is concerned with the competency of individuals in their present job as well as in future positions (see Figure 8-2). The aims of training are the individual's improvement in knowledge, attitude, and skills, resulting in increased productivity.

A common way of identifying training needs is during the performance appraisal. As we have seen in Chapter 7, appraisals serve different purposes, one of which is to develop managers. When performance is not according to plan, attempts should be made to identify the reasons for the deviation. If it is due to managerial deficiencies, training should be directed to overcome them. For example, in one savings and loan association performance was substantially below standards. The problem, it was found, was not so much the actual performance, but poor forecasting on which objectives were based. The president made wrong assumptions by extrapolating past performance into the future without taking into account the signs of an impending recession. But the president assumed the responsibility for his mistake and learned the skills of forecasting. This is an example in which developmental effort was directed to overcome specific deficiencies.

But to focus the training and development efforts only on deficiencies would be shortsighted. One has to prepare for the future, and it will not be the same as the present or the past. Thus it is necessary to develop skills that may be demanded several years from now.

The estimated potential of individuals also serves as the basis for identifying future development needs and for designing programs to meet the long-term needs of individuals. Take the case of a first-line supervisor with the ambition to become a division manager, who may realize the need for a master of business administration degree. To obtain such a degree is a long-term effort that requires several years of part-time study. Therefore, managers should set two kinds of development objectives relating to short-term improvements as well as to the long-term career.

Individual needs and plans should become the basis for organiza-

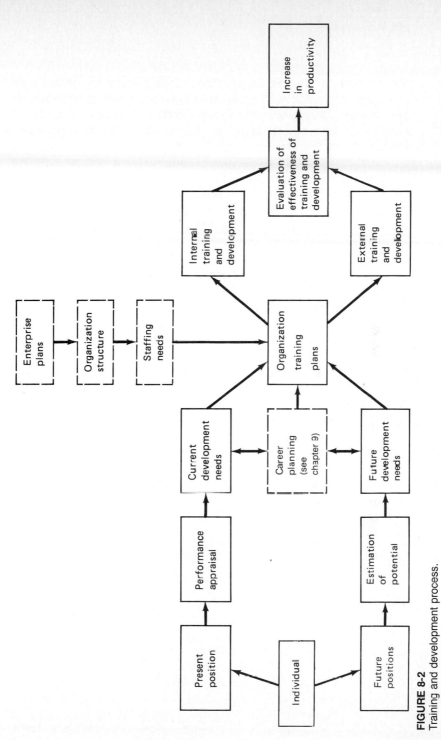

FIGURE 8-2
Training and development process.

tion training and development plans. The company must also consider its present and future staffing needs, which are derived from the enterprise plan and the organization structure, as shown in Figure 8-2. Training objectives determine the methods to be used. On-the-job training programs may range from job rotation to serving on committees known as "junior boards." These boards give the trainees exposure to problems that concern the whole organization. Thus, trainees may be asked to evaluate the feasibility of developing a new product and then report to the executive committee. Another internal training approach is the day-to-day coaching of subordinates. The personnel department may assist managers in developing their subordinates, but it does not relieve managers from their responsibilities to help subordinates to grow.

Managers may also attend special training sessions conducted either within the organization, by outside educational institutions such as universities, the American Management Association, or by consulting firms. To make these programs productive two things are required. First, the program should be related to training needs; second, the effectiveness of the programs should be evaluated and conscious attempts must be made to transfer the acquired knowledge or skills to the job.

The last two aspects in the training and development model, Figure 8-2, focus on the importance of the evaluation of the effectiveness of training and the impact on productivity. Often little effort is made to evaluate the effectiveness of training and development. To measure any difference in behavior of performance requires the setting of learning or training objectives. The evaluation process may involve the following steps:

1 Set learning, training, or development objectives.

2 Give the trainee a test to establish the level of knowledge or skills at the beginning of the training session.

3 Conduct the training.

4 Give the trainee a test after the training and note the difference between the results of the posttest and the pretest.

5 Assure the transfer of knowledge and skills to the work situation. Unfortunately, this transfer is not easy because what was learned may not always be directly applicable to the job or the firm's environment. In one of the sensitivity training sessions, a participant clearly met the seminar's objectives of open communication and "levelling." However, these objectives were incongruent with the firm's autocratic approach and top-down communication pattern.

Clearly the incompatibility of the training with the organizational climate should have been noted before the training. The transfer of knowledge and skills is facilitated when the training objectives are clearly established and fit the individual *and* organization needs.

6 The next step in the evaluation process is a follow-up to assess the effectiveness and appropriateness of the training as well as improvements in performance and productivity. Admittedly, it is rather difficult to attribute specific productivity increases to training. But a goal-oriented approach to managing and training is a step in the right direction despite its limitations.

7 If it is found that behavior, performance, or productivity has improved, and if it is believed that the change is due to the training efforts, reinforcement is essential. What is not reinforced is forgotten and discontinued.

The training and development model gives an overview of the process. But other aspects must also be considered to make training productive.

Making Training and Development Effective

A study of effective management development programs found that they differ widely among companies. Furthermore, the programs also differ for managers at various organizational levels. This is understandable because of the various skill requirements for positions in the hierarchy. It was also found that most of the training and development is on the job. Finally, this study concluded that training is the responsibility of all managers.[8]

These, then, are some guidelines for improving training and development.[9]

1 It should be directed toward the organizational purpose.

2 It should be systematic, based on an objective identification and analysis of organizational and individual needs.

3 It should require the involvement of managers rather than becoming the responsibility of the training department. This means that a great deal of development is through coaching on the job.

4 It should be congruent with the value system and the managerial style of top managers.

5 Although development is aimed at change, it usually cannot be completely incongruent with the organizational climate. Also, the pace of change should be appropriate. While there have been dramatic organizational changes occurring within a short timeframe, especially if they were initiated by top management, it is more likely that change efforts extend over a long period.

6 Top management's commitment to major training and development efforts is necessary. If feasible, executives should be directly involved in the program.

7 Training objectives should be set so that progress can be measured against the criteria.

8 Productive training requires that from among the various training methods the most suitable ones are selected to achieve the objectives.

9 The effectiveness of the training and development efforts must be periodically assessed.

10 Training and development efforts should contribute to improvement of short-term and long-term performance and productivity.

In Chapter 5 we stressed the importance of verifiable objectives and the advisability of including personal and professional development objectives. Here are some sample objectives that are measurable.

- Obtain an MBA degree from an accredited university by June 1, two years from now.
- Attend a seminar of personal computers by March 30.
- Read two books on management by June 30.
- Participate in a plant visit to learn about quality circles by May 15.
- Complete a course in public speaking by December 31.

IMPLICATIONS FOR MANAGERIAL PRODUCTIVITY

One of the keys to unlock people's potential for increasing productivity is the effective management of human resources. This chapter focuses on two main aspects of managing people: human resource planning and management development.

Human resource planning is an integral part of the managerial process.[10] The organizational demands must be matched with the available people, either from the inside or the outside of the organization. This requires recruitment, selection, placement, and promotion. Since one cannot rely on the supply of personnel from outside and the organization has a responsibility to develop its own employees, systematic training programs must be developed. Frequently a shortage of qualified managers is the crucial constraint in preventing the enterprise to grow.

Traditional training programs have not lived up to expectations. To overcome some of the weaknesses, a systematic process is suggested for making managers more productive in their present job as well as preparing them for future positions. The training needs of managers are matched with staffing needs derived from organizational plans. The training plans include external and internal programs. In general, a great deal of training occurs within the organization; therefore, every manager must be a coach.

Training must be evaluated in terms of its effectiveness and its contribution to productivity. The emphasis of goal setting in the development efforts allows measurement against verifiable training objectives. The linkage of training and productivity is a tenuous one. Most managers are aware of this linkage, but it is difficult to establish clear cause-effect relationships. However, to ignore training and development because of this difficulty in measurement would be a serious mistake in the quest for improving productivity.

NOTES

1 *Productivity in the Changing World of the 1980s– The Final Report of the National Center for Productivity and Quality of Working Life* (Washington, D.C.: National Center for Productivity and Quality of Working Life, 1978) p. 36.
2 The importance of people in increasing productivity is discussed by R. A. Sutermeister, *People and Productivity* (New York: McGraw-Hill, 3d ed., 1976).
3 Adapted from H. Weihrich, "The Management of Human Resources," *Arizona Business,* vol. 26, no. 6 (June-July 1979), pp. 17–23. *Arizona Business* is published by the Bureau of Business and Economic Research, College of Business Administration, Arizona State University, Tempe, AZ 85287. Used with permission.
4 The concept of outplacement has been discussed by J. L. Mendleson, "Does Your Company Need Outplacement?" *S.A.M. Advanced Management Journal,* vol. 40, no. 1 (Winter 1975), pp. 4–12.
5 G. S. Odiorne and E. L. Miller, "Selection by Objectives: A New Approach to Managerial Selection," *Management of Personnel Quarterly,* vol. 5, no. 3 (Fall 1966), pp. 2–10.
6 Some of the first authors linking management development and training to management by objectives were J. W. Humble, *Improving Management Performance* (London: Management Publications, Ltd., 1965) and

G. S. Odiorne, *Training by Objectives* (London and New York: MacMillan, 1970).

7 This approach was developed by H. Koontz, *Appraising Managers as Managers* (New York: McGraw-Hill, 1971). The questions are taken from the cassette recording *Measuring Managers—A Double Barreled Approach* (New York: AMACON, A Division of the American Management Association, 1980).

8 L. Digman, "How Well-Managed Organizations Develop Their Executives," *Organizational Dynamics,* vol. 7, no. 2 (Autumn 1978).

9 Some of these guidelines are discussed by G. S. Odiorne, *MBO II* (Belmont, CA: Fearon Pitman, 1979) and Odiorne, *Training By Objectives,*

10 M. A. Von Glinow, M. J. Driver, K. Brousseau, and J. B. Prince, "The Design of a Career Oriented Human Resource System," *Academy of Management Review,* vol. 8, no. 1 (January 1983), pp. 23–32.

CHAPTER 9

ACHIEVING PERSONAL EXCELLENCE THROUGH STRATEGIC CAREER MANAGEMENT*

The last chapter discussed human resource planning and managerial development. Human resource planning is the macroaspect of using people productively, primarily from an organizational perspective. Managerial development and training attempts to match organizational demands with developmental needs of individuals. This chapter continues with the same theme, but with even greater emphasis on individuals and their need for professional growth.

Although the successes of management by objectives (MBO) are numerous, there are also many failures.[1] What has gone wrong? The answer may be, in part, that insufficient attention has been given to the question of many MBO participants: "What is in it for me?" People want to know how they can benefit from a new managerial approach such as MBO. One way to integrate organizational demands and individual needs is career management, which consists of career planning and development. Both aspects have been neglected in most MBO programs. By giving greater attention to the aspirations of individuals, greater productivity may be achieved.

*Adapted from H. Weihrich, "Strategic Career Management—A Missing Link in Management by Objectives," *Human Resource Management,* vol. 21, no. 2 (Summer-Fall 1982), pp. 58–66. Used by permission of John Wiley & Sons, Inc. Copyright © 1982.

CAREER MANAGEMENT—THE NEGLECTED ASPECT IN THE MBO PROCESS

It is somewhat surprising that career management has not received more attention from practicing managers since management development, one aspect of career management, is occasionally mentioned in the MBO literature. Peter Drucker emphasized participative goal setting, self-direction, and self-evaluation.[2] Clearly, self-direction implies that managers can integrate their career path with MBO while at the same time contribute to the organization. Douglas McGregor, who called attention to the shortcomings of traditional appraisals that focused on personality traits, saw MBO as a means for self-development.[3] Specifically, according to McGregor, subordinates set short-term performance goals for themselves and agree with their superiors on the objectives. Performance is then evaluated against these standards. This process is essentially self-appraisal with the potential for self-development.

In his book *Management by Objectives,* George Odiorne devoted a whole chapter to the setting of personal development goals.[4] Similarly, John Humble, a well-known management consultant in Europe, made management development a critical part of his MBO model.[5] Other authors focused on the motivational aspects of MBO. Specifically, MBO is seen as integrating individual objectives with organizational aims. Again, the utilization of individuals' potential and the development of individual strengths within the framework of career development is implied.

Although there are references in the MBO literature to career development, in practice there is little evidence that career development plays an important part in MBO. One study showed that management development, which is closely related to career development, was hardly mentioned as one of the advantages of the MBO program in a large bank.[6] Another study showed that of the many purposes an MBO program serves, the development of managers— a response that would come closest to career planning—received a very low index of importance.[7] What accounts for the low importance attributed to career development in the MBO program? One reason might be that MBO programs focus on the demands of the organizations only and do not pay sufficient attention to the needs of individuals and their careers. This situation is illustrated in Figure 9-1, which shows a low degree of integration of individual needs and organizational demands. In such a situation employees will perform at the minimum acceptable level.

This situation can be illustrated by some typical examples. As

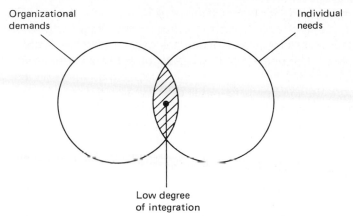

FIGURE 9-1
Low degree of integration of organizational demands and individual needs.

shown in Table 9-1, the organizational demands are often quite different from individual needs and career goals. The company, naturally, is concerned about effective and efficient operation, about profit, and about productivity. Not that these organizational concerns are unimportant to the individual, but they are secondary to the

TABLE 9-1
POTENTIAL CONFLICTS BETWEEN THE ORGANIZATION AND
THE INDIVIDUAL

Organizational needs and demands	Individual needs and career goals
1 Concern for effective and efficient operation, profit, and productivity	1 Concern for self-fulfillment and self-actualization
2 Concern for all members of the organization	2 Concern for self
3 Need to fill the roles in the organization structure	3 Need for self-fulfillment and self-actualization
4 Need for skills to fill all positions	4 Interested in challenging work only
5 Need for some specific, well-developed skills	5 Bored by routine work using specific skills
6 Best utilization of all talents within the organization	6 How to utilize own potential within or outside the enterprise
7 Manager to work in geographic location best for the organization	7 Location most suitable for self and family

individual's concern for self-fulfillment and self-actualization. To complicate matters further, the organization that wants to provide career opportunities for its employees has to recognize the needs of *all* employees. Unfortunately, the needs of some individuals are often in conflict with those of other individuals in the same firm. For example, one person's need for expanding the area of operation may conflict with the area of authority and responsibility of others. The enterprise must fill all the roles in the organization structure. Yet, some roles may be restricting the freedom of individual managers who want to utilize their capabilities and potential. Similarly, some jobs are simply boring—such as doing required paperwork—and these tasks are neither challenging nor interesting. Some jobs may be narrowly defined, requiring specialized skills. Unfortunately, this routine work may be incongruous with the individual's need for growth and development. Especially during times of slow business activity, there may be an oversupply of talented managers, and the organization may attempt to use the potentials of *all* managers, as far as this is possible in such a situation. The individual, however, is only interested in using his or her potential. Finally, some managers have to be assigned to locations where their specific knowledge and skills are needed. For example, good managers may be required for setting up a plant in a less-developed country. Yet, this location may be unsuitable for raising a family. But how can these conflicts, shown in Table 9-1, be resolved?

The aim of MBO is to achieve a high degree of integration of organizational demands and individual needs, as shown in Figure 9-2. To achieve complete congruency is unrealistic. Yet, a rational analysis of the situation often results in creative solutions to seemingly unsolvable problems. Integration should not be achieved through power struggles between the organization and the individual, nor even among individuals. Instead, both the organization and the individual have to give and take, and the first step in this direction must be a systematic analysis of the demands of the organization and the needs for development of individuals. Since managers are often not quite sure how to go about it, this chapter is written to fill this need to some extent.[8]

FORMULATING THE CAREER STRATEGY

Career planning and development must not be done in isolation. Rather, they must be integrated with the enterprise's need to fill organizational roles with competent managers who work toward the

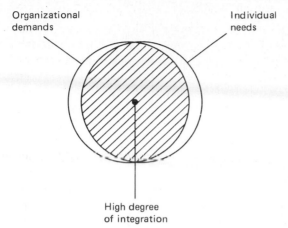

Organizational
demands

Individual
needs

High degree
of integration

FIGURE 9-2
High degree of integration of organizational demands and individual needs.

achievement of the firm's aims. The strategy is to match individual strengths and organizational opportunities. Specifically, a successful career-planning process involves the steps shown in Figure 9-3, which we'll now discuss in greater detail.

Step 1 Preparation of a Personal Profile (Know Thyself)

Perhaps one of the most difficult, yet essential, tasks is to gain insight into oneself. Are we extroverted, with attention directed toward our environment? Or are we introverted, with an inward focus? What is our life position toward ourselves? Are we OK or not OK? What is our position toward others? Are they OK or not OK? What do we value and what is dear to us? What are our attitudes toward time, achievement, work, material things, and, finally, toward change? A clarification of values will help to determine the direction of personal and professional development.

Step 2 Development of Long-Range Personal and Professional Goals

One of the failures of personal and professional development efforts is that managers are not clear what their development goals are and how they fit the aims of the organization. No ship could leave the harbor without a clear destination, yet how sure are managers about

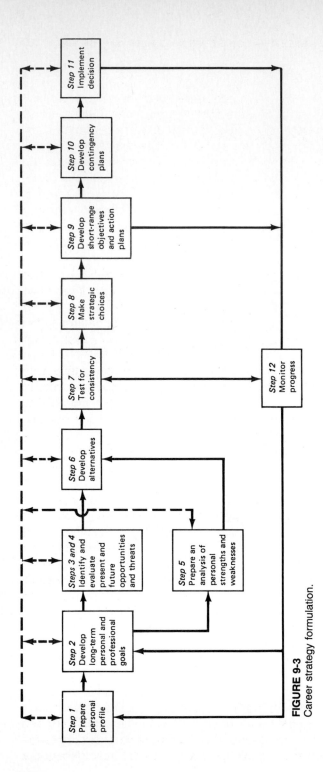

FIGURE 9-3
Career strategy formulation.

162

the direction of their lives? But people resist goal setting because it requires commitment. It requires choosing from alternatives, which means that when we select one goal we implicitly reject others. By choosing to become a chemist, one foregoes the opportunity of becoming a banker. People also resist setting goals because the environment is uncertain. The lack of knowledge about the future makes it difficult to make commitments. There is also the fear of failure to achieve the goals, and the nonachievement of aims is a blow to one's ego. Goal setting also requires self-confidence in oneself; it implies that one has some control of the environment rather than being a helpless victim of it.

By recognizing the factors that inhibit goal setting one can take steps to increase commitment. First, when setting performance goals becomes a part of the managerial process, then setting career goals is easier. Moreover, one does not set goals that determine the future in one sitting. Instead, it is a continuing process that allows revising goals in the light of changing circumstances. A second factor that reduces resistance to goal setting is the integration of long-term aims with the more immediate actions. For example, keeping in mind the aim of becoming a doctor makes it easier to study boring subjects. A third factor that facilitates goal setting is a supportive atmosphere and encouragement. For instance, writing a book is a long-term effort that requires discipline and self-denial. An understanding and supportive family atmosphere is necessary for the required sustained effort.

How far in advance should one plan? The answer may be found in the commitment principle in management. It states that planning should cover a period of time necessary to foresee the fulfillment of commitments involved in a decision made today. Therefore, the time frame will differ with the circumstances. For example, if one wants to become a professor it is necessary to plan for university studies of seven to nine years. On the other hand, if the career goal is to become a taxi driver, the time frame is much shorter. At any rate, the longer-term objective has to be translated into short-term objectives. Before we do this, however, we will have to make a situational analysis, that is, a careful assessment of the external environment with its threats and opportunities.

Step 3 Analysis of the Environment: Threats and Opportunities

In the analysis of the environment within and outside the organization, many diverse factors need to be considered. These factors are economic, social and political, technological, and demographic, and also include the labor market, and competition. They provide opportunities as well as threats.

The general state of the *economy* certainly affects the formulation of a career strategy. A recession and a low level of business activity can threaten one's position. Yet, this problem can also become an educational opportunity. During periods of high levels of unemployment, people often go back to school to continue their education.

Social and *political* factors may influence the career strategy as illustrated by the equal employment opportunity law, which may open up career paths that were not available to women or minorities. Similarly, new *technology* provides opportunities and threats. For example, computer technology is threatening to managers unfamiliar with it. At the same time, new applications of computers have created new jobs. *Demographic* factors can also affect careers. The geographic shifts in the United States, such as movement of people to the sun belt, have created an oversupply of labor in some areas. This may be threatening to some people. At the same time, the relocation of companies to the sun belt may result in new opportunities for obtaining a job in a particular field.

There are still *other factors* that must be considered when making strategic choices. Joining an expanding company is most likely to provide more career opportunities than working for a mature company that is not expected to expand. Similarly, working for a mobile manager increases the probability that the position of the superior will become vacant, or that one may ride on the coattails of the competent mobile manager. At any rate, successful career planning requires a systematic scanning of the environment for opportunities as well as threats.

Step 4 Identification of Future Opportunities and Threats

To collect the information about the environment is, to say the least, a tedious task. Singling out the factors critical to one's career is equally difficult. To make things even more complex, we have to be concerned not only about the present but also we have to forecast the future. One thing about the future is sure: it will never be the same as the present. Since there are many factors that need to be analyzed, planning one's career necessitates being selective and concentrating on those factors critical for personal success. Thus, one must anticipate the future and forecast changes in the environment that will critically affect one's career, one's ambitions, and one's life.

Step 5 Analysis of Personal Strengths and Weaknesses

For successful career planning, the environmental opportunities and threats must be matched with the capabilities of the individual. The strengths and weaknesses differ greatly among people. They may, however, be conveniently categorized as technical, human, conceptual, and design skills.

Technical skills pertain to knowledge and proficiency in using methods, processes, and procedures. Human skills are the ability to work with people and to create an environment in which people, as a team, work willingly and enthusiastically toward group goals. Conceptual skills are the ability to see the "big picture," to recognize significant elements in a situation, and to understand their relationships. Design skills are the ability not only to conceptualize a problem, but also to work and find practical solutions to the problem.

In assessing one's strengths and weaknesses, it is important to recognize that the relative importance of these skills differs for the positions in the organizational hierarchy. Technical skills, as shown in Figure 9-4, are very important at the supervisory level. At this level, human skills are also crucial because of the required interactions with subordinates. At the middle-management level the need for technical skills decreases while conceptual and design skills gain importance. Human skills are still important at this level, as they are for top management. Conceptual and design skills are especially important at the top level where there is relatively little need for technical skills. When making an analysis of their current skills and those required in the future, managers should recognize that these skills vary with the organizational level.

Step 6 The Development of Strategic Career Alternatives

Essentially, an individual can select from four sets of strategic alternatives based on the analysis of the threats and opportunities in the environment and on personal strengths and weaknesses. The

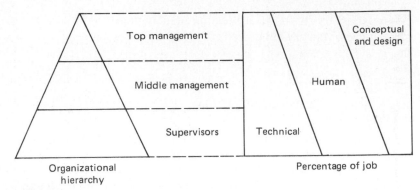

FIGURE 9-4
Variations in importance of skills at different organizational levels. [*Adapted from H. Koontz, C. O'Donnell, and H. Weihrich,* Management, *8th ed. (New York: McGraw-Hill, 1984), p. 403. Used with permission.*]

aim is to utilize one's strengths to overcome one's weaknesses, to take advantage of opportunities, and to cope with threats.

Conceptually, as shown in Figure 9-5, we have a threats-weakness strategy (TW), an opportunities-weaknesses strategy (OW), a threats-strengths strategy (TS), and an opportunities-strengths (OS) strategy. This may seem abstract and we therefore want to illustrate the concept below. Before making a strategic career choice, it is important to test the alternatives for consistency.

Step 7 Consistency Testing and Reevaluation of Career Goals

While developing the various strategies (TW, OW, TS, OS) they must be tested for consistency and compared with the personal profile. The rational choice based on the TOWS analysis is not always best. Specifically, the strategies must meet the test of personal values and interests (Step 1). Some may prefer the "do nothing strategy." Those managers, being fearful of change and risk taking, may make this choice rather than utilizing their full potential. Some managers may find great satisfaction in specialization, while others prefer to broaden their knowledge and skills. The point is, the rational decisions based on strengths, weaknesses, opportunities, and threats have to be tested for consistency with personal preferences and may require a reevaluation of career goals.

Step 1* Prepare a personal profile: (a) your values,   (b) your interests,
(c) your self-concept.
Step 2   Prepare long-range personal and professional goals.

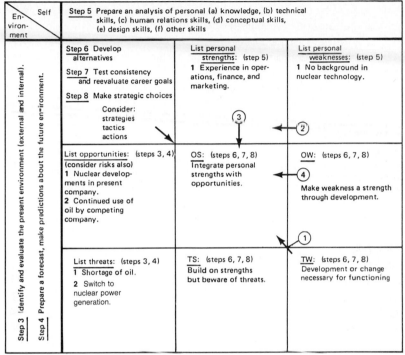

*The steps are suggestive and may vary.

FIGURE 9-5
Situation analysis for a career strategy.

Step 8 Evaluating and Choosing from Alternatives

The foregoing analyses of strengths, weaknesses, opportunities, and threats are the basis for a strategic choice that usually requires tradeoffs. Some alternatives involve high risks, others low risks. Some choices require action now; other choices can wait. Timing certainly is crucial. The rational and systematic analysis is just one step in the career-planning process, for a choice also involves personal preferences, personal ambitions, and above all, personal values.

Let us now turn to an illustration of how a career strategy can be developed using the TOWS analysis.

An Illustration of Career Strategies

A brief review of Figure 9-5 shows that the external threats are exemplified by the shortage of oil and a switch to nuclear energy for power generation. Specifically, the developing nuclear technology not only threatens the individual's job within the organization (let's say it is a utility company), but it also reduces the demand of current skills in the market place.

As is so often the case, problems can become opportunities. Consequently, a systematic environmental analysis indicates in our example great *opportunities* for careers related to nuclear energy technology, not only within the company but also outside the firm.

But threats and opportunities must be seen in light of the individual's weaknesses and strengths. Let us say, as an illustration, a professional manager's *weakness* is that he has no background in nuclear technology. The manager's *strength* is that he has broad managerial experience in a variety of areas such as operations, finance, and marketing. Based on the analysis of the situation, several career alternatives are available.

The Threats-Weakness Strategy (TW)   The current and future oil shortage poses a serious threat to the person in a supervisory position which, let's say, requires managerial and technical knowledge and skills. However, his or her weak background in nuclear energy technology does not qualify him or her for advancement. Several career choices are available. The individual could recognize his or her limitations and accept a demotion and an assignment to another department if his or her position is going to be eliminated by the switch to nuclear energy. Another strategy would be to escape the threat within the company and join another company which still uses oil for generating energy, an area of strength of the manager. This is indicated by arrow number ① in the model (Figure 9-5). Still another career strategy would be to undertake efforts to overcome his or her weakness (lack of nuclear knowledge) and make it a strength through continuing education efforts. This would mean a directional effort indicated by arrows numbered ② and ③ in the model. In other words, weaknesses are transformed into strengths to escape the threats and to take advantage of opportunities in the nuclear field.

The Opportunities-Weaknesses Strategy (OW)   This is a situation where a manager is not directly threatened by the environment, let's say the utility company still uses oil for generating electricity, but the manager sees long-term opportunities in the nuclear field. The new nuclear energy developments may increase the demands for managers with a nuclear knowledge background, thus providing great potential for advancement and increased remuneration. Such a manager's strategy could be developmental, with the aim of overcoming weaknesses and transforming them into strengths through additional education. This strategy is shown by arrow number ④.

Threats-Strengths Strategy (TS)   This strategy can be illustrated by a manager who has demonstrated competence in the current job over the years. That manager has a solid managerial experience and the technical knowledge required for generating electricity with oil. But there may be prospects for converting to nuclear energy. The career choice using the TS strategy is not so obvious and depends on many factors, such as the forecast of the nature, extent, and severity of the threat. Furthermore, the career strategy is also dependent on the availability of alternative choices. For example, if the use of nuclear energy is only supplemental to the use of oil within the company, the threat of becoming obsolescent is reduced. Similarly, as long as other utility companies are not expected to convert to nuclear energy, the individual with a great amount of knowledge, skills, and experience still has the choice of escaping the threat within the company by joining another utility firm.

Opportunities-Strengths Strategy (OS)   In general, this strategy is based on a very favorable situation. A manager with great strengths in all essential aspects will focus on opportunities within the enterprise as well as outside. The strategy will be one of identifying, evaluating, and choosing from among the many opportunities and matching them with capabilities, interests, and career goals. It is building on strengths to choose the career yielding the greatest satisfaction.

The strategies selected for the four situational positions (TW, OW, TS, and OS) are illustrative only. Certainly there are other alternatives available to a manager preparing his or her career plan. However, it is important to remember that a careful analysis of opportunities and threats in the environment, as well as a realistic assessment of one's strengths and weaknesses, provides a sound basis for selecting distinct career strategies based on four rather different sets of factors.

Step 9 Development of Short-Range Objectives and Action Plans

Up to this point our concern was with the process of giving direction to the career. Now we focus on short-range objectives and action plans that facilitate the achievement of the general aim.

As we have seen in Chapter 5, setting objectives is a complex and difficult task. A statement "to improve one's education" is a platitude, not a verifiable objective. But to say that the short-term goal is to complete the course "Fundamentals of Management" by June 30, with a grade of "A," is measurable. It states what will be done, by what time, and that the course should be completed with the highest grade (quality).

Although the emphasis here is on short-term career objectives, they may have to be supported by action plans. The above-mentioned example of the objective of completing a course in the MBA program may require specific action plans. For example, one may have to identify the tasks necessary to achieve this objective, schedule the time for attending class and doing the homework, and obtain the agreement from family members who may suffer because attending classes demands time that may otherwise be spent with the family. In short, then, the long-term strategic career plan needs to be supported by short-term objectives and action plans.

Step 10 Development of Contingency Plans

Career plans are built on uncertainty; the future cannot be predicted with accuracy. Consequently, contingency plans based on alternative sets of assumptions should be prepared. In our previous example, career plans were built on the assumption of the feasibility of using nuclear energy for generating electricity. Yet, the mounting opposition to nuclear power plants in recent years may make the whole plan impossible to implement if no such plants are being built. Wise managers certainly would not plan their entire lives on a single set of assumptions. Instead, they prepare alternative plans based on different sets of assumptions.

Step 11 Implementation of the Career Plan

From the organizational point of view, career planning must become an integral part of managing. Or, as we suggest, it must be a part of MBO, which we view as a system of managing that integrates many key managerial activities.

Career planning may start during the appraisal interview. The evaluation of past performance is only one of the aspects of the appraisal meeting. Certainly, the individual's growth and development should also be discussed and objectives related to one's career should be set. This way the career goals and personal ambitions can be considered in selecting, promoting, and designing training and development programs.

Step 12 Monitoring Progress

The monitoring process involves evaluating the progress toward the previously established goals and correcting undesirable deviations. An opportune time for assessing career development progress would be at performance appraisal. This is the time to review not only performance against objectives in operating areas, but also to review the extent to which milestones in professional development have been achieved. The superior, in the role of a counselor, can assist subordinates in their career development. However, the manager really concerned about the career development of subordinates will not wait for the periodic appraisal reviews. Instead, such a manager will continuously reinforce professional behavior and growth in subordinates.

These steps provide a logical framework to career planning and development. In practice, however, the sequence may vary. For example, one may start with an analysis of personal strengths and weaknesses or with the evaluation of opportunities and threats in the environment and then proceed with setting long-term, professional goals. Whatever the specific sequence, effective career management usually requires dealing with the variables in the model shown in Figure 9-3.

IMPLICATIONS FOR MANAGERIAL PRODUCTIVITY

Management by objectives can result in greater productivity if more attention is given to the potential conflict between individual needs and organization demands. To reduce this gap, integration between organizational and individual objectives is suggested by making career planning an essential aspect of the MBO process.

Effective career planning requires self-knowledge and a clarification of values. These, in turn, facilitate the selection of long-range personal and professional goals. The environment is scanned for threats and opportunities that hinder or facilitate career paths. Not only the present environment is evaluated, but also predictions must be made about the future environment. A thorough analysis of one's strengths and weaknesses becomes the basis for strategic career alternatives. These alternatives, then, must be tested for consistency with personal values and the long-term career goals. After careful evaluation of career alternatives, the best course is selected. To bring action into plans, short-term objectives are set. Since the environment is in a state of flux, contingency plans are developed. To implement a career plan, it is important to integrate it with the company's human resource plan. Finally, effective career planning demands monitoring the progress toward career goals.

A goal-oriented management system such as MBO can indeed give direction to the organization, the division, and the individual. At the same time, MBO must serve both the organizational requirements and individual needs. One such need is the development of a systematic approach to career planning. As we have seen in this discussion, career management can utilize many concepts of strategic planning. Thus, the matching of individual strengths and weaknesses with environmental opportunities and threats becomes the basis for long-term aims and for allocating the individual's physical and psychological resources so that people can be more productive and contribute effectively and efficiently to the organization.

NOTES

1 H. Levinson, "Appraisal of *What* Performance?" *Harvard Business Review,* vol. 54, no. 4 (July-August 1976), pp. 30–36, 40, 44–46, 160 and S. Singular, "Has MBO Failed?" *MBA,* vol. 9, no. 9 (October 1975), pp. 47, 48, 50.

2 P. F. Drucker, *The Practice of Management (New York: Harper, 1954).*

3 D. McGregor, "An Uneasy Look at Performance Appraisal," *Harvard Business Review,* vol. 35, no. 3 (May-June 1957), pp. 89–94.

4 G. S. Odiorne, *Management by Objectives* (New York: Pitman, 1965).

5 J. W. Humble, *Improving Business Results* (Maidenhead, England: McGraw-Hill, 1968).

6 H. Weihrich, "Management by Objectives—Does It Really Work?" *University of Michigan Business Review,* vol. 28, no. 4 (July 1976), pp. 27–31.

7 H. Weihrich, P. G. Decker, and S. D. Wood, "Is Management by Objectives Maturing?" *Industrial Management,* vol. 20, no. 5 (September-October 1978), pp. 5–9.

8 For alternative approaches to career development see the thorough discussion by M. T. Hall, *Careers in Organizations* (Santa Monica: Goodyear, 1976), a collection of excellent articles by M. Jelinek, *Career*

Management (Chicago: St. Clair Press, 1979), and more theoretical articles by T. P. Ference, J. A. Stoner, and E. K. Warren, "Managing the Career Plateau," *Academy of Management Review,* vol. 2, no. 4 (October 1977), pp. 602–612, and M. A. Von Glinow, M. J. Driver, K. Brousseau, and J. B. Prince, "The Design of a Career Oriented Human Resource System," *Academy of Management Review,* vol. 8, no. 1 (January 1983), pp. 23–32.

CHAPTER 10

MAKING ORGANIZATIONS PRODUCTIVE— THE MACROAPPROACH TO IMPLEMENTING MBO PROGRAMS

This chapter is about the macroapproach* to implementing goal-focused managerial productivity programs in organizations. Most people realize that productivity improvement is not a one-time task; rather it is an ongoing process for which every manager is responsible. Peter Drucker stated several years ago:

> The continuous improvement of productivity is one of management's most important jobs. It is also one of the most difficult; for productivity is a balance between diversity of factors, few of which are easily definable or clearly measurable.[1]

We will begin by showing that MBO can be implemented in stages over several years. In introducing a new program one must be aware of political factors that may hinder its effective implementation. What also has become increasingly clear is that a program cannot be superimposed on the existing organization with disregard of special circumstances. For example, it makes a great deal of difference if the predominant leadership style is authoritarian or participative. Therefore, we will recommend an organization development approach that takes into consideration situational factors such as those identified in

*The microaspects of implementation were discussed in Chapter 6.

Likert's four systems of management, ranging from the autocratic to the participative. Another approach shows how data-based research can improve an existing program. Finally, we will show how team building can be used to improve productivity in a government agency. Despite the importance of tailoring the goal-oriented productivity program to the needs of the organization, guidelines based on experience can help make MBO programs productive.

EFFECTIVE IMPLEMENTATION OF MBO DEPENDS ON THE SITUATION

To say that organizations are different appears unnecessary. Yet, many managers search for a program package accompanied by a guaranty of instant success. Experience has shown that effective programs must be planned and tailored to the needs of the organization. Often, then, implementation proceeds in stages.[2] As we will see, however, the stages may differ.

Stage Models for Implementing MBO

Some authors have suggested a four-stage sequential model for the implementation of MBO.[3] The first stage prepares the organization for the new managerial approach by focusing on strategic purposes and goals for the total enterprise. This involves top managers in the process who not only set the firm's direction but also its climate. The outcomes of the first stage should include written objectives, a thorough understanding of the process and the philosophy of MBO by top managers. Moreover, top management must demonstrate their commitment to the program in a way that is visible to subordinates.

The second stage includes goal setting and review sessions for subordinate managers. These coaching sessions may be between the superior and the subordinate, or they may include several managers. At any rate, through frequent feedback this process becomes institutionalized. At the end of the second stage, then, goal setting and review should be well established and the network of objectives should improve the planning process. Finally, roles of managers are also clarified.

In the third stage, other subsystems begin to be integrated with the MBO process. Some of the subsystems that may be affected include budgeting, the management information system, and performance appraisal. A great deal of training is necessary for understanding the relationships among the various aspects of MBO.

The fourth stage is called "the mature systems integration." This integration strengthens strategic and long-term planning introduced in the first stage. It is in this final stage that the monetary system is linked with the MBO process.

The sequential model of MBO implementation has several advantages. First, it minimizes the shock that might be caused by a hasty implementation of a comprehensive program. Second, it improves planning and clarifies roles and expectations. Third, it links compensation to MBO only *after* the program has been perfected. Fourth, it provides opportunities for understanding the system. Finally, it gives top management opportunities to show their commitment to MBO and reinforces the new way of managing.

But the process of implementing MBO may differ from the four sequential stages. It has been suggested that enterprises usually go through three stages that may take four to five years.[4] In the first stage the focus is on performance appraisal; the program is usually implemented by the personnel department. In the second stage, the emphasis is on the integration of organizational objectives and those of individual managers. Objectives are usually set for no longer than one year. The third stage includes long-range planning with a concern for the whole organization. These stages are quite different from the sequential model discussed earlier, which starts with strategic planning. In this three-stage model, long-range planning is the last step in the evolutionary process of MBO. Examples can be found for both models. One utility company introduced MBO to supplement performance reviews and salary administration and made the link to strategic planning at a much later time.[5] On the other hand, a large bank started an MBO program when it became aware of the need for better planning and the setting of corporate objectives for strategic decisions.[6] We can conclude, then, that there is no one best way to implement an MBO program, but it depends on the situation and even on organizational politics, the topic discussed next.

Political Aspects of Implementation

Three approaches to implement MBO have been identified.[7] The first one is based on authoritarian directives, the second relies on persuasion, and the third emphasizes educational programs, the most successful approach. But whatever approach is selected, it is important to recognize and deal with organizational politics. Since MBO programs require changes, they can alter power relationships inside the organization, which, in turn, affects some managers adversely. Second, MBO, especially when it is based on participation, requires the sharing of power. Third, the changes initiated by MBO may result in organizational conflicts and countermoves by those whose power base is being threatened. Fourth, there is also group loyalty. While people are asked to contribute to the overall organizational objectives, they may have difficulties in doing so because of their concern for the welfare of their own department. Fifth, MBO may be seen as a constraining factor imposing procedures, rules, and conformity on the individual. For example, schoolteachers often see MBO as being inappropriate for their position. They feel that such a program impinges upon the freedom they enjoy as professionals. MBO should not be politicized, yet one cannot ignore the political realities in an organization.

Organizational Factors in Improving Productivity

In an effort to identify the factors of productivity, scales for measuring organizational variables have been developed.[8] The variables include such factors as leadership styles, selection, formal and informal communication, performance feedback, monetary and nonmonetary (for example, social satisfaction) reward systems, job design, working conditions, technology, labor management cooperation, training, company characteristics (programs, job security, reputation), and company demographics (such as ownership, location, and others). These variables were used to study twelve firms, including companies such as Hewlett-Packard, Lincoln Electric (a company known for its innovative bonus system), and General Motors. The scale for General Motors is illustrated in Figure 10-1. It should be noted that the findings in the twelve companies suggest that these productive firms seem to have commonality only on the macrolevel of analysis. In the analysis of specifics one finds considerable differences among the firms. Most of the organizations that were studied contended that they can improve productivity through specific policies, programs, and decisions that must be suited for their company.[9] This suggests that the implementation of programs to improve productivity—including the MBO approach—must be tailored to the situation and the specific needs of the organization.

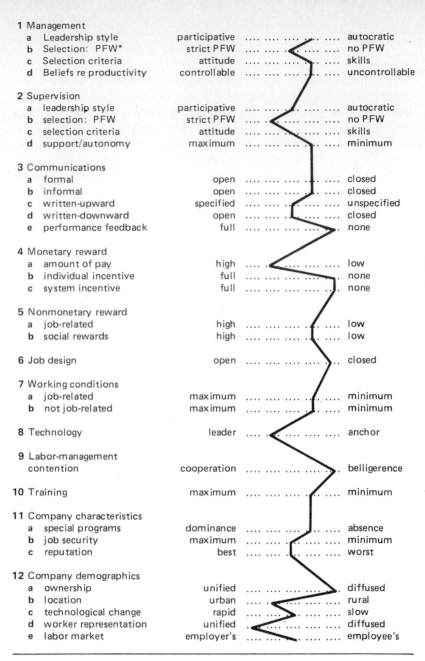

1 Management
  a Leadership style   participative .... autocratic
  b Selection: PFW*   strict PFW .... no PFW
  c Selection criteria   attitude .... skills
  d Beliefs re productivity   controllable .... uncontrollable

2 Supervision
  a leadership style   participative .... autocratic
  b selection: PFW   strict PFW .... no PFW
  c selection criteria   attitude .... skills
  d support/autonomy   maximum .... minimum

3 Communications
  a formal   open .... closed
  b informal   open .... closed
  c written-upward   specified .... unspecified
  d written-downward   open .... closed
  e performance feedback   full .... none

4 Monetary reward
  a amount of pay   high .... low
  b individual incentive   full .... none
  c system incentive   full .... none

5 Nonmonetary reward
  a job-related   high .... low
  b social rewards   high .... low

6 Job design   open .... closed

7 Working conditions
  a job-related   maximum .... minimum
  b not job-related   maximum .... minimum

8 Technology   leader .... anchor

9 Labor-management
contention   cooperation .... belligerence

10 Training   maximum .... minimum

11 Company characteristics
  a special programs   dominance .... absence
  b job security   maximum .... minimum
  c reputation   best .... worst

12 Company demographics
  a ownership   unified .... diffused
  b location   urban .... rural
  c technological change   rapid .... slow
  d worker representation   unified .... diffused
  e labor market   employer's .... employee's

*PFW = promotion from within

FIGURE 10-1
Scales of measurement for General Motors Corporation. (W. A. Ruch and J. C. Hershauer, "Factors Affecting Worker Productivity," *Occasional Paper Number 10,* Bureau of Business and Economic Research, College of Business Administration, Arizona State University, Tempe, Ariz., 1974, p. 86. Reprinted by permission.)

ORGANIZATION DEVELOPMENT

In the discussion of the stage models of MBO we saw that there are different ways of introducing an MBO program in an organization. A program cannot simply be superimposed on the existing managerial system without adaptation to the existing situation. One approach is to use organization development (OD). But there is no general agreement on what OD involves. One of the widely used definitions is that "Organization development is an effort (1) planned, (2) organizationwide, and (3) managed from the top, to (4) increase organization effectiveness and health through (5) planned interventions in the organization's 'processes' using behavioral knowledge."[10]

Organizational effectiveness concerns the achievement of objectives, which clearly is the focus of MBO. But the objectives are obtained at a cost, a frequently ignored aspect in many MBO programs. Thus, an organization should achieve objectives at the minimum cost or undesired consequences. Organizational productivity, as used in this book, is concerned with both effectiveness and efficiency. A weakness in the above definition of OD is that the interventions are largely confined to the use of behavioral knowledge. Clearly there are other ways of making enterprises more productive, as Harold Koontz from UCLA stated: "But many of these (OD) scientists are now beginning to see that basic management theory and techniques, such as managing by objectives and clarifying organization structure, fit well into their programs of behavioral intervention."[11] I suggest, therefore, the following definition:

Organizational development is a systematic, integrated, and planned approach to improve the short- and long-term productivity of an enterprise and its human resources, using a variety of approaches.

Development implies growth and dynamic adaptation to the changing internal and external environment. The systematic approach requires a diagnosis and a rational analysis of the organizational situation (which often has one or more problems), a sharing of the findings with members of the organization, a plan for solving problems and improving productivity, the implementation of the improvement plan, the monitoring and assessment of the plan, and the taking of corrective actions as required to achieve organizational productivity. Organization development is also an integrative approach, usually involving persons from different functional departments who contribute to organizational productivity. Not only people are integrated, but also processes and techniques.

Organization development is also a planned approach that is based on the analysis of the situation. Planning requires developing, evaluating, and choosing from among alternative courses of action. Many improvement programs focus on short-term results that, however, may be obtained at the expense of the long-term health of the enterprise. To obtain managerial support for OD, some improvements should, if possible, be visible rather soon. But, more important, the OD efforts should result in sustained productivity over a long time. The definition of OD emphasizes productivity rather than effectiveness alone. Achieving the goals (that is, being effective), has always been stressed in MBO and this is how it should be. But the achievement of ends should not be done at any cost; rather it should be accomplished with minimum costs (and the term "cost" is used in a broad sense, including, for example, human or psychological costs) or undesirable consequences. Thus, OD is not only concerned about the productivity of the enterprise but also its people. Finally, OD is eclectic because it selects from a variety of approaches. To be sure, the effective use of people is often the key to productivity, but it may also be essential to create a structure and an environment in which people can productively contribute to organizational aims and at the same time satisfy their needs for professional development.

Toward System Four Through
Organization Development*

Some of the traditional approaches and techniques of OD include laboratory training, team building, building of intergroup relationships, the managerial grid, role playing, force field analysis, transactional analysis, and the Kepner-Tregoe's approach to decision making.[12] One book of readings on OD includes virtually any imaginable managerial topic including job enrichment, analysis of personal values, organizational design, line-staff relationships, motivation, corporate planning, time management, performance appraisal, and so on.[13] While OD purists would probably not include many of

*Adapted from H. Weihrich, "MBO in Four Management Systems," *MSU Business Topics,* vol. 24, no. 4 (Autumn 1976), pp. 51–56. Used with permission.

these topics, the book indicates that OD is difficult to define and that many approaches can be used to make organizations more productive.

Although many of the largest companies in the United States now use MBO, only a few have realized its full potential because it is often considered as "just another program." As currently practiced, MBO is frequently superimposed on the existing organization without sufficient effort to evaluate the organizational climate and to make changes so that the managerial system is congruent with the goal-oriented orientation. For most organizations, MBO requires a change in managerial style, and a new way of managing. Likert's model of four systems of management facilitates the assessment of the existing organizational environment. The purpose of this section is to approximate the relationships between these four managerial systems and the steps in the MBO process.

MBO in the Four Systems of Management

Likert and his associates thoroughly studied many organizations and their effectiveness. Managerial styles and their related organizational factors were identified and grouped into four systems. Likert named System 1 exploitative-authoritative; System 2 benevolent-authoritative; System 3 consultative; and System 4 participative group.[14]

System 1 is highly autocratic with little trust and confidence. Motivation is through fear, threat, and punishment. Communication is downward and decisions are made almost entirely at the top of the organization.

System 2 is marked by a condescending approach to management. Motivation is through rewards and some punishment. Communication is still mostly downward. Although there is some delegation, policy control is at the top.

System 3 management is characterized by substantial, but not complete, confidence in subordinates. Motivation is through rewards and involvement but there is also some punishment. Communication flows down and up, and subordinates are generally consulted in decisions related to their jobs.

System 4 management is highly participative, with a great deal of confidence and trust in subordinates. This system is marked by effective teamwork and individuals feel motivated to achieve the goals of the organization. Communication is downward and upward, as well as with peers. Decision making is well integrated at all levels of the organization. Goals are set primarily by the group, with little or no resistance to the aims.

These different systems of management do have an impact on the steps in the MBO process, as shown in the following conjectural discussion and summarized in Table 10-1.

Management by objectives is a process that requires interaction among superior, subordinate, and peers. It involves managerial leadership, effective motivation, open communication, decision making, and measuring of performance.

MBO in System 1: Exploitative-Authoritative   In this system, management has no trust in subordinates, uses mainly threats and punishment, has very little real communication, makes decisions basically at the top, issues orders to lower levels, and concentrates control at the top. This environment leaves a distinct mark on the way the steps of MBO are carried out.

Step 1 Setting Objectives   In this kind of organization, objectives are set at the top, or by the superior in an autocratic manner. Subordinates, therefore, have little or no opportunity to set their own objectives. Nor do they provide any inputs to the departmental aims. In general, top management determines objectives, which may or may not be communicated down the organization structure. The set of objectives is rather limited and only a few alternative aims are considered. If some objectives are set by organizational units, they seldom are coordinated with other departments.

The set of individual objectives usually pertains to performance only and does not include personal development objectives. Because managers do not see how they personally benefit from MBO, there is a great deal of resistance to writing down objectives and making commitments.

Step 2 Action Planning   As in the goal-setting process, superiors are very directive. They determine the tasks and develop action plans for their subordinates. There is little awareness that in most situations there are alternative courses of action that can be taken to achieve objectives. Also, the superior establishes the timeframe for the tasks with little input from those who have to carry out the activities. Consequently, there are often severe problems in coordinating and timing the tasks of the various organizational units, especially when the activities are interdependent. And even if extensive action plans are developed, they are not communicated to all who contribute to them or who will be affected by them.

Step 3 Implementation   Top management and superiors deter-mine the implementation of plans. Subordinates are simply required to follow orders. Thus, subordinates may be indifferent to MBO or they may even boycott the efforts of upper management. The program is mechanistic and rigid, with heavy emphasis on filling out forms and meeting the bureaucratic requirements. There is an emphasis on activities and on busy work rather than on results. Individuals overtly or covertly resist MBO and take little initiative to utilize the potential benefits of the system. It is evident that such an organization does not manage in a way that is congruent with the MBO philosophy, which places responsibility on the subordinate and encourages initiative.

Step 4 Controlling and Appraising   Organizational control is rigid and concentrated at the top. Moreover, control standards are externally imposed on departments and individuals. Consequently, inappropriate standards—that is, those that measure the wrong things—may be set and pursued.

Performance appraisal provides little opportunity for self-control or self-development. Instead, the superior is viewed as a judge who acts in a punitive manner. Subordinates, of course, have a low degree of trust in their superiors. In the appraisal meeting, attention is given only to past performance, although the past cannot be changed. Feed-forward control, which is designed to prevent unde-sirable deviations from occurring in the future, is completely ignored. Yet, it is the future that provides opportunities for individual as well as organizational growth and development.

MBO in System 2: Benevolent-Authoritative   In a System 2 environment, management has a condescending confidence in subordinates. Rewards and some punishment are used to motivate individuals. The flow of information is still primarily downward. Although there is some delegation, policy decisions are made at the top. Comments are invited when establishing objectives. Control is exercised to a great extent at the top.

Step 1 Setting Objectives   There is a condescending use of authority. Objectives are usually set by the superior, but some inputs from subordinates are invited. There may even be some participation in setting objectives. But objectives are still communicated from the top of the organization downward with only limited upward informa-tion flow. There are some alternative objectives of different organiza-tional units. If personal development objectives are considered, they are set mostly by superiors.

TABLE 10-1

MBO IN FOUR MANAGEMENT SYSTEMS

System Steps in MBO	System 1—Exploitative- Authoritative	System 2—Benevolent- Authoritative
1 Setting objectives	Autocratic approach. Little or no participation in goal setting. Objectives set by top management and communicated downward. Few or no alternative objectives considered. Little coordination of objectives. (Not in tune with rest of the organization.) No personal development goals. No commitment.	Condescending use of authority. Objectives set by superior with some input from subordinates. Some participation in goal setting. Communication of objectives mostly downward with some upward flow. Some alternative objectives considered. Some effort made to coordinate objectives. Personal development goals may be set by superior.
2 Developing action plans	Superior very directive. Superior determines tasks and develops action plans for subordinates. Few or no alternative action plans developed. Superior establishes time frame for tasks. Severe problems in coordinating tasks of organizational units. Poor timing. Action plans are not communicated.	Superior condescending in determining tasks and responsibilities for subordinates. Subordinates give few inputs to plans; mostly downward information flow. Some problems in coordinating plans. Few contingency plans are developed.
3 Implementation	Top management determines implementation. Subordinates required to follow directions. No commitment to MBO. Rigid, mechanistic program. Emphasis on filling out forms. Management by activities rather than results. Considerable overt or covert resistance. Little initiative. MBO philosophy not understood.	Benevolent attitude of superiors. Subordinates largely follow direction without real commitment. Communication flow inhibited. Problems in coordinating activities of organizational units. Some covert resistance. No genuine commitment to MBO.
4 Controlling and appraising	External, ridgid control concentrated at the top. Inappropriate standards may be set and pursued. No self-control, nor self-development. Superior acts punitively as a judge. Low trust. Focus on past performance.	Control primarily at the top. Some control standards are inappropriate. Superior plays active part in appraisal. Use of reward and punishment. Little participation of subordinates in appraisal process. Hardly any self-appraisal.

TABLE 10-1 (Continued)

System Steps in MBO	System 3—Consultative	System 4—Participative group
1 Setting objectives	Subordinates are consulted in important matters. Considerable participation in goal setting. Considerable vertical and horizontal communication of objectives. Coordination of objectives is good. Considerable number of alternative objectives are evaluated. Personal development objectives set by subordinates, but changed at times by superior.	Supportive environment. Great deal of participation in setting goals. Integration of organization and individual objectives. Commitment to objectives. Many alternative objectives evaluated. Objectives communicated to all who need to know. Objectives coordinated throughout the organization. Synorgistic effect. Individual sets high performance standards congruent with aims of the group.
2 Developing action plans	Subordinate is consulted in developing action plans. Considerable participation in decision making. Two-way communication of plans. Fairly good coordination of tasks and responsibilities. Contingency plans are considered by superior and subordinate.	Active participation in identifying, evaluating, and deciding on tasks and alternatives. Individual plans are integrated with organizational plans. Team effort in developing action plans. Effective coordination of tasks and activities of different organizational units.
3 Implementation	Subordinates are consulted. Considerable commitment to MBO. Fairly good communication flow vertically and horizontally. Inputs from subordinates considered in decision making.	Individuals at all levels actively participate in MBO. Great deal of commitment. Opportunities for personal growth. Integration of organizational demands and individual needs. Organization as an interlocking system. Frequent and open communication. Effective conflict resolution. True team approach.
4 Controlling and appraising	Control at different points in the organization. Standards fairly accurate. Moderate participation by subordinates in appraising own performance. Some problem solving attitude. Some degree of concern for the future.	Control at critical points throughout the organization. Analysis of deviations. Development of forward-looking controls. Primarily self-control. Superior as a helper. Primary focus on the future and how to prevent deviations. Plans for development. Free information exchange. Fair evaluation of organizational and individual performance.

Step 2 Developing Action Plans   Tasks and responsibilities are determined mainly by the superior, although subordinates provide some inputs to the plans to achieve the objectives. But the information flow is mostly downward, and some problems in the coordination of plans may develop. In such an organization there may even be some plans for contingencies.

Step 3 Implementation   The implementation of MBO is characterized by a benevolent attitude on the part of superiors. Subordinates, then, largely follow direction without a real commitment to the MBO program. Because of the limited amount of upward and horizontal communication, some difficulties may develop in the coordination of activities within the organizational unit as well as among departments. Some covert resistance to MBO also may be encountered. If MBO is accepted, it is only with superficial commitment.

Step 4 Controlling and Appraising   Control is still primarily at the top and upper management, with insufficient responsibility placed on subordinates. Inappropriate standards for control may be set and pursued. During appraisal, the superior plays an active part, using rewards and punishment. There is little participation by subordinates in the evaluation of their own performance. In such an environment, self-appraisal is usually not feasible.

MBO in System 3: Consultative   System 3 is characterized by considerable trust, rewards, and occasional punishment, an up-and-down information flow, and a moderate amount of teamwork. Although top management makes general decisions, more specific ones are made at lower levels. The control function is moderately delegated to lower levels.

Step 1 Setting Objectives   Subordinates are consulted on important matters, and there is considerable participation in setting goals. Also, objectives are fairly well communicated, both vertically and horizontally. Consequently, there is usually a good coordination of objectives. Goals are set by subordinates in consultation with their superiors, who may, however, reserve the right to make changes.

Step 2 Developing Action Plans   Subordinates are consulted in developing the action plans. Moreover, there is considerable participation in deciding on the course of action. Plans are quite well communicated to those who need to know. Consequently, there is a fairly good coordination of tasks as well as responsibilities. Plans for contingencies are developed in consultation with subordinates.

Step 3 Implementation   In the implementation phase, subordinates are consulted and there is a moderate commitment to MBO in most parts of the organization. The information flows reasonably well, both vertically and horizontally. In operational decision making, inputs from peers as well as subordinates are given serious consideration.

Step 4 Controlling and Appraising   Controls are installed at different points in order to measure performance. The standards give a moderately accurate picture of organizational accomplishments. There is considerable participation by subordinates in the evaluation of their own performance, and some problem solving occurs during the appraisal meeting. Although the focus is on past performance, some attention is given to preventing undesirable deviations of performance in the future.

MBO in System 4: Participative Group   In System 4 there is extensive trust and confidence in subordinates. Moreover, people at all levels feel responsible for results and share the control function. With a great deal of teamwork and free flow of information, decisions at various levels are well integrated.

Step 1 Setting Objectives   The supportive environment is conducive to real participation in setting objectives. This results not only in an integration of personal objectives and organizational demands, but it also elicits commitment toward the achievement of aims. Before the set of objectives is finalized, many alternatives are considered. Also, objectives are not set in isolation, rather they are communicated to all who have a need to know. The effect is a well-coordinated network of goals throughout the organization, resulting in a synergistic effect. The organizational climate encourages individuals to set high performance standards that are congruent with the aims of the team.

Step 2 Developing Action Plans   In almost all situations, alternative courses of action can be taken to achieve the objectives. System 4 fosters creativity and is conducive to identifying, evaluating, and deciding on the tasks and activities necessary to achieve results. Individual and organizational plans are integrated; system optimization is accomplished through the team effort of individuals whose tasks are seen as being interrelated.

Step 3 Implementation   Managers—and even nonmanagers— at all organizational levels are committed to the achievement of common goals. With the goals set, individuals can use their creativity in finding better ways of doing things. Consequently, there are many opportunities for personal and professional growth. The organization is seen as an interlocking system. If conflicts occur—and they do in any organization—they are effectively resolved through open communication based on trust and confidence. Rather than individuals pursuing their own, sometimes conflicting, goals, it is a true team approach that results in synergistic effects.

Step 4 Controlling and Appraising   In the System 4 environment, control of performance is at critical points in the organization. Deviations from standards are analyzed and steps are taken to prevent undesirable ones from reoccurring in the future. In fact, the focus is on forward-looking controls that attempt to prevent deviations rather than having to correct them later.

During appraisal, the superior does not sit in judgment over subordinates. Instead of acting as a judge, the superior is like a coach interested in helping subordinates to improve their performance. Appraisal, then, is primarily self-appraisal aimed at promoting professional development, and the free flow of communication results in a fair evaluation of individual performance.

Implications

Although management by objectives is one of the most widely used approaches to managing, not all organizations have been successful in implementing MBO. Indeed, it may fail when it is superimposed on the organization without proper understanding of the existing climate. It is, for example, unrealistic to expect that managers who have operated for many years under System 1 can suddenly become participative team members (System 4). In fact, forcing these drastic changes without coaching may disturb the organizational equilibrium in a way that results in undesirable consequences.

To effectively implement MBO, it must be understood that MBO is a process as well as a philosophy of managing. If this philosophy is completely incongruent with the organizational climate, problems will occur. What is needed is a systems approach to organizational development that focuses on both the organizational climate and the MBO steps of setting objectives, action planning, and implementing, as well as controlling and appraising.

An alternative to the traditional "try and hope for the best" approach to implementing MBO is *data-based organizational development.* This involves the measurement of critical organizational characteristics such as those suggested by Likert. The data derived by using his questionnaire facilitate the grouping of organizational factors into System 1 (exploitative-authoritative), System 2 (benevolent-authoritative), System 3 (consultative), and System 4 (participative group). Likert and his colleagues found that over a period of time organizations that moved *toward* System 4 became more effective. Similarly, I suggest most organizations will become more effective when the steps in the MBO process are carried out in ways moving toward System 4. But this change will have to come gradually and must be accompanied by changes in the organizational environment. The framework of the four systems and the relationships to the steps in MBO as discussed in this chapter can facilitate this change process.

The practicing manager, of course, is interested in making this new approach operational when implementing MBO. Although there are different ways, the focus here is on the action research model that may involve: (1) Collection of data and diagnosis of the organization. Based on this information, a profile of organizational characteristics can be developed and grouped into Systems 1 to 4. (2) Discussion of these findings within the organization and a comparison with the characteristics of the four steps in the MBO process. (3) Joint planning of actions to change the organization and the MBO process in the direction of System 4. This also requires the teaching of the MBO concepts as well as MBO philosophy. (4) These three processes are then repeated until MBO becomes an integral part of dynamic organizational development.

The approach suggested here differs substantially from traditional ones that often superimpose MBO on the organization. There are several advantages to this new approach for implementing MBO. First, it is a systems approach that recognizes many critical organizational variables. Second, it is data-based, starting with the existing organization and moving toward an "ideal" one in a planned manner. Third, it is dynamic, flexible, and tailored for a particular organization. Fourth, the emphasis is on collaborative management with a great deal of team effort. Fifth, it is an ongoing process that continuously aims at improving the organization.

In conclusion, to be effective, MBO must be congruent with organizational characteristics. It is suggested that the manner in which the steps in the MBO process are carried out will differ for the four management systems. The wise administrator will collect data on the existing managerial system and develop a change strategy that takes into account both MBO and the organizational environment. Effective implementation of MBO requires time and effort, but the results can be rewarding.

IMPROVING AN EXISTING MANAGEMENT-BY-OBJECTIVES PROGRAM

There is evidence that MBO can be advantageous,[15] but there is also evidence that some companies have had disappointing experiences.[16] There are many reasons why MBO has not lived up to its expectations. Improper implementation is often cited as the main reason. Furthermore, MBO is a dynamic system that needs continuous attention. It is the theme of this book that to be effective, MBO has to be viewed as a way of managing that integrates many key activities into a system. But too often only selected aspects of the managerial job are emphasized. Managers who subscribe to the systems approach and who want to improve their MBO program find little help in the literature about how to achieve improvements. Let us therefore look at a utility company that collected and analyzed data for a research-based developmental strategy for improving its MBO program.[17]

The utility company had considerable experience with MBO. The program was introduced eleven years before the study was made as a supplement to performance review and salary administration. Over the years the program went through evolutionary stages with continuous efforts to improve the process. Although considerable progress had been achieved, top management felt the need to examine the program with the aim to further improve it.

Information was collected on the company's existing program in respect to the degree of integration of MBO with major managerial activities. Similar data were also obtained about an "ideal" program. The findings were then fed back to managers at all organizational levels, ranging from the chief executive officer to a selected group of first-line supervisors. The focus of the improvement was on those key managerial activities that showed the greatest differences between the existing and the ideal program. Closing this gap was the aim of the OD efforts. Specifically, workshops were conducted with top management, middle management, and lower-level managers in a problem-solving atmosphere. Different strategies were developed to close the gap between the existing and the ideal MBO program. It became rather clear that to be effective, MBO had to become a system of managing, or in other words, a part of the manager's job.

THE TEAM-BUILDING PROCESS AT THE U.S. FOREST SERVICE

An important aspect of organizational development effort is team building. There are different ways to improve the interactions among people in an organization, and the approach taken by the U.S. Forest Service can serve as one illustration.[18] For many years this organization searched for ways to increase productivity. Managers found that one of the most effective approaches was their work planning and performance review (WPPR) program. To make WPPR productive, the team approach was used to deal with concerns of employees, such as giving and receiving feedback, clarifying expectations and goals, and giving recognition for jobs that are well done.

Although the specific team-building approach must fit the situation, the process discussed here may be typical and could be adapted by other organizations.

1 The initial step was to conduct interviews and to prepare members for the team-building program.

2 The groups met to clarify expectations and they learned about transactional analysis (discussed in Chapter 6).

3 The teams then identified communication problems, using transactional analysis and other tools.

4 Team members prepared job profiles in terms of expected behavior and personal profiles that identified operating styles preferred by individuals.

5 In the next step, problems as well as opportunities for improvement were identified and shared with team members. In addition, short-range objectives were set in key result areas.

6 Groups also dealt with leadership styles in terms of orientation toward the task (to get things done) and the relationship with other persons in the organization. This led to discussions of attitudes in respect to delegation of authority. For example, some managers had difficulties in giving subordinates the freedom needed to do their work. Yet, the concept underlying a goal-oriented management approach is to facilitate self-control without losing accountability.

7 The two-day sessions were concluded with a review of the accomplishments and an agreement on a follow-up session.

The follow-up was usually scheduled 90 days after the initial meeting. The purpose of this session was to assess the progress of the team and to reinforce commitment to the new managerial approach. Another meeting was generally held a year after the team building began. The combination of team building and the WPPR program may indeed increase productivity, because it deals with human factors that often stand in the way of effective cooperation and performance. But it is also evident that the direct impact of team building on productivity is a process that does not lend itself to easy measurement. There are also other factors—many beyond the control of managers—that impact on productivity.

GUIDELINES FOR MAKING MBO PRODUCTIVE

Experience tells us that improving managerial productivity requires an analysis of the organizational environment and the adaptation of the MBO program to the situation. Yet, experience with many programs has also shown that some guidelines can help to utilize the advantages derived from MBO while avoiding its pitfalls.

1 *The MBO and productivity improvement program must be carefully planned.* This is especially important when it is to be used throughout a large, complex organization. Even a small mistake in the implementation is difficult to correct at a later time. In fact, an organization may benefit from testing the program on a limited basis before extending it to the entire organization.

2 *Participants in the program must be prepared.* This can be difficult for a company with managers located in different geographic areas. To be effective, the MBO philosophy—emphasizing self-control—as well as the formal aspects of MBO must be understood. Naturally, participants are vitally interested in how they are affected by the new managerial system. Active participation in the design and implementation is generally desirable. MBO is more than filling out forms; it is a new way of managing that first requires unlearning the customary way of doing some things. MBO means also a shift of focus from activities to results. This new orientation demands frequent reinforcement of the desired behavior.

3 *Participants need guidelines for setting goals.* Although it appears simple, setting goals is a difficult task. It requires identification of the key result areas in order to set meaningful, reasonable, yet challenging goals. Objectives set too high may frustrate participants; when set too low they provide no challenge. Although goal setting is a major advantage of MBO, it can also be one of the major difficulties.

4 *The network of objectives must be understood.* Individual objectives should fit into an overall network. Setting goals in a vacuum without a clear understanding of how the manager's goals affect other organizational units can have undesirable side effects. Managers often comment that through the use of MBO they gain a better awareness of the broader organizational objectives. This is important because people generally want to contribute to organizational goals, but this is possible only if they know what these goals are.

5 *Achievement of objectives may not accurately indicate performance.* Managers may miss or overachieve their objectives as a result of bad or good luck. Changes in the economy may make it impossible to reach the agreed-upon target. Even within the same organization, individual managers may be affected differently by external circumstances. For example, a bank branch office located near aerospace installations may not reach the goal of attracting savings at a time of high unemployment in that industry.

Markets and environments are different, and universal standards for all organizational units would be inequitable and unfair, fostering resistance to the program. When measuring performance against standards, environmental factors over which the manager has no control must be taken into account. Obviously, objectives must not be set arbitrarily.

6 *The time perspective of objectives is important.* Focusing on a twelve-month or even shorter time period (as most MBO programs do) may be myopic. Managers may be able to shift their best performance into the year that counts most as far as rewards are concerned. This can become especially critical if a bonus plan depends on earnings in a particular year. To avoid shortsightedness and suboptimization, goal-oriented productivity programs should not necessarily be restricted to a one-year time perspective but should recognize a pertinent cycle, be in agreement with the implementation of a major project, and be congruent with long-range plans.

7 *The MBO administrator can be very valuable in the difficult task of setting objectives and implementing the program.* The relatively swift implementation of the MBO program can certainly be facilitated when the person in charge is a well-respected and able individual on, let us say, the vice-presidential level. It should be pointed out, however, that subordinates must remain accountable primarily to their immediate superior. The administrator should function only in an advisory role and should not undermine the authority of the line manager.

8 *Tying MBO directly to an incentive system may have negative side effects.* Managers may learn to play the game to maximize their rewards by neglecting important activities that are not directly related to their objectives, or by setting low standards that can easily be achieved. It is interesting that financial incentives are often mentioned as an important advantage of MBO and, at the same time, can be one of the vexing problems. Therefore, the wise administrator should carefully consider the pros and cons of relating monetary rewards directly to the achievement of objectives.

9 *There is also the possibility of inflexibility.* When properly applied, MBO should promote flexibility. A goal-oriented management approach facilitates planning and gives direction. But planning should be a continuous process that requires reevaluation of plans in light of changed circumstances. For example, for a bank a change in money rates may require a change not only in objectives but also in strategies and tactics.

To pursue obsolete objectives for the sake of achieving agreed-upon results is absurd. But goals should not be changed lightly, either. If nonachievement is corrected by changing the standards, then goal setting is meaningless. A periodic review is needed to see whether the assumptions underlying the plans have changed. If so, goals should be adjusted to fit reality.

10 *The system should be monitored and should be kept simple at least at the beginning.* One of the major problems often mentioned by managers is the complexity and the administration of the program. Managers operate under a time constraint, and a complex system that requires too much paperwork causes resistance. It is a sure way to kill MBO. The success of MBO and productivity programs require continuous monitoring and evaluation of their effectiveness. The Detroit Edison Company, for example, benefitted greatly from its periodic reviews that compared actual productivity improvements with preselected objectives.

11 *The overall objectives, set through active involvement by top management, must be communicated to lower levels in the organization.* It is not easy, especially in large organizations, to communicate the plans to all who have a need to know. Yet, it is essential for individuals to be informed about the direction of the company so managers can set their objectives to fit the overall plan. Effective communication is a prerequisite to cooperation not only among departments but also between labor and management. At Buick's Factory 81, for example, labor and management decide together on organizational changes, and on quality, as well as productivity improvements.

12 *Managerial productivity needs to be measured.* In the past, the focus was on productivity of workers, equipment, the assets of the firm, and more recently, the effective use of energy. We draw attention to a new aspect: the productivity of knowledge workers with an emphasis on managers. To be sure, it is easier to count the products coming off the production line than to measure accurately managerial productivity. But MBO is a tool as well as a process that makes measurement possible.

13 *The organizational climate must be supportive of productivity efforts.* People must be constantly made aware of the importance of productivity. This, for example, was done at Hughes Aircraft Company, where managers were made aware how productivity would be measured. In addition, people were assisted in their efforts to improve productivity.

14 *Top management must be committed to MBO and productivity improvements.* There is general agreement that a successful MBO program requires top management's commitment. Every consultant and every observer of such programs will tell you so. But what is overlooked is the need for top management's involvement in productivity programs. Generally, this task has been delegated to lower-level managers, mostly first-line supervisors. Yet, it is interesting to note that Japanese managers see it as their responsibility to assure high quality of their products and a high level of productivity.

15 *Finally, MBO must be viewed as a managerial system.* It should not be a burdensome addition to the manager's job, but rather a way of managing. Then, and only then, can the advantages of such a program be fully realized and problems overcome. The purpose of MBO is to make managers more effective and promote the achievement of their professional potential.

IMPLICATIONS FOR MANAGERIAL PRODUCTIVITY

Effective implementation of a productivity program such as MBO requires a systematic approach tailored to the needs of the organization and the characteristics of the situation. An MBO program may be implemented in sequential stages. One such model starts with the strategic purposes and goals of the enterprise and continues with more detailed goal setting, review sessions, inclusion of subsystems into the MBO process, and culminates in a comprehensive approach by integrating many key managerial activities (including the linkage of rewards) into a system. Another stage model begins with performance appraisal, continues with the integration of individual and organizational objectives, and eventually links MBO with strategic planning. Support can be found for both models. Whatever the program for improving managerial productivity, it has to be adapted to the situation—including the political power structure in the organization—and one approach to accomplish this is OD.

Organization development implies measurement, yet a Conference Board Study concluded that the measurement of OD effectiveness is one of the greatest weaknesses.[20] On the other hand, those factors that do not lend themselves to easy quantification are often crucial for group and organizational productivity. As pointed out, OD uses a variety of approaches; we focused on three: (1) Likert's four systems of management and the relationship to the essential steps in MBO, (2) the improvements of an existing MBO program by identifying the differences between practiced and the "ideal" MBO program, and (3) the team-building process to improve the interactions among people in the organization.

Likert's four management systems range from the highly autocratic approach (System 1) to the highly participative one with a great deal of confidence and trust in subordinates (System 4). To be effective, MBO must recognize the existing managerial system and improve upon it. We suggest that the manner in which the steps in the MBO process are carried out will differ for the four systems. The wise administrator will collect data on the existing managerial system and develop a change strategy that takes into account both aspects of MBO and the organizational environment.

The second approach to OD involves the improvement of the existing MBO program by measuring the degree of integration of MBO with key managerial activities as it is practiced and how it should be practiced. The third approach to improving productivity focuses on team building at the Forest Service, which illustrates that the concern for productivity is not restricted to profit-oriented or product-producing companies but extends to governmental and service organizations. Although productivity improvements depend on the situation, research and experience provide some guidelines for making MBO programs effective and efficient. MBO is not a cure-all, nor can it be bought as a package ready to be installed in the organization. Rather, MBO is a results-oriented, dynamic managerial system designed to improve productivity.

NOTES

1 P. F. Drucker, *Management: Tasks, Responsibilities, Practices* (New York: Harper & Row, 1973), p. 111.
2 R. Babcock and P. F. Sorenson, Jr., "A Long-Range Approach to MBO," *Management Review,* vol. 65, no. 6 (June 1976), pp. 44–49.
3 Ibid.
4 R. A. Howell, "Managing by Objectives—A Three Stage System," *Business Horizons,* vol. 8, no. 1 (February 1970), pp. 41–45.
5 H. Weihrich, "Management by Objectives: Toward a Situational Approach," Faculty Working Paper MG 80-15, Bureau of Business and Economic Research, College of Business Administration, Arizona State University, 1980.
6 ———, "A Study of the Integration of Management by Objectives with Key Managerial Activities and the Relationship to Selected Effectiveness Measures," doctoral diss., University of California, Los Angeles, 1973.
7 G. S. Odiorne, "The Politics of Implementing MBO," *Business Horizons,* vol. 17, no. 3 (June 1974), pp. 13–21.
8 W. A. Ruch and J. C. Hershauer, *Factors Affecting Worker Productivity* (Tempe, Arizona: Bureau of Business and Economic Research, Arizona State University, 1974). See also W. A. Ruch and J. C. Hershauer, "Productivity in People-Oriented Organizations," *Arizona Business,* (May 1975), pp. 11–20.
9 Ruch and Hershauer, *Factors Affecting Worker Productivity,* chaps. 5 and 6.
10 R. Beckhard, *Organization Development: Strategies and Models* (Reading, Mass.: Addison-Wesley, 1969), p. 9.
11 H. Koontz, "The Management Theory Jungle Revisited," *The Academy of Management Review,* vol. 5, no. 2 (April 1980), p. 185.
12 For a good discussion of OD see H.M.F. Rush, *Organization Development: A Reconnaissance* (New York: The Conference Board, 1978).
13 A. C. Beck, Jr. and E. D. Hillmar, *A Practical Approach to Organization Development Through MBO—Selected Readings* (Reading, Mass.: Addison-Wesley, 1972).
14 R. Likert, *New Patterns of Management* (New York: McGraw-Hill, 1961); R. Likert, *The Human Organization* (New York: McGraw-Hill, 1967); R. Likert and J. B. Likert, *New Ways of Managing Conflict* (New York: McGraw-Hill, 1976).
15 The advantages of MBO are discussed by A. P. Raia, "Goal Setting and Self-Control," *Journal of Management Studies,* vol. 2, no. 1 (February 1965); H. L. Tosi and S. J. Carroll, "Managerial Reactions to Management by Objectives," *Academy of Management Journal,* vol. 13, no. 4 (December 1968); H. Weihrich, "Management by Objectives: Does It

Really Work?" *University of Michigan Business Review,* vol. 28, no. 4, (July 1976), pp. 27–31.

16 A. P. Raia, "A Second Look at Management Goals and Controls," *California Management Review,* vol. 13, no. 1 (Summer 1966); F. E. Schuster and A. F. Kindall, "Management by Objectives: Where We Stand—A Survey of the Fortune 500," *Human Resource Management,* vol. 13, no. 1 (Spring 1974).

17 H. Weihrich, "Management By Objectives: Toward a Situational Approach," Working Paper MB 80–15. Bureau of Business and Economic Research: Arizona State University, 1980.

18 S. R. Atkinson, L. S. Beck, and B. A. Courtright, "Team Building: An Important Element in Work Planning and Performance Review," *1981 Proceedings, IX Annual Management by Objectives State of the Art Conference,* Washington, 1981, pp. 1–6.

19 One of the most thorough discussions of the role of the advisor can be found in E. J. Seyna, *Organizational Change in Complex Organization: A Case Study in MBO* (Ann Arbor: University Microfilms International, 1982).

20 Rush, op. cit.

CHAPTER 11

SPECIAL SITUATIONS: IMPROVING GOVERNMENT PRODUCTIVITY AND APPLYING JAPANESE MANAGEMENT PRACTICES

For many years, goal-oriented management approaches have been used in the private sector. Less recognized is the application of MBO in the public sector. Any organization, large or small, manufacturing or service, high-tech or low-tech, has to achieve its mission and MBO facilitates this process. But in government, some special constraining factors exist and they are discussed in the first part of this chapter.

No discussion of productivity would be complete without mentioning Japanese management, which has been credited with achieving an astonishing success in productivity improvements. This chapter compares and contrasts Japanese and United States managerial practices.

PRODUCTIVITY THROUGH GOAL-ORIENTED MANAGEMENT IN THE PUBLIC SECTOR

If productivity is our national concern, as it should be, then one cannot overlook the opportunities for improvement in government. About 17 percent of the work force is now employed by government at the federal, state, or local level. Moreover, government spending is now over one-third of the gross national product, the total value of goods and services produced in the nation. Therefore, even small improvements in government productivity can have great effects on total productivity.

The Introduction of MBO in the Federal Government

Concern about effective government is not new. Every United States president in recent history has been concerned with government productivity. Under Presidents Kennedy and Johnson—with the driving force of Robert S. McNamara—Planning, Programmming, Budgeting (PPB) was introduced. Although this was an effective technique, considerable resistance to it was experienced. Many government agencies were simply overwhelmed by the amount of paperwork involved.

On April 18, 1973, another attempt was made to make government more effective. President Nixon issued an executive order requiring each of twenty-one agencies to submit a list of ten to fifteen of their most important objectives. The order read as follows:

> As an additional measure to help us ensure that we are continually running the machinery of government in the people's interest, I am now asking each department and agency head to seek a sharper focus on the results which the various activities under his or her direction are aimed at achieving.
>
> To this end I would appreciate your preparing an outline of major goals and objectives for your organization to be accomplished during the coming year. Some of these objectives will be part of longer range strategies to be carried out by the end of my administration. In these cases you should indicate both the long-term goal, and, as a short-term objective, that portion which can be accomplished within the next year.

The next day, the director of the Office of Management and Budget (OMB) issued a memorandum, elaborating on the new approach to management. Perhaps without the Watergate investigation, MBO would have had more support from the president, who, naturally, had to direct his attention to more personal problems. But MBO did not disappear under the new administration of President Ford, who stated when he took office: "As one of my first undertakings in the Presidency, I have reviewed your accomplishments for the past year and the objectives you have set for the current fiscal year."[1]

During the Carter administration zero-base budgeting (ZBB) became the dominant managerial tool. Simply stated, zero-base budgeting, which was developed at Texas Instruments, requires a re-evaluation of all programs. Conceptually, ZBB is not new. Peter Phyrr, considered the driving force behind ZBB, stated in an interview that "...it takes many well-accepted management tools that are normally used in isolation and wraps them into the budgeting process—for instance, identification of objectives, now widely called management by objectives, or MBO."[2] While one would have to agree with Phyrr that budgeting is an important part of managing governmental organizations, it appears that the more appropriate approach is to use the comprehensive goal-oriented management system as the basic framework in which budgeting (not necessarily ZBB) is only a subsystem for achieving objectives. Essentially, ZBB requires a breakdown of the entire annual budget into packages that are ranked in order of their priority. Decisions are then made on the basis of the priority ranking and the justification of the package. But this approach has been called a fraud by Harvard Professor Robert N. Anthony.[3] He pointed out that in the federal government the large numbers of decision packages make ZBB unmanageable. Besides, the budgeting process is very time-consuming.

In the Reagan Administration, MBO is back in style (although MBO was never discarded during the Carter administration, as I found out in interviews in 1977). At the White House Conference on Productivity in 1983, it became clear that some of the more effectively managed departments used MBO concepts. But at that time the Office of Management and Budget did not have a grand design for MBO. Instead, the emphasis was on the bottom-up approach in which individual departments take the initiative in applying goal-oriented management concepts. But let us look back at the time when MBO became the official managerial system in the federal government.

What Has Been the Experience with MBO in the Federal Government?

To install MBO in an organization as large as the federal government was not easy. The Department of Health, Education and Welfare (HEW), which used MBO rather early, experienced considerable dissatisfaction with MBO. Some people in the agency felt that it is difficult to set quantifiable objectives for their tasks. Under the direction of Frederic Malek a study was undertaken to find out what needed to be done to make the department more effective. The findings showed the need for long-term as well as short-term specific objectives, clear delegation of authority, and identification of responsibilities. In addition, Malek identified the need for control and monitoring performance to see to what extent objectives were obtained and whether corrective actions were taken. He stated:

> If the executive branch of government is to be managed effectively, it clearly needs a system for setting priorities, pinpointing responsibility for their achievement, requiring follow-through, and generating enough feedback that programs can be monitored and evaluated from the top.[4]

These are precisely the key aspects of the MBO process.

Another frequently mentioned concern was the amount of paperwork involved in managing by objectives. There was also the fear that the managerial experts and the Office of Management and Budget (OMB) would set objectives rather than the managers themselves and that MBO might be used to concentrate power at OMB. Roy Ash, the budget director, attempted to dispose of these fears by emphasizing that MBO facilitates decentralization and the diffusion of power.

Then there was the problem in enforcing the directives for the MBO program. In an attempt to reduce resistance to the new managerial system, Roy Ash assured the managers that the Office of Management and Budget would not take any action against agencies that did not achieve their objectives. Did this, then, render MBO meaningless? Not necessarily. It could be argued that the identification of deviations from standards could—and should—result in positive steps to correct the deviations. Furthermore, guidance can be given to those agencies that do not measure up to their potential so that they will be able to improve their performance in the future.

Another difficulty often encountered in government pertains to the measurement of organizational performance. In a business organization, executives are held accountable for results such as profits, return on investments, market share, and similiar criteria. Most of these measures are not available in the public sector and often less precise standards have to be used. With this limitation in mind, it can be argued that even if the measurements are not as precise as in most business organizations, consciously thinking of results rather than mere activities will, in general, result in better management.

An additional problem in government is that most executive appointees hold their position for only a short period of time. Harold Steinberg of the Office of Management and Budget pointed out that in 1983 the average tenure of political appointees was less than two years. They may, therefore, not feel accountable for results. Yet, it could be argued that even if an appointee resigns, the goals set by the predecessor will give the successor an indication of the direction of the organization.

Perhaps the biggest problem in government is the reward system, which does little to benefit managers who are productive and achieve cost savings. More recently, gain sharing (an old idea in business organizations) is being introduced to a new audience, the federal government.[5] The gain sharing plan in the U.S. Army Supply Depot in Chambersburg, Pennsylvania, contributed to productivity increases ranging from 4 to 40 percent. But the results-pay linkage is still a novelty in government and only the future will show whether such a program can be applied on a broad basis.

Let us now turn to a more detailed discussion of the important topic of strategic planning in the public sector.

The Need for Long-Range Planning in Government

It appears that one of the greatest weaknesses in managing governments is the lack of vision and the lack of planning for crisis. For example, there was ample evidence of the coming of an energy crisis—long before 1973. Indeed, some experts warned about the impending energy problem in the 1950s. Yet, nothing was done until the crisis actually happened. This led, naturally, to crisis management and the establishment of the Federal Energy Administration (FEA). Yet, this massive organization, at least in its early stages, had no clearly defined objectives. By and large, government is run by politicians and "short-lived" political appointees who often have insufficient concern about the long-term effects of their decisions. Yet, history shows that when we as a nation put our mind to do something we can, as evidence by our commitment to having the first man on the moon. But note, our space explorations were again a response to a crisis, created by the Russian Sputnik. Although we achieved our goal, that is, we were effective, it will long be debated if it was worth the cost—that is, if it was productive. In the 1950s, the United States had an abundance of resources, but now things have changed, increasing the concern about the effective and efficient use of available resources.

Frederic Malek, who served Presidents Nixon and Ford as Special Assistant to the President and as Deputy Director of the

Office of Management and Budget, made keen observations about the workings of the government and what can be done to improve it. He stated: "The problem in the United States today is that we know we are on a great journey into the future but are not really certain where we are going."[6] Government, and this is true for all levels of government, does very little long-range planning, even though attempts have been made, but with questionable outcomes. In 1969 President Nixon wanted to strengthen domestic strategic planning by creating a National Goals Research Staff with the task of identifying goals. But the well-prepared report contained recommendations that were not congruent with the short-term needs of the administration. The result was that the recommendations were not implemented and the staff was dissolved. One of the basic problems in government is that the short-term orientation is usually hindered by the political process itself. Elected politicians usually do not get re-elected because they are good administrators, but rather, because of how they cope with crises. Also, it is very difficult to hold political leaders accountable for the long-term consequences of their decisions. Finally, the complexity of problems, the fragmented organizational structure, and the overlapping of authorities and responsibilities all contribute to the lack of strategic planning in government.

Implementing MBO in the Military

Organizational and personal changes are frequently the result of events in the environment. Consider the effects of the Civil Service Reform Act (CSRA, 1978) on Major Harold Bolton and his organization.[7] He was in command of the U.S. Army Depot System, an organization that employed over 37,000 people (mostly civilians). His immediate task was to implement two new appraisal systems, based on the CSRA, for 600 executives in twenty-four different locations. After deliberation, a decision was made to use an MBO-based approach involving three essential steps: (1) identifying group values (for example, integrity, responsiveness, purposefulness), (2) establishing norms of behavior, and (3) clarifying the mission.

The approach was guided by a philosophy of participative management that is in sharp contrast to a Theory X orientation discussed in an earlier chapter. This new way of managing freed Major Bolton to use his time more productively by spending 30 percent on MBO, 30 percent on people issues and the implementation of CSRA, 30 percent on productivity issues and future improvements, and the remaining 10 percent on mission performance and other tasks.

This experience shows that an external event, such as the Civil Service Reform Act, requiring the installation of a new performance appraisal system based on results, often demands other changes also. In this case, the demand was for a new managerial style based on participation with a focus on results.

The concepts of managing by objectives are sound and can be applied in government. To be sure, some of the objectives are difficult to state in terms of results—but, this complaint is also heard from business. Certainly the political environment contributes ·to power plays between agencies—but, this is also true to some extent in business (although it is usually not along party lines). It should be noted, however, that the rapid turnover in personnel in appointed positions in government organizations may require a renegotiation of objectives with new office holders. New managers will find it easier to take over a job because the stated objectives give them guidance for the new assignment.

CAN THE JAPANESE APPROACH TO MANAGING BE APPLIED IN THE UNITED STATES?

In the beginning of the book we noted that the United States had one of the smallest productivity increases of any industrialized nation, while Japan had the highest. It is not surprising that we look to Japan to find the answer to our productivity crisis. Japan's phenomenal success in increasing productivity is often attributed to its managerial approach, as briefly pointed out in Chapter 1. Indeed, there is an abundance of literature on this topic, and two such books even made the best-seller list,[8] but there are other books[9] and many more articles. Although there is considerable agreement on the basic characteristics of Japanese management, there is less agreement—and certainty—about the transferability of the *practices* (not science) of management to other cultures and the possibility of convergence of Japanese and American management approaches.[10]

In the 1960s scholars and practitioners were very much concerned about the universality and transferability of management, which is considered a critical factor for organizational success and economic growth. A great deal of controversy centered on the question as to whether management is culture-bound. Some scholars seem to suggest it is,[11] while others point at the universality of management.[12] UCLA's Harold Koontz, who developed one of the most comprehensive models of comparative management, concluded that the opinion differences about the universality of management can probably be attributed to the fact that management as science—organized knowledge—has universal application, but the practice of management is an art and as such must be adapted to the situation.[13]

Comparisons of Japanese and United States Management Practices

The most common way of organizing managerial knowledge is to classify key activities into the functions of planning, organizing, staffing, leading, and controlling.[14] This framework will also be used for comparing and contrasting the managerial approaches in Japan and the United States, as summarized in Table 11-1.

At the outset, a word of caution is in order. It is obvious that not all American firms are managed the same way as illustrated in Table 11-1 and discussed in this section. The same is true for Japanese managerial practices. We must also realize that very few empirical studies exist on the subject and that most of the available literature is descriptive. Many writers point out the differences in the managerial practices in Japan and the United States, or in the West in general. But others report that, for example, no differences have been found in participation in the decision-making process[15] or in job satisfaction in Japan and elsewhere.[16] Therefore, the contrasting managerial approaches are suggestive and need to be substantiated by additional research.

Comparisons in Planning[17]

In Japan, planning is greatly aided by the cooperation between government and business. After World War II, Japan developed policies promoting economic growth and strength as well as international competitiveness. These policies harmonized monetary and fiscal policies within the industrial structure, thus creating an economic environment relatively predictable for planning purposes.

Planning is choosing the purpose and objectives of the organization as a whole or a part of it and selecting the means to achieve those ends. Planning requires making decisions. The Japanese, in general, have a longer-term orientation in planning than American managers. There are several reasons for this. In Japan, banks are the primary providers of capital and their interest is the long-term health of the enterprises. In contrast, U.S. managers are often under pressure by stockholders to show favorable financial ratios each time they report them. Unfortunately, this may not encourage investments that have a payout in the more distant future. Also, Americans usually stay in their managerial positions only a relatively short time

TABLE 11-1
PROPOSITIONS ABOUT THE COMPARISON OF JAPANESE AND UNITED STATES MANAGEMENT APPROACHES*

Japanese management	United States management
Planning	
1 Long-term orientation.	1 Primarily short-term orientation
2 Collective decision making ("ringi") with consensus.	2 Individual decision making.
3 Many people are involved in preparing and making the decision.	3 Few people are involved in making and selling the decision to persons with divergent values.
4 Decision flow is from the bottom to the top and back.	4 Decisions are initiated at the top and flow down the organization.
5 Decision making takes a long time. Implementation of the decision is fast.	5 Making a decision is fast. Implementing the decision takes a long time and requires compromise, and often results in suboptimal decisions.
6 People share decision power and responsibility.	6 Decision power and responsibility vested in designated individuals.
7 Individual goal ambiguity.	7 Individual goal clarity.
8 Operational decisions are strategic.	8 Operational decisions are tactical.
Organizing	
1 Collective responsibility and accountability.	1 Individual responsibility.
2 Ambiguity of decision responsibility.	2 Clarity and specificity of responsibility.
3 Informal organization structure.	3 Formal bureaucratic organization structure.
4 Common organization culture and philosophy are well known. Competitive spirit toward other enterprises.	4 Common organization culture lacking. Identification with profession rather than with the company.
5 Changing processes in the organization with emphasis on consensus. Use of internal change agent.	5 Changing goals in the organization. Confrontation. Frequent use of external change agent.

(continued)

TABLE 11-1 (*Continued*)

Japanese management	United States management
Staffing	

Japanese management	United States management
1 Hiring young people out of school. Hardly any mobility of people among companies.	1 Hiring people out of schools and from other companies. Frequent company changes.
2 Slow promotion through the ranks.	2 Rapid advancement highly desired and demanded.
3 Loyalty to the company.	3 Loyalty to the profession.
4 Very infrequent performance evaluation for new (young) employees.	4 Frequent performance evaluations for new employees.
5 Appraisal of long-term performance.	5 Appraisal of short-term results.
6 Rewards for long-term performance.	6 Rewards for short-term results.
7 Small differences in pay increases.	7 Substantial differences in pay increases (especially for top managers).
8 Rewards for group and company performance.	8 Rewards for individual achievements.
9 Promotions based on multiple criteria.	9 Promotion based primarily on individual performance.
10 Training and development considered a long-term investment.	10 Training and development undertaken with hesitation because employee may switch to another firm.
11 Broad intracompany career paths. Exposure to many enterprise functions.	11 Frequently narrow career path within the organization. Expertise in specialized enterprise functions.
12 Lifetime employment common in large companies.	12 Job insecurity prevailing.

Japanese management	United States management
Leading	

Japanese management	United States management
1 Leader as a social facilitator is part of the group.	1 Leader as decision maker is heading the group.
2 Paternalistic style.	2 Directive syle, strong, firm, determined.
3 Common values facilitate cooperation.	3 Often divergent values. Individualism may hinder cooperation.
4 Avoidance of confrontation may lead to ambiguities. Emphasis on harmony.	4 Clarity valued; face-to-face confrontation.
5 Confluence of working and private life.	5 Separation of working and private life.
6 Bottom-up communication.	6 Communication primarily top-down.
7 Emphasis on face-to-face communication.	7 Emphasis on written communication.

TABLE 11-1 (*Continued*)

Japanese management	United States management
Controlling	
1 Control by peers.	1 Control by superior.
2 Control focus on group performance.	2 Control focus on individual performance.
3 Save face.	3 Fix blame.
4 Extensive use of quality control circles.	4 Limited use of quality control circles.
5 Suggestion box considerable success.	5 Suggestion boxes with limited success.

*Source: H. Koontz, C. O'Donnell,, and H. Weihrich, *Management,* 8th ed. (New York: McGraw-Hill, 1984.) Used with permission.

and myopic decisions can seldom be traced to the manager who had made the decision but in the meantime got promoted or even changed companies.

One of the most interesting aspects of Japanese management is the way decisions are made. In a typical organization, several levels are involved in making the decision. Actually, the most important part of the process is the understanding and the analysis of the problem and the development of various alternative solutions. The final authority for making a decision still rests with top management. But before a proposal reaches the executive's desk, the problem and the possible solutions have been discussed at various levels in the organizational hierarchy. Top management still has the option to accept or reject a decision. But, more likely, a decision is returned to subordinates for further study, rather than being rejected outright. A proposal is confirmed through the "Ringi" process. The "Ringi-Sho" is a proposal document prepared by a staff member. This paper is circulated among various managers before it goes to top management for formal approval. The document, which is usually initialled by those involved in or affected by the decision, elicits cooperation and participation of many people. This, in turn, assures that the problem or the decision is examined from different perspectives. This decision-making process is very time-consuming. But after a consensus is reached, the implementation of the plan is swift because of the understanding of the plan, the clarification of the problem, the evaluation of the different alternatives, and the involvement of those people who will implement the decision. The sharing of the decision power and responsibilities can also result in a problem so that no one feels individually responsible for the decision.

In United States organizations, decisions are made primarily by individuals and usually only a few people are involved. Consequently, after the decision has been made it has to be "sold" to others, often to people with different values and different perceptions of what the problem really is and how it should be solved. In this way, the making of the decision is rather fast, but its implementation is very time-consuming and requires compromises with those managers holding different viewpoints. It is true that decision responsibility can be traced to individuals, but at the same time, this may result in a practice of finding scapegoats for wrong decisions. In summary, in United States companies the decision power and the responsibility are vested in designated individuals, while in Japan people share both decision power and responsibility.

There are other characteristics in the planning process that should be considered. On the individual level, goals and objectives are rather vague and ambiguous for Japanese managers and they are seldom used for measuring performance against verifiable objectives.[18] In contrast, in the United States, MBO goals are considered to be most useful when they are clear and precise and can serve as standards against which performance can be measured.

One researcher observed that successful Japanese firms make operational decisions in connection with strategic planning by considering the long-term implications of such plans.[19] It is argued that operational decisions, such as setting up a production facility, involve investment in capital goods that are to be used for a long time. Moreover, it is rather difficult to change operational decisions within a short time. Finally, operational decisions are strategic because they influence the strategic position of the firm. In contrast, American managers treat operational decisions as tactical moves, or simply as means for implementing a general plan.

Comparisons in Organizing[20]

Organizing involves setting up a structure to coordinate human efforts so that people can contribute effectively and efficiently to the aims of the enterprise. This requires determining roles, responsibilities, and accountability.

In Japanese companies, largely due to the search for consensus in decision making, the emphasis is on collective responsibility and accountability. Individual responsibilities, then, are implied rather than explicitly defined as the organization structure is rather ambiguous. Although this may discourage placing the blame for an incorrect decision on individuals, it can also create a great deal of uncertainty. Another characteristic found in Japanese firms is a common organizational culture and philosophy, placing a high value on unity and harmony within the organization. At the same time, there is a competitive spirit toward other enterprises. Organizational change is accomplished by changing processes, with the aim of maintaining harmony among those affected. The change agent (OD consultant) is virtually always an employee of the company.

Organizations in the United States emphasize individual responsibility, with efforts to clarify and make explicit who is responsible for what. Often specific job descriptions clarify the nature and extent of individual responsibilities. Indeed, many organizations, especially those operating in a stable environment, have been rather successful in using the formal bureaucratic organization structure. As far as the climate is concerned, not many managers make special efforts to create a commonly shared organization culture. This may indeed be difficult because professionals—managers as well as technical people—often have a closer identification with their profession than with a particular company. In addition, the work force often consists of people with different values derived from a diverse heritage. Many American firms have a high employee turnover rate, which is partly due to the great mobility of the people in this country. With a relatively short duration of employment with any one company, the loyalty toward the firm is frequently rather weak.

Organizational change is often accomplished by changing goals instead of processes. But, organizations using change agents with a behavioral science orientation often focus on interpersonal processes to reduce conflicts and to improve performance. In the United States it is quite common to employ organization development consultants from outside the firm, which is almost never done in Japan.

Comparisons In Staffing[21]

Staffing requires identifying the human resource needs and filling the organization structure, and keeping it filled, with competent people. It is in the management of human resources—besides the decision-making process—that the Japanese approach to managing differs greatly from that of United States companies. The Japanese educational system, recruitment practices, and the training system all promote a system of cliques within the organization and demphasize the identification of the employees with their profession.[22]

In Japan, people are hired out of school and for a young man, choosing the company is one of the most important decisions he makes besides selecting a spouse and a university. After a person has joined a large company, there is hardly any opportunity to find employment in another firm. Within the company, promotion is rather slow, and for most young people the career paths during the first fifteen or twenty years with the company are rather similiar. Still, employees develop a strong identification with the company which, in turn, takes care of them. Employees repay with their loyalty. After joining the company, performance of employees is evaluated very infrequently. In fact, it may take ten years before a formal performance evaluation is made. This does not mean, however, that the progress is not monitored. But it is done on an informal basis. Working together with others in an office, without walls separating employees and superiors, leaves little doubt about how well individuals perform. Furthermore, infrequent appraisals, encompassing a long period of time, reduce the probability that luck or misfortune influence the evaluation. What is evaluated is the overall, long-range success and decision capability of the individual. This practice facilitates linking rewards to effective long-term performance. Still, the differences in pay increases are very small and rewards are essentially based on group and company performance rather than individual contributions.

Because the employees are an integral part of the corporate community, promotion practices must be considered by all as being fair and equitable. The criteria for promotion is usually a combination of seniority and merit. Also, the educational background plays a role in promotion decisions. Japanese companies invest heavily in the training and development of their employees and the practice of job rotation throughout the working life leads to a broad career path in which employees get exposed to many different enterprise activities.

Perhaps the most pervasive impact on managerial practices is lifetime employment. Japanese companies make every effort to ensure a stable employment until retirement age (around 55). At times of economic slow-down, companies usually dismiss part-time or seasonal employees who are not considered members of the permanent work force. Also, rather than laying off permanent employees, companies often transfer them to organizational units that are in need of additional help. But the practice of life-long employment seems to become less important. In an interview Japanese executives suggested that life-long employment is very costly to the company, resulting in a top-heavy organization structure, and therefore may have to be slowly modified.

The management of human resources in the United States is quite different from Japan. American firms also recruit employees from schools; but, they also hire employees from other companies. For example, the high turnover rates among those who recently received their master of business administration degree is quite notorious. Rapid advancement is expected and if it is not forthcoming, an employee may change companies. Professionals, such as engineers or accountants, often identify more with their profession than with their company, and jobhopping is not unusual.

A common practice in American companies is to appraise the perfomance of new employees rather soon after they join the company. If the performance does not meet the company's expectations, employment may be terminated. But even for those who have been with a company for many years, performance is evaluated at least once a year and in many cases performance is reviewed periodically during the year. In general, the focus of performance appraisal is on short-term results and individual contributions to the company aims. Moreover, differentials in pay increases based on individual performance may be substantial, especially at upper levels of management. Promotions in United States companies are based primarily on individual performance. Although progressive companies provide for continuous development, training is often undertaken with hesitation because of the cost and the concern that the trained person may switch to another firm. Thus, employees are often trained in specialized functions resulting in a rather narrow career path within the firm. Finally, in many American companies, employees feel that they may be laid off during economically hard times, which naturally contributes to job insecurity.

Comparisons in Leading[23]

Leading involves the process of influencing people so that they contribute to organizational aims; it is concerned with leadership, motivation, and communication. Japanese managers are seen as social integrators who are a part of the workgroup. Using a paternalistic leadership approach, managers show great concern for the welfare of their subordinates. Common values and team spirit facilitate cooperation. The role of managers is to create an environment of esprit de corps, and they are willing to help out in doing the same work their subordinates do. In an attempt to maintain harmony at almost any cost, managers avoid face-to-face confrontation. This also means that things may be purposely left ambiguous. Leadership requires a following and managers are aided by the fact that individuals are expected to subordinate their self-interest to that of the group and the organization. While managers may not be very directive, influence is exerted through peer pressure. In fact, close personal relationships are nurtured not only by working together on common tasks, but also by meeting and associating outside the work environment. The result is a confluence of organizational and private life.

Communication patterns parallel decision making with an emphasis on bottom-up communication. In one study it was found that in Japanese companies communication was initiated much more often at lower levels than in American firms.[24] This communication pattern is also promoted by Japanese managers who take a great deal of time communicating with their subordinates, emphasizing face-to-face contact rather than memos.

The managerial function of leading is carried out quite differently in American companies. Leaders are seen as decision makers heading the group; they are expected to be directive, strong, firm, and determined. Their task is to integrate diverse values, but the emphasis on individualism in the society in general and in organizations in particular may hinder cooperation. It is expected that managers take decisive actions and clarify the direction of the group or the enterprise even if this requires face-to-face confrontation with those who may disagree. Although managers work hard, they value their private life and separate it from their working life. Within the organization, the communication pattern is to a great extent from the top down with considerable emphasis given to written communication.

Comparisons in Controlling[25]

In the view of Western managers, controlling involves setting standards, measuring performance, and correcting undesirable deviations. But to the Japanese this process is more indirect. As we have noted in the discussion of decision making, the group, with its dynamics and its pressures, has a profound impact on the managerial process. In an open-office design, peers are well aware of the performance of their colleagues. Moreover, managers are a part of the work group rather than separated from employees in their offices. The measurement of individual performance is not against specific, verifiable objectives; instead, emphasis is placed on group performance. Also, the Japanese approach of letting subordinates "save face" would be incongruent with fixing the blame for deviations from plans on individuals. The emphasis of control is on process, not numbers. The Japanese are well-known for their concern for quality. Yet this has not always been the case. In the 1950s and 1960s Japanese products had an image of shoddy workmanship and quality. As we all know, this image has changed and good quality is one of the characteristics now associated with Japanese products. This is due, in part, to the success of quality control, which requires grassroots involvement with very active participation in quality control circles.

Control in the United States often means measuring performance against pre-established precise standards. Management by objectives, as widely practiced in this country, requires the setting of verifiable objectives against which individual performance is measured. This way the superior can trace deviations to specific individuals, which frequently results in fixing the blame. In an attempt to maximize individual results, group performance may suffer. We all can think of examples in which the self-interest of individuals was placed before group or organizational interest. The use of quality control programs is not new. Hughes Aircraft Company, for example, had such programs for a long time under the name of zero defects and value engineering. Many of these programs were developed in this country and later used by the Japanese in the improvement of their product quality and productivity.

In summary, the managerial practices in carrying out the functions of planning, organizing, staffing, leading, and controlling show considerable differences between the United States and Japan. With the success of increasing productivity in Japan, there is the tendency to look across the ocean for answers to our productivity crisis. Some say that Japanese management practices are culture-bound and cannot be adopted any place else. Others suggest that we should simply copy Japanese management to increase productivity. Both views are probably wrong. The impact of the external environment, especially the sociocultural impact, cannot be ignored. Yet, it should not be overestimated either. The proper way of action may be to analyze carefully which aspects of the managerial process can be transferred to the United States environment and then make the necessary adaptations.

ON THE TRANSFERABILITY OF JAPANESE MANAGERIAL PRACTICES TO THE UNITED STATES

In the foregoing discussion we contrasted and compared Japanese management with that of the United States. The Japanese success at increasing productivity at an astonishing rate certainly raises the question about the transferability of these practices to the United States. Earlier we noted that the extensive literature on Japanese management largely lacks the support of substantive research. It is, of course, rather difficult to make crosscultural comparisons. The fact that cars, for example, can be produced with less cost in Japan may be due to a variety of factors. To isolate them and label them as causes for productivity is not easy to do. But even if this could be accomplished, it still does not answer the question of whether Japanese managerial practices are transferable to western countries. One approach, then, is to look at the way Japanese subsidiaries operate in the United States. In an attempt to demonstrate the effectiveness of Japanese managerial approaches, success stories of Japanese firms have been cited.[26] Workers at San Diego's Sony television plant are said to produce as well as workers in Japan.[27] But there is also evidence that Japanese managers have to adapt their style to fit the United States environment.[28] One author even called the performance of Japanese firms operating in the United States a "mixed bag."[29] Despite the limitations associated with the study of Japanese firms operating in the United States, we can gain some knowledge about transferability. In the discussion that follows we will draw from descriptive literature on Japanese and American management. But, because of the lack of solid research evidence, we will discuss the Japanese managerial practices and their transferability (largely following the summary shown earlier in Table 11-1) in terms of propositions.

Propositions on Planning

The national concern for productivity in the United States raises the question of what could be adopted from the Japanese to improve productivity. For one, we need to pay more attention to the long-term implications of managerial decisions. In most organizations, managers get rewarded for short-term performance. Unfortunately, this short-term orientation can lead to decisions that are detrimental to the company in the long run. Some successful American firms have recognized the need for rewarding managers for strategic decisions that may have a payout in the distant future. Such actions may require making large capital Investments in labor-saving machines, or developing new product lines, or investing in research and development. Texas Instruments serves as an example of integrating short-term results with long-term aims.[30] The firm's objectives, strategies, tactics system (OST System) requires and rewards decisions that balance the concern for both the short and the long term. Moreover, some American companies are now developing, in a systematic way, strategic plans that demand a long-term orientation. Traditional management-by-objectives programs have focused on short-term results, usually one year or less. But modern programs now integrate strategic planning into the MBO process. If strategic planning is to succeed, managers must be rewarded for investing the firm's resources in a way that is beneficial for the firm in the more distant future. To be sure, one cannot ignore short-term performance, but immediate results must not be achieved to the detriment of the long-term productivity of the firm.

One of the distinct characteristics of the Japanese is consensus decision making. It may be true that the Japanese culture is more conducive to participative management than the environment in the United States. Yet, effective teamwork is not peculiar to Japanese managers. In fact, they may have simply adopted the research findings of American scholars such as Rensis Likert and his associates at the University of Michigan, who found that as organizations moved toward System 4, the participative management approach, they became more effective, as discussed in the previous chapter.[31] In System 4, decisions are made at various levels throughout the organization. Furthermore, subordinates are fully involved in decisions related to their work. It was also found that this kind of decision making substantially contributes to motivation. In short, then, what often is attributed to Japanese management may not be restricted to their culture. What may be required is to look at our research findings, draw conclusions from them, and apply what we have learned.

In Japan, goals for individuals are usually not clearly identified in specific and verifiable terms. In contrast, in the United States the popular management-by-objectives approach emphasizes verifiable goals that, in turn, serve as a way of measuring the contributions of individuals to the organization's endeavor. Perhaps companies have overemphasized individual goals at the neglect of group goals and group performance. Many organizations are engaged in complex and interdependent tasks that would favor the setting of group goals, as suggested by the team approach to MBO (see Chapter 10), in which objectives are set, not only for individuals, but also for the work group.[32] This approach, among other things, facilitates the identification of conflicts among individual goals. Furthermore, through group problem solving, the contributions of individuals to the group as a whole can be carefully assessed. Finally, individual and group objectives are integrated with the goals of other teams and thus contribute to the overall aims of the organization with a minimum of conflicts among objectives.

Propositions on Organizing

Organizing involves setting up a structure of roles for people so that they can contribute effectively and efficiently toward the aims of the enterprise. Japanese organizations have been called organic type and American organization, system type.[33] The Japanese organization is portrayed as one in which managers perform multiple functions; the delineations of each are not quite clear. Thus, the organization is marked by ambiguity, informal relationships, and a common organization culture. Organizational change is accomplished by obtaining consensus. But the distinctions between Japanese and American management in organizations do emphasize individual responsibility, clarity of decision responsibility, and a formal structure. At the same time, there are many kinds of organizations (for example, research and development firms) that do have characteristics of organic organizations.

In his classic book *The Practice of Management,* Peter Drucker emphasized the need for building a true team, directing individual efforts toward a common goal, and seeing the organization as a whole. Furthermore, he highlighted the need for self-control and self-direction, assuming that people would direct their activities toward the common good.[34] In an overemphasis on accountability (perhaps promoted by the application of MBO to performance appraisal), many companies may have neglected to remember that organized effort is, in the final analysis, team effort. On balance, then, I think that we should take another look at the underlying philosophy of MBO—emphasizing teamwork and self-control—and make greater use of it. It appears feasible for American firms to obtain a better balance between group and individual responsibilities. Currently the latter may be emphasized at the expense of the former. To this extent, the Japanese example can be very valuable. At the same time, our culture, which places a great value on individuality, may not be very conducive to tolerating excessive ambiguities in assigning responsibility. I suggest that flexibility and contingency theory in organizational design may provide guidance for managers. The research at Harvard and other institutions indicates that organizations with dynamic environments call for organic types of organizations.[35] In these kinds of enterprises teams may be used to integrate activities. On the other hand, stable environments may be more conducive for the use of more mechanistic organizations that, for example, emphasize hierarchical relationships for coordination and direction. In designing organizations, it is therefore advisable to give attention to the environmental factors. It appears, then, that American managers should not blindly adopt organizing practices of Japanese firms but rather look carefully at our organization theory research.

Propositions on Staffing

The managerial function of staffing is carried out quite differently in Japan and the United States. Recruiting, selecting, promoting, appraising, and training differ greatly and some of these practices may be difficult to apply in our environment. Others work surprisingly well. It was a generally held opinion that Americans would find little attraction in long-term employment with extraordinary emphasis on job security. Yet, Japanese companies in the United States have found that their American employees value stable employment. Furthermore, recent labor contracts now give a higher priority to job security. But it is unlikely that most American employees would forego employment opportunities elsewhere and not change to another company out of loyalty. In our mobile society it is difficult to imagine that young employees would join a firm with the intent of a lifelong commitment to that company. Nevertheless, companies in the United States may benefit from taking the employment contract more seriously by providing employees with an objective assessment of career opportunities within the firm. On the other hand, employees need to learn about the company *before* joining. Unnecessary turnover is detrimental to sustaining high productivity.

The Japanese practice of slow promotion through the ranks may be difficult to accept by employees in this country, especially when opportunities for fast advancement are offered by other companies. Similarly, loyalty to the company will be difficult to achieve as long as employees have a closer identification with their profession than with their company. For this and other reasons, high turnover may continue, especially at times of a low supply of managers and employees and a high demand for their services.

It is also unlikely that employees would be content with infrequent performance appraisals. Because the emphasis in our culture is on individual accomplishments, people want to know where they stand. On the other hand, it appears to be quite appropriate to appraise and reward employees for short-term achievements and for working toward long-term goals. For example, managers should get recognition when they develop a new product or when they engage in research and development that may be profitable only in the more distant future. Whether or not individual pay increase differences should be small, as in Japanese firms, or substantial is difficult to assess. Rewarding individual performance without recognition of group performance may lead to actions based on excessive self-interest of individuals without concern for the welfare of the firm. Consequently, group and organization performance, in addition to individual performance, should influence the level of rewards.

Promotions in Japan are based on multiple criteria, while in the United States performance is the primary determinant for advancement. Performance, especially short-term performance, should be supplemented by an evaluation of managers as managers, that is, how well they carry out their managerial activities. Such an approach was suggested several years ago in which seventy-three key managerial activities, grouped into functions of planning, organizing, staffing, directing, and controlling, were used as criteria for evaluating managers.[36] To be sure, these measurements are not as precise as when measured against verifiable objectives (which was also one set of appraisal criteria), but they draw attention to the essentials of managing that contribute to long-term managerial productivity and development.

In Japan, training and development are considered long-term investments because employees stay with the firm for a lifetime. The broad career path, which gives the employee a great variety of experience, is quite similar for all employees for the first fifteen to twenty years of their working lives.[37] In the United States, with a high mobility of employees, investments in training and development are often made reluctantly. As a consequence, career paths are usually rather narrow, leading to expertise in a specialized area. Since many firms are in need of general managers, broad training and development is called for. At the same time, the cost of such an approach must also be considered. It is therefore rather difficult to come to a conclusive judgment about the advisability of adopting these Japanese practices in the United States.

Propositions on Leading

The managerial function of leading has to do with leadership style, motivation, and communication. Like staffing, the practice of leading is rather strongly influenced by sociocultural factors. A widespread assumption is that the Japanese management style works well in their cultural environment but does not work anywere else. However, commonly held assumptions are often incorrect. Since many Japanese companies have now opened production facilities in the United States, we can look at the effectiveness of the style of their managers. For example, Matsushita Electrical Industrial has taken over Motorola's TV production of the Quasar line; Marubeni has set up a textile mill in South Carolina; NTN Bearing is producing bearings in Illinois; YKK has established a new factory in Georgia; and Sony is producing TV sets in California.[38] It is interesting that these companies not only use their capital and their technology with great skills, but also their managerial style.

Japanese managers are often seen as social facilitators who become a part of the work group. American workers in Japanese subsidiaries report that they like the fact that their suggestions are considered seriously by their Japanese managers. Moreover, Japanese managers do their part to promote an informal atmosphere and they do not hesitate to help out with manual tasks that are normally carried out by workers. A Japanese manager at the YKK Zipper Company reported that he works twelve hours a day and then frequently entertains other managers so that they can discuss in an informal atmosphere subjects such as work ethics or the company's philosophy. In contrast, most United States managers feel rather strongly about separating their work life from private life.

The paternalistic style common in Japan elicits mixed reactions from American employees working in Japanese subsidiaries in the United States. While cooperation in Japan is facilitated by shared values, divergent values and individualism in the United States may hinder close cooperation. Also, Americans like to see their managers as being firm, strong, and decisive. Clarity in direction is appreciated, even if it means face-to-face confrontation. Evidently the Japanese style, with an emphasis on harmonious relationships, is quite different. Managers avoid confrontations, even if that leads to ambiguity. Thus, cultural differences may hinder the transferability of Japanese leadership practices to American firms.

Japanese management is not only known for bottom-up decision making, but also for bottom-up communication. Surprisingly, though, one study found that Japanese companies in the United States did *not* have more upward communication than American companies.[39] Still, there was somewhat more participation in decision making in Japanese enterprises. Also, managers in Japanese firms showed more concern for the feelings of their subordinates than managers in American companies.

Japanese managers emphasize face-to-face communication, while American counterparts often rely on written communication. On the other hand, MBO, as advocated in the United States, encourages face-to-face and upward communication. However, these discussions are less concerned about personal feelings and more concerned with a rational analysis of individual performance. It appears, then, that Japanese communication practices, with an emphasis on upward communication, could increase understanding and consensus in American firms.

Propositions on Controlling

Controlling is making events conform to plans. In Japan, control is exercised by peers and the emphasis is on the measurement of group and organizational performance. In the United States, with control exercised largely by the superior, it would be difficult to rely on group control. On the other hand, if the team approach to MBO is applied, group interaction and pressure would facilitate informal control. Still, the relatively high mobility of the work force in the United States and the high value placed on individualism are not conducive to group control. But, the practice of letting subordinates save face in case of deviations from standards may be a managerial art that could be more widely practiced by American managers.

The use of suggestion boxes and quality control circles is nothing new to American companies. Indeed these concepts do have their origin in the United States and there should be no problem of re-emphasizing these managerial tools in American industry. Eastman Kodak started their suggestion system in 1898 and during the course of its operation received 1,000,000 suggestions.[40] What the Japanese have done, and this may be the primary lesson for us, they have done extremely well. They have taken a concept or an idea, adapted it to their environment, and then made great efforts to perfect it.

IMPLICATIONS FOR MANAGERIAL PRODUCTIVITY

With the increasing role of governments—federal, state, and local—improving productivity in the public sector is essential. At the federal level a public law[41] established a White House Conference to increase productivity in the public as well as the private sector. But in government, managers concerned about productivity face additional constraints. Not only the size of the organization makes it difficult to implement a comprehensive program, but also the change in administrations, each with its own ideas, makes it hard to implement an enduring managerial system. The short tenure of political appointees compounds the problem. Yet, experiences in departments that are committed to criteria-based performance approaches have achieved remarkable results. What is needed, however, is to make the short-term achievement congruent with long-term aims that still are largely missing in public organizations.

Management, once considered an American challenge to Europeans, has become, in the minds of many, a Japanese challenge to managers in the United States. Whether the perception of the superiority of Japanese management practices is correct—and there are some doubts—remains to be seen. Although management science and theory may be universal, its practice is not. Managerial practices in planning, organizing, staffing, leading, and controlling are different in the United States and Japan. Some may be transferable but others are not. The environment, especially sociocultural factors, does influence practice. But its impact may have been overstated. Toji Arai, the director of the Japanese Productivity Center, pointed out to me that young people in Japan engage in many sports that favor individualism (judo, karate, swimming, and gymnastics) while in the United States the popular sports such as football, baseball, and basketball all require team effort. Yet the Japanese managerial practices emphasize teamwork while U.S. managers value individualism. Those who discard Japanese managerial approaches as being cultural-based—not being applicable in the U.S.—should be open to new ways of managing.

It is also interesting to note that an American, W. Edwards Deming, referred to as the father of quality control, taught the Japanese after World War II how to produce high-quality goods. Yet, he is hardly known in this country.[42] Perhaps it is time to rediscover techniques that had their origin in the United States but were improved by the Japanese.

NOTES

1 J. Havemann, "Executive Report/Ford Endorses 172 Goals of 'Management by Objective' Plan," *National Journal Reports* (Oct. 26, 1974), pp. 1597–1605.

2 "Zero-Base Budgeting—Peter Pyhrr Defends His Brainchild,"*MBA,* vol. 11, no. 4 (April 1977), p. 25.

3 R. N. Anthony, "Zero-Base Budgeting Is A Fraud," *Wall Street Journal* (April 27, 1977).

4 F. V. Malek, *Washington's Hidden Tragedy* (New York: The Free Press, 1978).

5 W. D. Ploger and M. C. Minahan, "Gainsharing in the Federal Government," in Panel Background Papers, *White House Conference on Productivity,* 1983.

6 Malek, op. cit.

7 J. H. Bolton, "Management by Objectives for Organization Results," *1981 Proceedings, 9th Annual Management by Objectives State of the Art Conference,* held in Washington, Aug. 23-26, 1981, pp.36–43.

8 W. G. Ouchi, *Theory Z* (Reading, Mass: Addison-Wesley, 1981); R. T. Pascale and A. G. Athos, *The Art of Japanese Management* (New York: Simon & Schuster, 1981).

9 E. F. Vogel, *Japan as Number One* (New York; Harper & Row, 1979).

10 R. T. Johnson, "Success and Failure of Japanese Subsidiaries in America," *Columbia Journal of World Business* (Spring 1977), pp. 30–37 and Y. Tsurumi, "The Best of Times and the Worst of Times: Japanese Management in America," *Columbia Journal of World Business* (Summer 1978), pp. 56–61.

11 See, for example, R. F. Gonzalez and C. McMillan, Jr., "The Universality of American Management Philosophy," *Journal of the Academy of Management* (April 1961), pp. 33–41; W. Oberg, "Cross-Cultural Perspectives on Management Principles," *Academy of Management Journal* (June 1963), p. 120.

12 The pioneers in comparative management taking this position include R. N. Farmer and B. M. Richman, *Comparative Management and Economic Progress* (Homewood, Ill.: Richard D. Irwin, 1965); A. R. Negandhi, "A Model for Analyzing Organizations in Cross-Cultural Settings: A Conceptual Scheme and Some Research Findings," *Comparative Administration and Research Conference* (Kent, Ohio: Bureau of Economic and Business Research, Kent State University, 1969), pp. 55–87; J. Fayerweather, *The Executive Overseas* (Syracuse, N.Y.: Syracuse University Press, 1959); H. Koontz, "A Model for Analyzing the Universality and Transferability of Management," *Academy of Management Journal* (December 1969), pp. 415–429. Koontz also cites in his article four unpublished doctoral dissertations.

13 Koontz, op. cit.

14 H. Koontz, C. O'Donnell, and H. Weihrich, *Management,* 8th ed. (New York: McGraw-Hill, 1984).

15 R. T. Pascale, "Zen and the Art of Management," *Harvard Business Review* (March-April 1978), pp. 153–162.

16 K. Azumi and C. J. McMillan, "Worker Sentiment in the Japanese Factory: Its Organizational Determinants," in L. Austin, ed., *Japan: The Paradox of Progress* (New Haven: Yale University Press, 1976), pp. 215–230.

17 Planning aspects have been widely discussed by P. F. Drucker, "What We Can Learn From Japanese Management," *Harvard Business Review* (March-April 1971), pp. 110–122; "Japanese Managers Tell How Their System Works," *Fortune* (November 1977), pp. 127–138; I. Hattori, "A Proposition on Efficient Decision Making in the Japanese Corporation," *Columbia Journal of World Business* (Summer 1978), pp. 7–15; R. T. Johnson and W. G. Ouchi, "Made in America (Under Japanese Management)," *Harvard Business Review* (September-October 1974), pp. 61–69; R. T. Moran, "Japanese Participative Management—Or How Rinji Seido Can Work for You," *S.A.M. Advanced Management Journal* (Summer 1979), pp. 14–22; W. G. Ouchi and A. M. Jaeger, "Type Z Organization: Stability in the Midst of Mobility," *Academy of Management Review* (April 1978) pp. 305–314;

S. C. Wheelwright, "Operations as Strategy Lessons From Japan," *Stanford GSB* (Fall 1981–82), pp. 3–7; C. Y. Yang, "Management Styles: American vis-a-vis Japanese," *Columbia Journal of World Business* (Fall 1977), pp. 23–31.

18 But Professor T. Cullen in "The International Manager and His Values," doctoral diss., Cornell University, 1983, pointed out that a study showed a higher level of satisfaction among middle-level managers when more concrete performance measures were used. His research also supports this finding, suggesting that the setting of specific goals, such as used in MBO, may work in Japan.

19 Wheelwright, op. cit.

20 Aspects of organizing have been discussed as follows: Johnson and Ouchi, op. cit.; Johnson, op. cit.; M. K. Kobayashi and W. W. Burke, "Organization Development in Japan," *Columbia Journal of World Business* (Summer 1976), pp. 113–122; Moran, op. cit.; Ouchi and Jaeger, op. cit.; W. G. Ouchi and R. L. Price, "Hierarchies, Clans, and Theory Z: A New Perspective on Organization Development," Organizational Dynamics (Autumn 1978), pp. 25–44; Tsurumi, op. cit.; Yang, op. cit.; M. Y. Yoshino, "Emerging Japanese Multinational Enterprises," in E. F. Vogel (ed.), *Modern Japanese Organization and Decision Making* (Berkeley: University of California Press, 1975), pp. 146–166.

21 Staffing aspects have been discussed by P. F. Drucker, op. cit.; *Fortune* (November 1977), op. cit. ; Hattori, op. cit.; Johnson and Ouchi, op. cit.; L. Kraar, "The Japanese Are Coming—With Their Own Style of Management," *Fortune* (March 1975), pp. 116–121, 160–164; Moran, op. cit.; Ouchi and Jaeger, op. cit.; T. Ozawa, "Japanese World of Work: An Interpretive Survey," *MSU Business Topics* (Spring 1980), pp. 45–55; Tsurumi, op. cit.; A. M. Whitehill and Shin-ichi Takezawa, "Workplace Harmony: Another Japanese 'Miracle'?" *Columbia Journal of World Business* (Fall 1978), pp. 25–39.

22 T. Cullen, "Development and Use of the Functional Informal Group in the Japanese Organization," in S. M. Lee and G. Schwendiman, eds., *Management by Japanese System* (New York; Praeger, 1982).

23 Leading has been discussed by P. F. Drucker, "Behind Japan's Success," *Harvard Business Review* (January-February 1981), pp. 83–90; *Fortune* (November 1977), op. cit.; Hattori, op. cit.; Johnson, op. cit.; K. Odaka, *Toward Industrial Democracy: Management and Workers in Modern Japan* (Boston: Harvard University Press, 1975); Ouchi and Jaeger, op. cit.; Ozawa, op. cit.; H. Takeuchi, "Productivity: Learning from the Japanese," *California Management Review* (Summer 1981), pp. 5–18; Tsurumi, op. cit.; Yang, op. cit.

24 Pascale, op. cit.

25 Controlling has been discussed by K. Koike, "Will America Regain Its Competitiveness?" *Economic Eye* (March 1981), pp. 26–32; Takeuchi, op. cit.

26 Johnson and Ouchi, op. cit.

27 Morgan, op. cit.

28 Tsurumi, op. cit.

29 Johnson, op. cit.

30 G. A. Dove, "Objectives, Strategies, and Tactics in a System," *The Conference Board Record* (August 1970), pp. 52–55.

31 R. Likert, *The Human Organization* (New York: McGraw-Hill, 1967); R. Likert and J. G. Likert, *New Ways of Managing Conflict* (New York: McGraw-Hill, 1976).

32 H. Weihrich, "TAMBO: Team Approach to MBO," *University of Michigan Business Review* (May 1979), pp. 12–17.

33 Yan, op. cit.

34 P. F. Drucker, *The Practice of Management* (New York: Harper & Row, 1954), chap. 11.

35 P. R. Lawrence and J. W. Lorsch, *Organization and Environment* (Homewood, Ill.: Richard D. Irwin, Inc., 1967); J. J. Morse and J. W. Lorsch, "Beyond Theory Y," *Harvard Business Review* (May-June 1970), pp. 61–68.

36 H. Koontz, *Appraising Managers as Managers* (New York: McGraw-Hill, 1971). See also the discussion in Chapter 7 in this book.

37 Johnson and Ouchi, op. cit.

38 Kraar, op. cit.

39 Johnson, op. cit.

40 V. G. Reuter, "Suggestion Systems Utilization, Evaluation, and Implementation," *California Management Review* (Spring 1977), pp. 78–89.

41 Public Law 97–367, Oct. 25, 1982, 97th Congress, An act to establish a White House Conference on Productivity.

42 M. Tribus and J. H. Hollomon, "Productivity...Who is Responsible for Improving It?" *Agricultural Engineering,* vol. 63, no. 7 (July 1982), pp. 10–20 and correspondence with Professor Tribus at MIT.

CHAPTER 12

PREPARING FOR THE FUTURE OF MANAGERIAL PRODUCTIVITY

The chapter is about the future of goal-oriented management for improving managerial productivity. In a sense it is also about the present because the future can only be estimated by understanding the present and to some extent, even the past. We will glance at expected developments of goal-oriented managerial approaches and suggest ways of responding to changes in future environments as predicted by Alvin Toffler's *The Third Wave* and John Naisbitt's *Megatrends.* A summary reviews the highlights of the book and suggests direction for the productive organization.

FUTURE DEVELOPMENTS OF MBO

Management practitioners and academicians often ask: "MBO—quo vadis? What is the next stage in the development of the goal-oriented management system?"

A study at UCLA by Gerard L. Rossy forecasts the future developments of MBO as follows:[1]

- A trend toward a more totally integrated management system

- An emphasis on group and qualitative goals with a greater influence of subordinates in the goal-setting process
- A greater emphasis on training and development
- The use of names other than MBO for a goal-oriented management approach
- Continued use of MBO in public and not-for-profit organizations, with its greatest application in the private sector

These predictions demand a closer analysis. From the discussions in previous chapters it has become clear that to be effective, MBO has to be viewed as a comprehensive managerial system that integrates many key managerial activities. Similarly, because of the interrelatedness of the managerial activities, setting verifiable goals for individuals independent of the network of aims is unproductive. Instead, individual goals must be supplemented by group goals and qualitative goals. The latter are especially important for upper-level managers, staff personnel, and public employees. The need for power sharing and greater participation by subordinates in the decision-making process is well recognized by those with experience in implementing MBO programs.

The term MBO sometimes has negative connotations. An English company, for example, experienced resistance to a program that was introduced with an MBO label. Later, essentially the same program was reintroduced under a different name and became generally accepted by managers. As pointed out in Chapter 1, the term MBO was used in this book with some reluctance because the term means different things to different organizations. But for convenience, and not to spread the semantic jungle,[2] we have continued using the acronym MBO for the comprehensive managerial system that focuses on goals and results.

Although Rossy's study forecasts the greatest growth of MBO in the private sector, public organizations increasingly use goal-oriented management approaches. The Bureau of Labor Statistics in Washington is developing a goal-oriented program by establishing labor productivity indexes for government agencies with 200 or more employees.[3] These efforts are significant since one out of every six members of the total work force are now employed by the government, and improving their productivity will have considerable impact on the nation's economy.

Let us now turn to the future by focusing on changes in the external environment and their impact on the organization.

MANAGERIAL PRODUCTIVITY IN THE FUTURE ENVIRONMENT

We all would like to know what the future will bring. Roger Evered at the Naval Postgraduate School assembled over forty pages of citations of books, articles, journals, periodicals, and newsletters dealing with futures planning.[4] In addition, he listed thirty-six organizations from around the world that were working on issues dealing with the future. This was in 1979. Today, with the rapid expansion of knowledge, such a list would probably be considerably longer.

Despite the efforts to predict the future, no one knows it: neither futurists, nor historians; neither planners, nor managers. Talking about the future is interesting and challenging—but our forecasts may also be wrong. At best, predicting the future can be an educated guess.

How to Respond to the Third Wave with Goal-Oriented Management

Alvin Toffler has written extensively about the future. In *The Third Wave* he makes a large-scale synthesis in which history is seen as a succession of intermingled waves rather than an abrupt change of periods.[5] The first wave was characterized by the rise of agriculture. In turn, this wave gave way to the second wave of industrialization that influences our lives today.

In Toffler's second-wave society, the drive in organizations was toward standardization. Frederick Winslow Taylor, the father of scientific management, contributed to productivity improvements by replacing the "rules of thumb" with science. The attempt was to maximize output by finding the best way of doing things. This is why we find the early productivity improvement efforts on the worker level, where it is relatively easy to measure inputs (wages or time) and outputs (items produced). This measurement was facilitated by the trend toward specialization. For example, the workers on the assembly line carried out very specific tasks, repeated over and over again. With the aid of time and motion studies apparent productivity could easily be measured: "apparent" because the human costs involved when treating workers as machines were often not taken into account when measuring productivity.

The third wave is not a linear extention of the second wave. Rather it is a distinct shift in direction characterized by dramatic changes in the economy, in technology, in communication, in education, in corporations, and in society in general. Some of these changes of the third wave include

- A widespread use of minicomputers at the work place and at home
- Working at home in the "electronic cottage"
- More part-time employment
- Educational experiences outside the classroom
- Increases in the proportion of white-collar workers to blue-collar workers
- Flexible work hours
- Greater decentralization in organizations
- A greater variety of organization structures and more transient work relationships
- Increase in transnational corporations
- Pressure on organizations to take into account the social implications of their decisions
- The application of the systems approach to managing with due consideration of the relationship of business and society

With increased diversity, greater complexity of tasks, more knowledge work, and the move toward the third wave, productivity measurement becomes more difficult. During the second wave the primary, and often the only goal of enterprises, was economic performance, usually expressed as profits. But increasingly organizations must consider the legitimate demands of many claimants, such as employees, consumers, suppliers, governments, and, of course, stockholders (see Figure 1-2). This means that organizations have to set social goals in addition to performance goals. The Chemical Bank of New York, for instance, bases 10 to 15 percent of their appraisal on social performance. Many companies now have special committees on the board of directors dealing with social responsibility issues. Father Theodore Purcell of Georgetown University strongly urges organizations to institutionalize ethics on the corporate board of directors.[6] Profit and return-on-investment goals (as discussed in Chapter 4) are certainly important, but even more crucial is that they are achieved in an ethical manner. The inclusion of noneconomic goals is not restricted to United States companies. In West Germany, for example, some twenty of the largest corporations now prepare social reports. It seems reasonable to predict that more and more companies will recognize their social obligations and set objectives in the area of social responsibility as suggested in Chapter 4.

Adapting to Megatrends with Goal-Oriented Management

We are in an age of major transformations affecting our society, our organizations, and our lives. In his best-selling book, *Megatrends,* John Naisbitt identifies the following ten trends[7]:

1 From industrial to information society

2 From forced technology to high tech/high touch (which means that technology is counterbalanced by a human response; such as relating to people)

3 From a national to a world economy

4 From a short-term to a long-term orientation

5 From centralization to decentralization (transformations in politics, business, and culture)

6 From institutional assistance to self-help (e.g. self-care, self-education, and so on)

7 From representation to participation (in politics and in organizations)

8 From organizational hierarchies to networking (which means sharing of information, resources, and ideas)

9 A shift of population and activity from the North to the South and the Southwest

10 From simple and limited options to multiple options

Managers, in any organization, may not change these trends, but they must recognize them and adapt to them. We will highlight possible managerial responses (summarized in Table 12-1) to some of these trends using the goal-oriented management system.

A brief look at the daily newspapers, the weekly magazines, the library shelves of newly published books, and the evening TV programs shows that we are becoming an information society. The computer found its way not only into our organizations, but also into our homes, and into all aspects of our lives. One frequently heard complaint of MBO participants is that they do not have sufficient information for setting objectives. But now a wealth of information can be tapped from a common data base. Computer terminals provide easy access to information that will affect the enterprise. Increasingly, company information is stored in a central computer from which managers can draw. For example, if projected sales figures need to be revised, the production manager and other affected persons can be easily informed through a computer-based information network. My research and that of others has shown that

TABLE 12-1
MANAGERIAL RESPONSES TO MEGATRENDS*

Trend toward	Managerial responses using the goal-oriented management system
An economy based on information	1 Communication system facilitates managerial process and links the organization with its environment (#1)** 2 Scanning of the external environment and use of a common data base (#1, 2, 3). 3 Gathering of information and forecasting the future (#2). 4 Career planning involves information gathering about the environment (#9).
High tech/ high touch	1 An important output of the system is human satisfaction (#1). 2 Top management creates appropriate climate for high-tech/high touch (#10). 3 Theory Y assumptions and team management (9,9 on the Grid) create high-touch organizational environment (#6). 4 Organization development (OD) uses high-touch behavioral science for making people productive (#10). 5 Quality circles is the high touch Japanese managerial response to high tech (#11).
A world economy	1 Scanning for opportunities around the world (#2, 3). 2 In a worldwide economy one can learn from other people in Japan and Europe (#11).
A long-term orientation	1 The systems approach demands taking the long-term, strategic view (#1, 2). 2 Determining the socioeconomic purpose, mission, and corporate objectives requires long-term orientation (#4). 3 Short-term objectives should be consistent with long-term aims (#5). 4 Career plan needs to focus on short- and long-term personal goals (#9). 5 Long-range planning is needed in government (#11).
Decentralization	1 Setting objectives and measuring performance against them facilitates decentralization (#4, 5). 2 Delegation by results is the basis for decentralization (#5).

(continued)

TABLE 12-1 (*Continued*)

Trend toward	Managerial responses using the goal-oriented management system
Self-reliance and self-care	1 The philosophy of MBO emphasizes self-control and self-evaluation (#1, 7). 2 Through career planning managers gain control over their lives (#9). 3 Setting of objectives by subordinates promotes self-reliance and self-control (#5). 4 Self-appraisal is the basis for self-direction and self-development (#7, 8).
Participation and democracy	1 Managers should set their own objectives (#1). 2 Bottom-up goal setting encourages participation (#4). 3 Participation is based on Adult-Adult transactions (in TA terms) (#6). 4 System 4 is a participative approach to managing (#10). 5 In Japan, the decision flow is from the bottom to the top and back (#11). 6 In Japan, bottom-up communication, participative decision making, and control by peers is quite common (#11).
Network structures	1 Action planning requires integration of tasks and activities with deemphasis on hierarchies (#1, 4, 5). 2 Network of aims provides basis for network structures (#4).
A shift toward the South	1 Strategic planning requires asking: "Where are our customers?" (#2). 2 Strategic management considers demographic factors (#2).
A multiple-choice society	1 Multiple goals of claimants need to be integrated (#1). 2 MBO requires multiplicity of objectives (#5).

*John Naisbitt, *Megatrends* (New York: Warner Books, Inc., 1982).
**Indicates chapter in the book.

one of the easiest ways to make an MBO program ineffective is to burden the managers with excessive paperwork. The computer can relieve this burden, giving managers more time to interact with people.

But high tech does not have to be at the expense of high touch, by which Naisbitt means a counterbalancing human response to the introduction of technology. One of the greatest benefits of MBO is the human interaction in activities such as deciding on the mission of the enterprise and setting of objectives by the superior and subordi--nates. In many Japanese firms, high-tech robotization of the work place is accompanied by high-touch quality circles. These circles are also increasingly used by U.S. companies such as IBM, General Motors, General Electric, and American Express for improving productivity. A quality circle (also called quality control circle because the emphasis was originally on control) is a group of people who participate voluntarily to work on problems that affect their performance. William Werther at Arizona State University cautions that an autocratic, top-down approach will not work for quality circles.[8] It appears that a high-touch organizational environment similar to System 4 (discussed in Chapter 10) may be conducive for the success of quality circles.

There is ample evidence that we move toward a global economy. A look at the products we buy should convince us that the economies of the world are closely interwoven with relatively free trade among the countries. At one time the interaction between countries consisted of exportation of goods or licensing agreements, but now we find joint ventures, subsidiaries, and multinational corporations operating in many countries. Thinking globally is common, but what about managerial practices? Can they be used internationally? Nations must not only adapt to, and live with, each other, but people must also learn from each other. At one time, American management was considered superior—and to some extent it still is today—but we realize now that some Japanese managerial practices may be emulated successfully for greater productivity.

Yesterday we admired American management approaches, today we study Japanese managerial practices for improving productivity. Tomorrow we may look at management practices in Singapore or China, or how about the concept of industrial democracy or co-determination, so popular in Europe? In the early 1950s a law was passed in Germany that required the participation of labor representatives on the supervisory board and the executive committees of large corporations. Not long ago the American Chrysler Corporation adopted a similar concept when it provided for labor's participation in managerial decisions. The point is simply this: Countries are interconnected and managers learn from each other. Management by objectives is now used in various forms around the world and its concepts seem universally applicable. However, the way MBO is practiced—such as the degree of participation in the goal-setting process—may vary with the culture and the peculiar situation in each country.

The fourth megatrend is toward a long-term orientation in making decisions. Since we discussed this topic at length in Chapters 1, 2, 3, and 4, little elaboration is necessary. Let us simply add that a clear mission and long-range and strategic plans are important but not sufficient. It is essential to build a support system that encourages decisions that have long-run benefits. Specifically, performance appraisal, promotion, and rewards need to be structured in a way to give a balanced emphasis to both short- and long-term performance. This requires a board of directors with vision to demand from top executives (who in turn set the climate for the organization) not only quarterly profit performance, but also decisions beneficial for the long-term health of the organization with sustained high productivity levels.

Another megatrend is a shift from centralization to decentralization, which is the tendency to disperse decision-making authority. This trend can be seen not only in the operations of large multinational corporations, but also in government, as shown by President Reagan's attempt to decentralize the federal bureaucracy, giving greater authority to state and local governments. Moreover, representatives of the Office of Management and Budget see decentralization of governmental agencies as a way to increased productivity.[9]

Another trend proposed by Naisbitt is the increasing participation of people at lower organizational levels in the decision-making process. Although he views this development from a sociopolitical perspective, an analogy can be drawn for organizations as it relates to the goal-oriented management system. As you will recall from previous chapters, the philosophy underlying the MBO process is based on genuine participation of subordinates in setting goals, evaluating performance, and implementing the program. Clearly Naisbitt's projections in respect to participation are, in effect, an extension of the present approach to managing by objectives.

The last megatrend to be considered is the shift from organizational hierarchies to networking, which means sharing of information, ideas, and resources. In Chapters 4 and 5, we discussed the importance of integrating objectives into a network of aims. This process requires vertical and horizontal information exchange, sharing of resources, and building on the ideas of managers and workers throughout the organization. People coordinate their tasks through open communication with a deemphasis on hierarchical authority relationships. Moreover, this networking needs to be extended beyond the boundaries of the organization, which, as an open system, interfaces with the external environment.

We can conclude from the discussion of the megatrends that if these predictions are correct—and they are to some extent already a reality today—the goal-oriented management system will assist managers to cope with these changes. Several years ago an article appeared with the ominous title "MBO—A Requiem is Due." The predicted death of MBO obviously did not happen because goal orientation is inherent in individuals, groups, and organizations. Even more important, the goal-oriented management system, if continuously updated and adapted to the changes in the environment, will help us to cope with the demands of the future.

TOWARD THE PRODUCTIVE ORGANIZATION—
A SUMMARY

The purpose of this book is to achieve management excellence through improved productivity of all organizational members, but especially managers and knowledge workers. Only a nation that can continuously better the output/input ratio, with due consideration to quality and time, can in the long run maintain a high standard of living in the very competitive national and international environment.

In the past, efforts to improve productivity were made on the worker level. But the trend in developed nations is from blue-collar work toward knowledge work. Yet little effort has been undertaken to measure and improve the productivity of knowledge workers in industry, government, and not-for-profit organizations. The goal-oriented management system, a refinement of the management-by-objectives approach, and for convenience called MBO, provides some hope for making knowledge workers more productive.

Critics have accused United States managers of a short-term orientation in decision making. The strategic planning model in Chapter 2 identifies the essential steps in strategy formulation. To ensure long-term productivity, strategic planning needs to be intergrated with traditional MBO programs. The dynamic environment needs continuous and systematic scanning by the managers. Specifically external threats and opportunities have to be matched with the enterprise's weaknesses and especially its strengths. The TOWS matrix in Chapter 3 provides tools for analyzing the situation and developing alternative strategies.

Every organizational unit, every manager, and every nonmanager should contribute to the purpose of the enterprise. The hierarchy of aims, introduced in Chapter 4, implies that each objective contributes to the next-higher-level goal and eventually to the mission of the enterprise. The aims of organizational units must not only be vertically consistent, but they must also be linked horizontally so that the goals of the functional departments are in harmony.

Although the hierarchy and network of aims provide an essential framework for goal-oriented management, they need to be supported by the systemic setting of group and individual objectives, particularly difficult aspects of MBO. This process is aided by the guidelines for setting verifiable objectives suggested in Chapter 5. But objectives must be supported by plans that state in greater detail the what, how, when, and who in bringing action into plans.

To implement plans and programs effectively and efficiently, the environment has to be conducive for utilizing the full potential of all employees. The understanding of the nature of people, the leadership style appropriate for the situation, and the application of transactional analysis concepts all can make managers more productive by facilitating the interactions among them and their subordinates (see Chapter 6).

The measurement of productivity requires comparing perfomance against verifiable criteria, and the objectives set in the planning process become the standards against which individual and organizational performance are measured. The most effective control, however, prevents deviations from plans before they occur. Thus, feedforward control, often overlooked by managers, is likely to be the most productive approach to control and appraisal (Chapter 7).

Excellence in managing requires staffing, and keeping staffed, the organization structure with people best suited for the job. This means integrating human resource planning into the goal-oriented management process (as discussed in Chapter 8), so that both organizational demands and individual capabilities are properly matched. Systematic recruitment, selection, placement, promotion, training, and development will benefit both individuals and the organization and will result in greater productivity.

Closely related to human resource management, but with greater emphasis on the needs and aspirations of individuals, is career planning and development, aspects generally not included in goal-oriented management programs. Strategic career planning, as suggested in Chapter 9, demands self-knowledge in selecting career and professional goals. Individuals' strengths and weaknesses are then matched with present and future opportunities to arrive at a satisfying career path.

To be effective, a goal-oriented productivity program must be tailored to organizational needs. Whether the program is simple or complex, mechanistic or organic, directed from the top or through the active participation of lower managers, introduced as an appraisal program or as a comprehensive managerial system, it must be adapted to the organizational situation. No prepackaged program, superimposed on the existing organization with disregard of its special characteristics, can be effective. Organizational development demands a systematic and planned approach to improve the productivity of individuals, groups, and the total organization, as was discussed in Chapter 10.

Managerial excellence is demanded not only from business managers, but also increasingly from government administrators. With a large portion of the work force now employed by the government, and with the huge budget deficits of the federal government, the public demand for productivity improvement becomes stronger. The response to these demands resulted in the 1983 White House Conference on Productivity, a first step in the right direction. While government now employs successful business techniques, business seeks some answers to their productivity crisis in the application of Japanese managerial practices. The comparison of United States and Japanese approaches to managing shows considerable differences. While some Japanese practices may be culture-bound, others can be transferred to the United States for improving the productivity of operation and the quality of products.

Although the systems approach to MBO is not a cure-all, it is an effective way to respond to third wave characteristics described by Toffler and to adapt to Naisbitt's megatrends. As we move toward an information society, a high-tech, high-touch technology, a global economy with increasing decentralization of organizations, and a society with multiple options, we need a system flexible enough to adapt to these trends.

The decline in productivity growth rates is a problem that probably will be with us for a long time as we move toward the twenty-first century. Americans have been at their innovative best in times of challenge. The productivity situation offers an opportunity for managerial excellence.

NOTES

1 G.L. Rossy, "The Future of MBO: Some Implications for Management and Research," presentation at the Western Academy of Management, Monterey, Calif., 1981.

2 The different MBO approaches constitute a kind of jungle. See H. Weihrich, "An Uneasy Look at the MBO Jungle—Toward a Contingency Approach to MBO," *Management International Review* (Europe), vol. 16, no. 4 (1976), pp. 103–109.

3 M.A. Mark, "Productivity Measurement of Government Services—Federal, State, and Local," in Panel Background Papers, *White House Conference on Productivity,* 1983.

4 R. Evered, *Futures Planning in Management: Bibliography and Information Sources* (Chicago : CPL Bibliograpies, 1979).

5 A. Toffler, *Future Shock* (New York: Random House, 1970) and *The Third Wave* (New York: Bantam, 1981).

6 See J. Weber, "Institutionalizing Ethics into the Corporation," *MSU Business Topics,* vol. 29, no. 2 (Spring 1981), pp. 47–52; T.V. Purcell, S.J. and J. Weber, *Institutionalizing Corporate Ethics: A Case History* (New York: The Presidents Association, The Chief Executive Officers' Division of American Management Association, 1979), Special Study No. 71; and T.V. Purcell, "The Ethics of Corporate Governance," *Review of Social Economy,* vol. 11, no. 3 (December 1982), pp. 360–370.

7 J. Naisbitt, *Megatrends* (New York: Warner Books, 1982).

8 W.B. Werther, Jr., "Productivity Improvement Through People," *Arizona Business,* February 1981, pp. 14–19.

9 White House Conference on Productivity—Preparatory Conference on Government Organization and Operation and the Role of Government in the Economy held in San Diego, July 19–21, 1983.

INDEX

242